BIND US T
. . . TO BE THE CHURCH TI

Bind Us Together

... to Be the Church that Jesus Really Wants

The Restoration Movement and its Message for the Church

JOHN FLEMING

THANKFUL BOOKS

First published 2007

Published by Thankful Books
c/o P.O. Box 2118, Seaford BN25 9AR.

ISBN: 978 1 905084 15 9

Book design and production for the publisher by
Bookprint Creative Services, <www.bookprint.co.uk>
Printed in Great Britain.

CONTENTS

ACKNOWLEDGEMENTS

First and foremost I would like to thank my wife Jean who endured, with patience, the many hours I spent in background reading and then huddled over my computer preparing the manuscript. The cups of tea and coffee were very much appreciated. I am also grateful to a number of others who helped and encouraged me. Meetings with David Lillie and Terry Virgo, both, in my view, heroes of restoration, were vital to building the historical overview of the subject. Thanks too to Jonathan Wallis who gave me a copy of the now out-of-print *Beyond Charisma*, on which the church model described in Chapter 13 is based. Interviews with leaders from Southampton Community Church were also valuable in getting different views on our own history. These included Ron Rothery, Tony Morton, Dave Adcock and, in particular, Roy Pearson who loaned me his meticulously kept diaries of the exciting days of our church's beginning. Others have been most helpful during the writing of the manuscript. My son Steve and his friend Dave Light, who both grew up as part of the movement, have read and commented on sections of the book. The positive feedback from members of the younger generation was a great encouragement. Dave Adcock and Meric Srokosz ploughed their way through an earlier and longer version of the manuscript, and in addition to making many helpful comments persuaded me to cut out some extraneous material. Billy Kennedy, the leader of our church also took the time to read the book and make encouraging noises. Di Moss has done a wonderful job in proofreading, which is so necessary for an author who finds his own typographical errors almost impossible to spot. David Nickalls and Tim Short of Bookprint have also been most helpful in easing the path through the process of publication. My final thanks, though, must be to Jesus himself, for his presence and sense of inspiration at all times.

INTRODUCTION

It has probably been true throughout history that when people reach middle age, they start to reflect on how things have changed during their lifetime. This is certainly the case for me looking back over the last 50 years. The rate of scientific and technological development has been astonishing. Probably the most notable achievement was sending a manned spacecraft to the moon, but when Neil Armstrong walked on its surface, he had never seen a PC, a DVD player or a mobile phone, and had probably never even considered the concept of Dolly, the cloned sheep, all of which have appeared since that date in 1969. The improvements in communication have led to the concept of the Global Village. Wars have sadly still continued, but there is unprecedented agreement amongst the major nations of the world to reason together. These positive changes have not made life easy for the church in the Western world. With man appearing to grow in stature and achieve so much, the need for God has seemed to diminish. The Christian influence in the thinking and morals of Western society has continued to decline, calling into question for many people the relevance of the church to today's society.

However, rumours that 'God is dead' have been greatly exaggerated in the past and his response to repetitions of this assertion over the last 50 years, has been equally positive. Exciting developments in church life have occurred throughout the world during this period, which loudly proclaim the message that God is still very much alive. The church in the United Kingdom has participated in these changes, and while we have not seen the revivals that have occurred in some countries, church life has been altered significantly during this period. God's Spirit has been poured out on Christians bringing a fresh vitality to their lives, and this has inevitably had an influence on our churches, as the new wine has required new wineskins.

The charismatic movement first emerged during the late 1950s and early 1960s. Christians from all denominations started to realise that the baptism and fullness of the Holy Spirit were not things of the past, and began to experience them in their own lives. The impact on individual Christians was very positive, drawing them closer to God and equipping them to serve more effectively in the church. Arthur Wallis, later to become a leader of the movement, was one of the first to receive the baptism of the Spirit outside a Pentecostal setting[1]. He describes his experience as follows:

Early in 1951 my friend, Oscar Penhearow, shared with me his concern for 'an enduement with power for service.' He had been reading R.A. Torrey. We decided that we would each seek God and search the scriptures. I went right through the New

Testament on this subject, and within three weeks we were both filled with the Spirit – for me it came alone on my knees, and without any contact with Pentecostals. The experience was revolutionary. It changed my prayer life, my preaching and my witnessing, though it was not until much later that I was to experience spiritual gifts.

At first, the impact of this on the Church as a whole was limited, as the majority of Christians did not initially accept this as a move of God. There was particular disquiet over the doctrine of the baptism of the Holy Spirit and the use of the gifts of the Spirit, such as tongues. At that time, evangelical Christians generally considered that the baptism in the Spirit was received at the time a person first became a Christian. They believed that the gifts of the Spirit had died out after about the first century, being unnecessary once the content of scripture had been officially established. This left a dilemma for the new charismatic Christians; should they stay in their denominations and try to influence things from within, or should they start up alternative churches giving freedom to accommodate all aspects of the new spiritual life that God was bringing? This sadly divided the charismatic movement into two parts, the renewal movement, those who stayed in their churches, and the restoration movement, those who left to start new fellowships.

The restoration movement was a central part of the Pentecostal/charismatic revival of the twentieth century. However, within this general movement of the Spirit, it had its own distinctive message regarding the nature and operation of the church. Its principal contribution has been to pioneer a return to a scriptural concept of church life unencumbered by denominational traditions. It has tried to recapture the spirit of a flexible New Testament church, which is adaptable both to changes in the world environment in which it finds itself, and to new directions from the Holy Spirit. This has been instructive to the church as a whole, both in demonstrating new models of church life, and in highlighting some pitfalls to avoid. The lives of many Christians have been revived; new churches have been established and many other churches positively changed. This has had the effect of drawing Christians of all denominations closer together with a new sense of a shared vital and exciting Christian life.

Much of the essential message of the restoration movement is neatly summed up in one of its songs[2].

There is only one God
There is only one King
There is only one body
That is why I sing

Bind us together Lord
Bind us together
With cords that cannot be broken
Bind us together Lord
Bind us together
Bind us together in love
  Extract taken from the song 'Bind us Together' by Bob Gillman
                    Copyright © 1977 Thankyou Music

It seems ironic that a theme song of a movement, which broke away from the existing church structures, is about Christian unity. When we sang that song in the early days of the movement, as we did repeatedly, our immediate thoughts were mainly about the tremendous sense of unity that we felt amongst ourselves, as those whom God was calling to be part of this new initiative. However, the song itself is about Christian unity on a broader scale and, although we were separating from the existing denominations, there was always a sense that we didn't want to form another denomination, but rather to be used by God to help bring his body together. I can remember a poignant term being used in our prayers at that time, that we would become a focal point of unity in the church.

Relatively little has been written on the restoration movement, with arguably the best-known book, *Restoring the Kingdom* by Andrew Walker[3], being written by someone outside it. Although this provides a good history of events, it does not convey the full heart of the movement, and towards the end presents quite a negative picture of its current state. One of the reasons for writing this book, is the belief that the restoration movement has made an important and valuable contribution to church life in the UK during the second half of the twentieth century. I believe that it was inspired by God, and conveys something of his heart. Church history over the last 500 years has been characterised by a number of different renewal movements. Each recovered particular scriptural principles that had previously been lost. The church has benefited greatly by hearing what God has said through these renewals, and responding appropriately. It is therefore important that the church in the twenty-first century does not lose the truths that have been re-emphasised in the restoration movement. As restorationists, we need to try and convey our message as clearly as possible. I hope that this book will accomplish this task, and go some way to being an apologetic for the movement.

The book will also look at the thoughts of writers from other streams of the Christian church, and consider their views of restoration. Two recent books are *The Glory and the Shame* by Peter Hocken[4] and *Charismatics and the New Millennium* by Nigel Scotland[5]. The former looks at both the Pentecostal and charismatic movements of the twentieth century through the eyes of a Roman Catholic, while the latter is by a Charismatic Anglican. Nigel Scotland presents a very balanced review of the charismatic movement, including a lot of detail about restoration. My aim is to complement these excellent books by presenting a view of the restoration movement from someone within it. Although it will be an inside view, my aim is to place the movement in the context of what is happening in the world and the rest of the Church. I have a passionate belief in the importance of the unity of the whole of God's church, and therefore wish to lay particular emphasis on trying to show how developments in restoration churches relate to other Christians. The vision of restoration was to encourage all God's people to be living in the abundant life we read of in the New Testament, and to see the life of the church reflect that vitality. I hope to assist in mutual understanding across all the various streams of the church.

Peter Hocken's book, *The Glory and the Shame,* covers both the good and bad aspects of the Pentecostal and Charismatic movements. While my aim is to stress the good things that have occurred within the restoration movement, it too has had its share of the shame. The creation of new churches and the transformation of existing ones have involved sacrifice and pain. Strain has been put on relationships and not all have been strong enough to withstand the pressure. I do not want to hide this aspect of the movement, but neither to dwell on it unhelpfully. Where lessons can be learned from past mistakes, then it is valuable to take note, but over-emphasis on the less attractive parts of its history that have now been confessed and forgiven, is not likely to lead to edification or encouragement of the reader.

What's in a Name?

As part of this brief introduction, it is worth discussing the different names given to the movement, which are somewhat varied and confused. The confusion has occurred, because the restoration movement has never become an official organisation. This has helped it to avoid being considered as a new denomination, but has made it difficult for people to know how to refer to it. I have chosen the term 'restoration', because I believe it best describes what the formation of these churches was trying to achieve. The principal purpose was not to introduce anything new, but to restore the things that had been lost, and move towards a church life aligned as closely as possible to New Testament principles. One disadvantage of using the term is that it could be construed as only relating to that part of the movement associated with the *Restoration* magazine, which circulated during the 1970s and 1980s. When I use the term here, it is meant to include all groups that have the vision of restoring the church according to scriptural principles. This includes groups that are sometimes referred to as house churches, new churches or new apostolic churches. These different terms reflect aspects of what God has been doing in recent days, but I think the term 'restoration' is the one that conveys most clearly the centre of God's heart for the church over this time.

The term 'new church' reflects the significant changes that were occurring during the second half of the twentieth century. The church was being seen as a dynamic organism, which will always be changing and becoming new. This concept is also implied in the term 'restoration', in that the New Testament church that is being restored, also displayed this ethos of adaptability. 'New', however, has the disadvantage of being very non-specific, and possibly also somewhat misleading. The restoration principle is not about bringing a new message, rather returning to the original. The term also implies that the new churches will be separate from the rest, whereas my understanding is that across all these groups, there is a longing to see God's whole Church functioning together in a biblically based fashion. The names 'house churches' and 'new apostolic churches' both express important components of the changes that have occurred in the church, but also seem less suitable than 'restoration', as they convey only part of the story of what God has done in the movement.

One other recent development in the UK church is the concept of 'emerging church', where people experiment with different ways of being church to find out what is successful in reaching out to non-Christians. While there are similarities to restoration, in the willingness to accept new ideas about church life, this is really quite a different concept from the scriptural emphasis at the heart of the restoration message. This important difference will be discussed in more detail later.

What is the Church that Jesus really wants?

This is the essential question that the book is trying to address. It is a question that has occupied me since I first became a Christian, as a teenager. Even before I had heard about the restoration movement, I had read of Jesus' desire for his people to be in unity, and it seemed to me, that the division of the church into various different denominations was not God's ideal. The restoration movement has certainly tried to address this problem. That it has done so imperfectly is clear. However, it has given us some important pointers, and as the church of today we must be careful to learn the lessons that God wants to teach us through it.

We often refer to ourselves as being on a journey in our personal lives. I believe that the church too is on a journey. It's a journey that has lasted two thousand years to date. Sadly, some of that time it has been travelling in the wrong direction. The restoration movement, like several other major reforms over the last 500 years, has helped to get us back on the right track. Alongside its development, there has been a growing desire among Christians across nearly all sections of the church, to recognise our unity in Christ. There is much to be optimistic about. However, we certainly have not arrived yet. I am keen that we do all we can to progress on our journey together in the right direction. I want to encourage Christians to have a clear vision for the church, and to be as excited about the journey of the church as they are about their own personal journey. If this book can fill us with a desire to work together to be the church that Jesus wants, then I'll be delighted.

The future vision for a unified church, which I present in the concluding chapter, represents quite a change from the current situation. It seems an impossible dream. However, I am encouraged that seemingly impossible dreams do sometimes happen in reality. How many people 25 years ago, longing for the Berlin Wall to come down, dreamt that this were possible? And yet it happened. How much more should we be able to hope in a dream for the church, that is based on what Jesus and the whole New Testament seem to point towards so clearly?

Summary of the Book

The book is divided into three parts. In that sense it's a bit like the *Star Wars* trilogy. It starts in the present, covering the story of the restoration movement in the UK church over the second half of the twentieth century. Then it goes back in time to consider the biblical viewpoint, God's heart for the church and how it began. Finally, the third part looks to the future. The book is also like *Star Wars* in that it is about a universal organisation, the Kingdom of God, and about a battle between good and evil forces. But here the similarity ends. *Star Wars* is pure fiction. The church is reality. This is a story about the central purpose of God in the universe to bring all things together under him, a story of the establishment of the Kingdom of God.

The book is written primarily from the perspective of the church in the UK, but the issues raised are not specific to a particular country, and can apply to the church in any location. I have tried to provide coherent arguments that will stand up to academic analysis. However, I have also tried to use everyday language in the hope it will be of interest to all Christians. I pray that it will encourage all who read it with a fresh heart and a fresh vision for the church that Jesus wants.

References

1. Wallis, Jonathan, 1991, *Arthur Wallis: Radical Christian*, Kingsway, Eastbourne (Quotation used by permission of Kingsway Publications, Lottbridge Drove, Eastbourne).

2. Gillman, Bob, *Bind Us Together* © Thankyou Music, Eastbourne, England.

3. Walker, Andrew, 1998, *Restoring the Kingdom – the Radical Christianity of the House Church Movement*, Eagle, Guildford, Surrey.

4. Hocken, P., 1994, *The Glory and the Shame: Reflections on the Twentieth Century Outpouring of the Holy Spirit*, Eagle, Guildford, Surrey.

5. Scotland, N., 2000, *Charismatics and the New Millennium: the Impact of Charismatic Christianity from 1960 into the New Millennium*, Eagle, Guildford, Surrey.

Part 1
A Brief History of Restoration

I always find the study of history fascinating. Trying to understand the reasons behind the things that happened is inevitably instructive. It's good, too, to look at the events from different angles. How helpful it is that we have four accounts of the life of Jesus, each bringing a view of his life from a different perspective. There have already been descriptions of the history of the restoration movement, notably *Restoring the Kingdom* by Andrew Walker[1]. This provides an excellent objective description of events, but it is written by someone outside the movement. In this part of the book, I summarize the development of restoration from the viewpoint of someone who has been part of it. I will also aim to interpret the events from a number of other perspectives.

One of the long-term visions of early restorationists, was that the movement would result in the whole church coming together and adopting New Testament principles of church life. It is therefore interesting to consider the history of restoration in the context of other developments in the UK church. How has the rest of the church influenced restoration, and how has restoration impacted the rest of the church?

The restoration story will also be viewed from the perspective of the typical church member. Most church history tends to describe events largely from the point of view of church leaders. This is natural, as they obviously have a key role in shaping what has happened. However, it is also important to think about things from the point of view of the ordinary 'man-in-the-pew' (or should we say 'man-in-the-armchair' when we are talking about house churches?). Such people comprise the bulk of the church and their response to leadership direction is a very important determining factor in church development. This aspect is all the more relevant in restoration churches, as one of the emphases of the movement, is on the importance of every member having a contribution to make as part of the body of Christ.

Finally, this description will be a personal view, as someone who has been part of restoration since the early days. I am aiming to present a balanced perspective on the movement, but inevitably what I write will reflect my own views on what has happened, and how things have developed. I am also a scientist by profession, and so that will influence my approach. I view things analytically. I want to understand what's going on. As a Christian, I'm very keen to understand God's purpose for his church. Overall, I feel that restoration has been a move of God with some very important lessons, both for those of us within the movement and for the church as a whole. I am keen for fellow restorationists to consider what has been achieved, to understand where we got it right, and to be honest about where we got it wrong. I have a great passion to see the whole church restored, and hope this reflection will help us all to see where God wants to take us from here.

Reference

1. Walker, Andrew, 1998, *Restoring the Kingdom – the Radical Christianity of the House Church Movement*, Eagle, Guildford, Surrey.

CHAPTER ONE

THE BEGINNINGS OF RESTORATION

The Historical Context

The twentieth century restoration movement can be seen as one of a series of changes that have occurred in the Church since the Reformation in the 16th century. Prior to this time, the Church as a whole had drifted some way from the basic teaching of the New Testament. A return to the biblical message of justification by faith, pioneered by Martin Luther and the other reformers, led to a revolution. The invention of the printing press around this time, and the subsequent general availability of the scriptures, also had a considerable influence in convincing people of this rediscovered truth. The early reformers, however, by no means recaptured all aspects of New Testament Christianity that had been lost, and the following 500 years have seen several more significant developments.

In subsequent Church history, each substantive change has been brought about by rediscovery of particular biblical truths. Believer's baptism, for example, was re-introduced as the scriptural initiation ceremony into the Christian faith. The teachings of Wesley brought church life out of special buildings, and into homes, just as is recorded in Acts. The idea of the 'priesthood of all believers', that all Christians have an important contribution to make as part of the church, was also emphasised by several groups, notably the Brethren. The realisation of these changes relied on the principle that faith comes by hearing and hearing by the Word of God (Rom 10:17). Men saw the truths in scripture and received them as God's word to them. This gave them vision and faith to initiate the change. The Holy Spirit was then released to allow the word to be realised in practice. It is interesting to reflect how this view of God's work in maturing the church, is very similar to the principle of growth in our own individual lives. God first speaks to us. When we believe it, and turn faith into action, the word becomes real in our lives.

Each of these changes challenged the status quo in the Church, and in almost every case the pattern of events was similar. The discovery of the new truth was accompanied by a period of revival, as the surge of faith released the Holy Spirit to move in power. The established church usually initially resisted the new move, causing many of its enthusiasts to leave to start their own group, where they could implement more fully what God was showing them. The new group then formed its own churches, leading to the emergence of a denomination having particular emphasis on the truth that had been recovered. The radical edge of the new group gradually dwindled, as a fence was placed around what they believed in the form of a doctrinal statement. The effect of this on the rest of the church was two-fold. The division resulting from the development of a separate denomination was disappointing, but the seed of the new truth was planted in the church as a whole. The initial negative reaction of the establishment gradually died down, and in many cases the new ideas gained acceptance over a period of time. In this way, developments based on the recovery of scriptural principles have had a significant positive influence on the global church. The Roman Catholic Church today, for example, has changed out of all recognition compared to that of the Middle Ages, in no small way due to the reformation in other parts of the church.

The Pentecostal Revival

These changes in the church continued and even accelerated during the twentieth century. Towards the end of the nineteenth century, Christians had begun to consider the possibility, that the baptism of the Spirit and the supernatural gifts of the Spirit, described in the New Testament, were intended for the contemporary church. This was accompanied by spontaneous outbreaks of revival in many different countries across the world during the first few years of the twentieth century[1]. One of these in Azusa Street in Los Angeles between 1906 and 1909, gave a focus to the gifts of the Spirit, and this provided the launch pad for the development of twentieth century Pentecostalism. At the same time as the events in Azusa Street, a revival was occurring in different parts of the United Kingdom, most notably in South Wales. Thousands of people became Christians, and the whole area was profoundly affected by the gospel. Although there were supernatural signs such as visions, trances, and the gift of discernment, the gift of tongues, a key part of the Pentecostal movement, was not originally in evidence. However, the revival had the effect of opening people's hearts to expect the tangible signs of the Holy Spirit in their lives. From among those who became Christians during the Welsh revival, some went on to become leaders of the Pentecostal movement in the UK.

The response to these new ideas was varied. Some Christians who received the Holy Spirit stayed in their own denominations, a notable example being Alexander Boddy, an Anglican vicar from Sunderland. However, this was the exception rather than the rule, and essentially the mainline churches rejected the movement. Events followed the typical pattern of church history, which has been outlined above, and new churches began to emerge. Sadly, there were disagreements between leaders of these churches, and they polarised into three main denominations, Elim, Assemblies of God and the Apostolic church. The formation of these groupings had the advantage of enabling stable churches to be established. However, the definition of the boundaries inherent in the creation of denominations, had the effect of stifling the growth of ideas, and also of cutting Pentecostals off from the other churches. Although these denominations grew, they did not take many believers from established churches, and they ceased to act as a provocation to change to the rest of the church. This situation remained until the 1960s. However, God's plan was for the church as a whole to be touched, and at this time he began to stir the hearts of Christians from all denominations throughout the country.

Preparing the Ground

The origins of the restoration movement can be traced back some years prior to the 1960s. In 1936 in South Africa, the legendary preacher, Smith-Wigglesworth, gave a prophesy to a young Pentecostal Minister called David Du Plessis.

> 'I have been sent by the Lord to tell you what he has shown me this morning. Through the old line denominations will come a revival that will eclipse anything we have known throughout history. No such things have happened in times past as will happen when this begins . . . Then the Lord said to me I am to give you a warning that he is going to use you in the movement'[2].

Although he remained in the Pentecostal movement, David du Plessis became involved in the early days of the World Council of Churches, and provided an important link between the Pentecostals and the emerging charismatic movement in other denominations.

Around this time things were already stirring in Britain. In the West Country, God began to speak to a young banker with a Brethren background, David Lillie, challenging him to consider whether the supernatural gifts of the Spirit were relevant for the twentieth century church[3]. The challenge came initially through a soapbox preacher in Tower Hill in London, when David worked in the city, and then by his own reading in the Acts. He soon found others to whom God had been saying the same things, and was encouraged to consider them further. However, the Brethren assembly that he attended was unhappy about his 'Pentecostal views', and he was given an ultimatum, that unless he renounced his interest in them, he could no longer take part in the assembly. He decided that leaving was the right thing to do, and joined up with about a dozen others, who shared fellowship together in their homes. Some time later David was filled with the Holy Spirit. He describes the experience in his book, *Restoration . . . is this still on God's programme?*[4]:

One February night, in the presence of several friends in Sister Violet's cottage, like John Wesley of old, 'I felt my heart strangely warmed', and as we continued in worshipping the Lord, I was given a new tongue with which to praise Him. It was an 'out of this world' experience, which, more than fifty years on, I still recall with a sense of awe. The gift of tongues I received at that time is still my precious possession.

The move thus started in a small way with generally only individuals or small groups being touched by the Holy Spirit. The blessing was nevertheless very real, and Christians were finding their lives revolutionised. In most cases, those being touched were part of churches, which either did not understand what was happening, or which were positively antagonistic to the move. For lay individuals to whom this happened life was not very easy; it was difficult to live out their newfound freedom in the Spirit in this environment. Some struggled on where they were in their denominational church, hoping for a change, while others moved, either to a Pentecostal church, or like David Lillie, to one of the new independent groups which were beginning to appear with increasing rapidity from the 1950s onwards.

Should I stay or should I go?

For church leaders, the decision was hardly any easier, particularly when the teaching on being filled with the Spirit was not accepted by the congregation. Some, however, who were charismatic both in character and in their acceptance of the gifts of the Spirit, were able to share their newfound experience with their church, and transform its ethos accordingly. David Watson and Colin Urquhart are two notable examples of Anglicans who brought renewal to their local congregations during the 1960s following their own experience of being filled with the Spirit. Both have written extensively on God's dealing with them and their churches[5]. David Watson describes what happened to him:

> We took the usual evangelical line that all such gifts were purely for the apostolic period and were not even meant for today. But then why were such specific instructions given for their use within the pages of the New Testament? And what about those strange Pentecostals whose growth in South America in particular had been one of the most remarkable movements of this century? Had they experienced the power and gifts of the Spirit that we were somehow missing? These became insistent, urgent questions that I could not escape. Next I studied again in the Acts of the Apostles and the conviction was steadily dawning on me that there was a normal spiritual dynamic about the early church that was almost entirely missing within the church today.

After much seeking and prayer David continues:

> Suddenly, I realised the missing link. I had been praying and praying to be filled with the Spirit; but when nothing seemed

to happen, I assumed that my prayer had not been answered. As I shared this with a friend, I remembered the example of the Virgin Mary. Once she accepted God's remarkable promise to her, she began to praise God that it was now already true, before the promise was confirmed in her own experience. I had been waiting for the experience before I believed that the promise had been fulfilled. It was entirely the wrong way round. I had to claim the promise of the Spirit, believe it to be true, start praising God that it was true and let the reality or experience of the promise follow in God's own way and God's own time.

Once again, I confessed every sin I could think of, and asked for God's forgiveness, even the sphere of my unbelief. I told him that I was willing to obey him, whatever the cost. I then asked him to fill me with his Spirit, and *began to praise him that he had now done it*. As I went on praising for perhaps ten to fifteen minutes, I had a quiet but overwhelming sense of being embraced by the love of God. There were no startling manifestations. I did not speak in tongues, and anyway I still believed that these had died with the apostles. But it seemed that the presence of God filled the room in which I was praying. I knew that I had been filled with the Spirit, and was bubbling over with new joy.

It is significant to note that the stories of both David Lillie and David Watson as well as that of Arthur Wallis, related in the introduction, all revolve around their willingness to take a fresh look at the scripture in a straightforward manner, and not to be constrained by the limited views of their denominational traditions.

These initial stirrings marked the beginning of what was to become known as the Charismatic movement of the twentieth century in the United Kingdom. Despite the similarities of the experience there were, however, different responses, which are typified by the two Davids, Lillie and Watson. David Watson sought to allow it to touch the Church of England where he was already placed, while David Lillie felt led by God to experience this new stirring of the Spirit in a small group setting. Thus two camps began to emerge, consisting on one side of those who considered that the new experiences could be accommodated within existing church structures, and on the other of those who felt the need for a completely new church context to fully express what the Holy Spirit was doing. These became known later as the renewal and restoration movements. We start by considering the restoration movement as this started a few years earlier than renewal.

Restoration

The Vision Emerges

Some spirit-filled Christians were convinced that the new wine of the Holy Spirit could only be contained in new wineskins, and this set the scene for the beginning of a separate movement. The negative response to the new teaching on the Holy Spirit in some denominational churches, was certainly a contributing factor. However, this development was more than just a group of disaffected charismatics, and during the 1950s and early 1960s a larger vision began to emerge. David Lillie was the leader of one of the earliest of these groups, which was located on the Countess Wear estate in Exeter. He was challenged by the important discrepancies he observed between church life as it was in the early 1950s, and the New Testament pattern. He wanted to do something to change the situation. Coming from a Brethren background where the concept of every member of the church having a part to play in church meetings was recognised, he was keen to see these ideas extended to embrace the gifts of the Spirit which he had been experiencing. His vision was for a restoration of all aspects of church life, going far beyond the confines of the charismatic movement, which focussed on the work of the Holy Spirit in the individual.

It was when David Lillie, with his vision for the church, met Arthur Wallis, a man full of zeal for God and a heart for revival, that these ideas were pressed forward[6]. In 1953 they started locally, with a series of small conferences held in David's home to discuss the Holy Spirit. Their ideas developed over the next few years, and in 1958 they organised a larger residential conference to discuss the theme of the church, which attracted a much wider audience. It was held in Exmouth and was entitled 'The Church of Jesus Christ – Its Purity, Power, Pattern and Programme in the Context of Today'. Among those attending the conference were Roger Forster, Graham Perrins and Cecil Cousen, who all became important figures in the subsequent development of the restoration movement. A further conference was held in 1961 in Belstone in Devon, where the concept of independent churches outside existing denominational boundaries began to crystallise. Jonathan Wallis's biography of his father contains much important detail about this conference, where many of the seed concepts of restoration were sown[7]. It was entitled 'The Divine Purpose of the Institution of the Church – an Enquiry'. The letter sent out to potential participants included the following:

More than three years have elapsed since a few of us met for a three-day conference at Exmouth. Many of us feel that we are far from seeing a dynamic New Testament Church in action either locally or on a wider scale. Where is the true Church of Christ? Must it continue to be obscured and dishonoured by all the impedimenta of denominationalism, by its unbelief, its worldliness, and its apathy?

Before us from the pages of the New Testament there rises THE CHURCH OF JESUS CHRIST, a glorious church, not having spot or wrinkle or any such thing. This surely is the Church which must arise at this hour through the mighty operation of the Holy Spirit! If this is our conviction, then we must be open, both individually and collectively to experience a mighty enduement of the Spirit of God in revival power. Feeling the need for this enduement and for clearer instructions regarding the function of the Church in the divine plan, it is felt that the time is ripe for some of us to come together to wait upon God and confer over these matters.

Around 40 people attended the conference. They were men who had already accepted scriptural teaching on the importance of the work of the Holy Spirit in their lives. Now they were facing the broader challenge of considering how other aspects of church life matched with the biblical description. Several key New Testament principles were discussed at this conference. The message was well summarised in a presentation by Arthur Wallis on 'The Divine Idea of the Local Church'. He spoke of the important picture of the Church as the body of Christ, pointing out the need to view it as an organism operating under God's design, rather than an organisation having a humanly devised structure. A key principle outlined in this talk was the view of the local church as a miniature version of the universal church, and that as such it should function as an independent body joined directly to Christ as the head. The following quote illustrates the way in which Arthur saw this operating:

> The church is to stand on its own feet and manage its own affairs. It is not to be dependent on outside control though warmly welcoming outside fellowship and holding loving communion with other believers and other fellowships of believers. The vital principle of self sufficiency under Christ of each local church could save us from the formation of another denomination, from which may the Lord deliver us.

The leadership of the local church was to consist of a group of elders who were to be appointed under the guidance of the Holy Spirit. The place of trans-local leaders such as apostles and prophets was in establishing the church and recognising the first leaders. The aim was then to allow the local eldership to mature and gradually assume the full responsibility of leadership. The elders ruling the church were to submit to God, seek unity between themselves, and avoid a dictatorial style. The functioning of the church was to be like that of the human body, depending on the correct operation of all its parts. Each member of the church was to be recognised as having a valuable contribution to make.

Leaders from both Brethren and Pentecostal backgrounds were involved in these early meetings. The teaching of both denominations influenced the development of ideas that emerged. It was felt that an environment was needed where the truths could be combined and extended. This led to a new concept of church, which would avoid putting a barrier around itself and becoming a new denomination, but rather, would be open to move as God led in new ways in the future. Many of the new concepts of church, which subsequently drove the restoration movement, are to be found in the records of this conference. The extent to which these ideas stemmed from the New Testament teaching, and the extent to which the movement adhered to them, will be discussed in subsequent chapters.

There was a further conference in the Exeter area in 1962, which was the first to be attended by Bryn Jones, another figure destined to play a key role in the development of the movement. However not long after this, Arthur left for what became an extended visit of two years to New Zealand. This resulted in some loss of the momentum that had been generated by the Exeter conferences.

Restoration develops

The departure of Arthur Wallis and Campbell McAlpine to New Zealand during 1963 and 1964 gave the opportunity for others to pick up the mantle, and in the unlikely setting of the sleepy seaside resort of Worthing, a series of Prayer and Bible weeks was initiated by Denis Clark. The first took place in the early weeks of 1964, and they ran annually for several years in the New Year period[8].

At this stage, the house church movement still had a low profile, with little co-ordinated leadership. Numbers of small groups began to emerge across the country, which attracted people for two main reasons. First, there were those who had a clear new vision of the church. They felt that the house group concept was very much in keeping with New Testament teaching on the church, and wanted to align

themselves with one of these groups. The second category of
people that joined the early groups, were those that found that
their experience of being filled with the Spirit was not
accepted by their church as being from God, and therefore felt
they had to move. It is important to remember that this was
the situation in the majority of non-conformist churches
during the 1960s. Christians that joined house groups at this
stage were of a pioneering spirit; it was a bold move of faith
to leave the security of a sound evangelical church, to join a
small group of people meeting in someone's living room, with
no formal leadership structure. The meetings themselves
were also often far removed from the experience of the
average Christian of the day, even those who had just
been filled with the Spirit. Things that are now regarded as
commonplace, such as speaking in tongues, words of
prophecy and exuberant worship were quite revolutionary. In
fact many people with a charismatic experience felt unsure
about the wisdom of such a move and, despite the opposition
in their current church, stayed where they were for the time
being.

There continued to be meetings of the leaders of the differ-
ent groups that were emerging. One of these occurred at
Westwatch in Sussex in 1967. This was organised by Maurice
Smith, and was attended by many of those who later become
nationally recognised leaders, such as Roger Forster, Graham
Perrins, Hugh Thompson, Peter Lyne and, of course, Arthur
Wallis.

Some of the groups were more co-ordinated than others.
The house groups that looked to Wally North as pastor
became known as the 'North Circular', and there were in
fact some of these groups not far from that road in

North London. The group at Chard in Somerset under Harry Greenwood and Sid Purse was also well developed. In addition, many of those who were to emerge as key leaders in the movement were setting up their own groups in towns throughout England. Bryn Jones had a small church in Bradford, Graham Perrins in Cardiff, Maurice Smith and Ted Crick in Canterbury and Gerald Coates in Cobham, Surrey. This 'ad hoc' growth of groups was soon to be dramatically affected by key events in the early 1970s.

Renewal

Running alongside the emergence of restoration, the move of the Spirit in the 1960s also began to touch denominational churches resulting in a variety of responses.

Renewal in the Church of England

The Church of England, while certainly not making any general acceptance of the charismatic movement, at least made room for it to happen where the appropriate leadership was in place. This was probably helped by the fact that churches, which underwent a charismatic transition, were usually successful in increasing numbers. It is also interesting to reflect that the acceptance of this new move demonstrates that some lessons of church history have been learnt over the years. If this development had occurred 200 years ago, the Church of England would almost certainly have opposed it, as happened with the revival of the eighteenth century under John Wesley.

Renewal grew rapidly in churches where strong charismatic leaders such as David Watson and Colin Urquhart

were able to bring their congregations through to an acceptance and experience of the fullness of the Holy Spirit. The
security for Christians coming into the experience within the
established church, was that it was still part of the denominational setting with which they were familiar. One important leader in these early days was Michael Harper, who had
been a curate at All Soul's Langham Place in London,
working with John Stott. He had been filled with the Spirit,
and had felt led to resign his position in the Anglican Church
in 1964, to set up an independent organisation, the Fountain
Trust. The aim was to encourage those in the Anglican
Church who were coming into a charismatic experience. The
Trust organised meetings primarily for Anglicans to explore
the new move of God. However, Michael had an interest in
bringing together Christians from other groups who were
similarly being touched by the Holy Spirit, and several
leaders of what was known then as the house church movement, were invited to meetings he organised. One such
meeting in January 1965 at High Leigh, was attended by
both Arthur Wallis and also Campbell McAlpine, another
leading light in the early days of restoration. Michael also
invited Arthur Wallis to be an adviser for the Trust. The Trust
established a publishing wing and produced a number of
influential books around that period. It helped in seeing
many churches revitalised during the 1960s and 1970s.
However Michael himself became disillusioned with the
doctrinal laxity in the Church of England, and joined the
Greek Orthodox Church. The Trust was disbanded in 1980,
but the momentum it had created was significant. Renewal
in the Church of England has continued to develop, and is
still ongoing at the time of writing.

Renewal in the Roman Catholic Church

The Roman Catholic Church was also somewhat surprisingly open to the new move of God. In fact, God's Spirit seems to have been clearly at work in the Catholic Church in preparation for the Second Vatican Council, which met between 1962 and 1965 under the leadership of Pope John 23rd. This represented the most significant restatement of the Catholic faith for some 400 years, when the Council of Trent had met between 1545 and 1563 to discuss the response of the Catholic Church to the Reformation. This Second Council brought wide-ranging changes to the Catholic Church, but one phrase was of particular prophetic relevance in the context of the Charismatic movement. In the prayer, which was to be said daily throughout the world during the Council, Pope John asked the Holy Spirit to 'renew your wonders in this day as a new Pentecost'. This new openness in the Catholic Church provided the basis on which God could bless many Catholics with the baptism of the Spirit, and renewal began to occur in the UK in the late 1960s and early 1970s[9].

The inclusion of the Catholic Church as part of the renewal was significant, in that it was the first time that Roman Catholics and Protestants had been part of the same move of God since before the Reformation. The catholic writer, Peter Hocken[10], has made a number of interesting observations regarding the nature of the renewal that are worth noting:

1. it was unplanned and unexpected
2. it had no one founder or one place of origin

3. there was no single way into the blessing
4. it occurred across all denominations

Although the renewal in the Catholic Church was a significant move, it still only involved a small minority of
members. It has continued to be marginalized by church
leadership, which has resulted in relatively slow growth
compared to the development of renewal in Anglican
churches.

Renewal in Non-Conformist churches

By contrast to the situation in Anglican and Catholic
churches, the non-conformist denominations were initially
much less accommodating to the charismatic movement.
Christians who had or were seeking a 'Pentecostal' experience, were very often shown in no uncertain terms that they
were not welcome. David Lillie's story is a good example.
This reluctance to accept the new move of the Spirit sadly led
to splits in many churches.

The response of the free churches also illustrated the relationship between the Pentecostal denominations and the
rest of the church in the middle years of the twentieth
century. They were regarded as being a separate group,
somewhat removed from mainline Christianity, involved in
teachings and practices that were not accepted by the other
denominations. When God's Spirit began to move in similar
ways in the historic denominations, the Pentecostals were
naturally enough somewhat surprised and sceptical.
However, as early as 1960, one of their leaders, Donald Gee,
included the following in his address at an Assemblies of
God conference[11]:

A new era appears to be dawning for a revival of the manifestations of the Holy Spirit that for the last fifty years has been associated almost exclusively with the Pentecostal movement. Can we rise by the grace of God to the challenge and responsibility of a new situation? We must shed our complexes, bred by the ostracism of half a century, and boldly take our place alongside our brethren in Christ in the older denominations who may now surprise us by their openness to new moving of God's Spirit. To share in such a new springtime of Pentecostal grace and power will be thrilling.

With such words of wisdom, the seeds were sown for the integration of the Pentecostal denomination into the mainstream of evangelical Christianity in the United Kingdom.

Relationship between Restoration and Renewal

Despite the similarities of the early renewal and restoration movements, and the fact that they were occurring more or less at the same time, there was relatively little interaction between them. There were some attempts to get proponents of the movements together. Several of the house group fraternity, such as Denis Clark and Campbell McAlpine spoke in denominational settings during this period. Michael Harper also ran several meetings to bring the two groups together, one example being the High Leigh conference in January 1965. However these did not all go smoothly and George Tarleton[12] remembers another of Michael's meetings, which got bogged down in denominational differences over speaking in tongues. It was gradually becoming clear, that although there was a great oneness of heart and spirit regarding the charismatic experience that was common to both groups, views on the Church were fundamentally different. It is as if they were moving along parallel lines, going in the same direction, but never meeting. It is quite astonishing that there is so little cross reference in the writings from both groups dating from this period, given the degree of common ground of the work God was doing in them.

A number of different authors have tried to analyse the relationship between renewal and restoration, arriving at a variety of conclusions. The most widely held view is that restoration was part of the charismatic movement that occurred in the latter half of the twentieth century[13]. This is reasonable, given that restorationists included teaching on the baptism in the Spirit and the gifts of the Spirit among the truths being restored to the church. However, some restorationists argue that their movement should be regarded as a separate from the charismatic movement for two reasons:

1. their ideas were being discussed in small groups before the charismatic movement started to make any impact in denominational churches, and
2. the main thrust of their message was about the church, which was very different from the emphasis in renewal[14].

It seems to me that restoration should be regarded as a natural extension of the charismatic movement. If God was restoring the teaching on the Holy Spirit that had been lost over the years, why would he not also want to restore other aspects of church life mentioned in the New Testament that were missing today? This idea incorporates the similarities of the two movements, while recognising the separate nature of the restoration message.

Concluding Remarks

Both restoration and renewal movements have had a significant positive impact on the church in the UK over the last 50 years. God has brought a distinct message through the restoration movement about the scriptural nature of church. We need to hear and understand this message if we are to realise the benefits that will ensue from responding to it appropriately.

References

1. Pratney, W., 1983, *Revival – Principles to Change the World*, Whitaker House, Springdale, PA, USA.
2. Scotland, N., 2000, *Charismatics and the New Millennium: the Impact of Charismatic Christianity from 1960 into the New Millennium*, Eagle, Guildford, Surrey.
3. Lillie, David, 1994, *Restoration: Is this still on God's programme?*, Phillips and Co (The Kyrtonia ExPress), Crediton, Devon.
4. *Ibid*.
5. Watson, David, 1978, *I Believe in the Church*, Hodder and Stoughton, London, and Urquhart, Colin, 1974, *When the Spirit Comes*, Hodder and Stoughton, London.
6. Walker, Andrew, 1998, *Restoring the Kingdom – the Radical Christianity of the House Church Movement*, Eagle, Guildford, Surrey.
7. Wallis, Jonathan, 1991, *Arthur Wallis: Radical Christian*, Kingsway, Eastbourne (Quotation used by permission of Kingsway Publications, Lottbridge Drove, Eastbourne).
8. Walker, *op cit*.

9. Hocken, P., 1994, *The Glory and the Shame: Reflections on the Twentieth Century Outpouring of the Holy Spirit*, Eagle, Guildford, Surrey.

10. *Ibid*.

11. Edwards, J., 1999, *Lord, make us one but not all the same*, Hodder and Stoughton, London.

12. Tarleton, G., 1993, *Birth of a Christian Anarchist*, Pendragon Press, Lymington.

13. Scotland, *op cit*; Hocken, *op cit*.

14. Lillie, *op cit*.

CHAPTER TWO

THE EVANGELICAL INFLUENCE

In parallel with the twentieth century Pentecostal and Charismatic movements, an equally important, although less contentious development had also been underway, the growth of Evangelicalism. In reviewing the history of the restoration movement it is necessary to consider its relationship to this key development.

Defined simply, Classical Evangelicalism is the belief that the Bible is the inspired word of God and is the primary source of our understanding of Christianity[1]. It centres on the death of Christ on the cross, as being the means by which we are made right with God. We can then enter into a relationship with him, through being born again in the Holy Spirit. In academic circles around the turn of the twentieth century, liberal theologians seriously attacked these beliefs in the authority of the Bible. This resulted in the teaching at many theological establishments during the first quarter of the century, being dominated by those who took a critical view of the Bible. Many aspects of central evangelical belief were challenged, and alternative doctrines were taught. Prospective church leaders were having their faith undermined during their training, and this inevitably had its effect on the church as a whole. Most denominations were influenced by this situation. Evangelicalism was regarded as not being an intellectually viable interpretation of the Bible.

Despite these developments, there were still a number of strong evangelical churches, and as a group they began to respond to the situation. They realised that they had often been rather narrow in their interpretation of scripture, and had a tendency to be critical of others. Things started to change from the 1930s onwards. Leaders with wisdom and vision, who were convinced of the evangelical stance, began to emerge. Development occurred initially through the creation of a number of para-church organisations. Many of these were in the field of education, significant examples being the London Bible College, which began in 1943, and the development of evangelically based Christian Unions in Universities. These helped to re-establish the evangelical position as being academically acceptable. Prominent individuals in this process were Dr Martyn Lloyd-Jones and John Stott, who represented the non-conformist and Anglican wings of the evangelical movement respectively. Lloyd-Jones was a medical doctor who gave up his career for the Christian ministry, becoming affectionately known in evangelical circles as 'the Doctor'. He was an excellent communicator of the evangelical position through his inspired teaching. John Stott began his ministry as curate at All Souls' Church in Langham Place in London, and was prominent in University missions in the 1950s. Both 'the Doctor' and John Stott have made arguably their most important contributions in their prolific output of books.

Another of the parachurch organisations that emerged was the Fellowship of Independent Evangelical Churches. This had been started before the Second World War by E. J. Poole-Connor, as a forum for advice and help for evangelical churches that were not linked to a particular denomination. In many ways, its concept reflected the New Testament idea that trans-local church relationships should be primarily for support and encouragement, rather than the governmental approach taken by most denominations. In this respect it had some similarity with the ideas of the restoration movement.

By the 1960s, many non-conformist and several Anglican churches held an evangelical stance, and evangelical Christian Unions were the primary Christian group in most universities. The strong adherence to the scriptures as the basis of faith, was an important factor in the development of the charismatic and restoration movements at this time, as it had been for the Pentecostal movement 50 years previously, and as it had been for the Reformation, 400 years before that. Nearly all the early adherents to the restoration movement came from an evangelical background. Despite that, relatively few evangelicals accepted the movement as being from God in the early days, and there was considerable antagonism towards it from many established churches. Among evangelical leaders, John Stott was firmly against the movement, while Martyn Lloyd-Jones, although never firmly aligning himself with it, had a much more accepting and encouraging attitude towards it, and his influence on its development is worthy of more detailed consideration.

The Doctor

As one browses the pages of the biographies and other writings of early renewal and restorationist leaders, one cannot escape the references to the London Bible College, and in particular to 'the Doctor', who lectured there for many years. Although very much a traditional evangelical institution, and therefore in the 1960s not at all charismatic, it had a significant impact on the renewal and restoration movements. The evidence points to 'the Doctor' as being a key catalyst in bringing this about. While training as a surgeon he was called to the ministry, and although soundly evangelical was also a radical thinker. He had been filled with the Spirit in 1949, shortly after the Hebrides revival, through contact with Duncan Campbell. From his position at London Bible College and Westminster Chapel, his teaching influenced a whole generation of nonconformist ministers. Some went on to become leaders of the restoration movement, such as George Tarleton and Terry Virgo. His faithfulness to the scriptures, combined with his willingness to accept them at face value, even if that meant violating accepted evangelical beliefs, was inspiring.

His influence was not restricted to the non-conformist community; he was accepted by Anglicans as well. David Watson acknowledges the important part the Doctor had in his own path to understanding the fullness of the Spirit[2]. He recalls, in particular, the famous sermon where the Doctor examines the evangelical dogma that all the fullness of the Spirit is received at conversion.

There are some who are guilty of quenching the Spirit by limiting in their very thinking the possibilities of life in the Spirit. I am convinced that there are large numbers of Christian people who are quenching the Spirit unconsciously by denying these possibilities in their very understanding of the doctrine of the Spirit. There is nothing, I am convinced, that so quenches the Spirit as the teaching that identifies the baptism in the Holy Ghost with regeneration. But it is a very commonly held teaching today. Indeed it has been the popular view for many years. They say that the baptism of the Spirit is non-experimental, that it happens to everybody at regeneration. So we say 'Ah, well I am already baptised with the Spirit, it happened when I was born again, it happened at my conversion; I've got it all'.

'Got it all? I simply ask in the name of God, why are you then as you are? If you have got it all why are you so unlike New Testament Christians? Got it all? Got it all at your conversion! Well where is it I ask?'

In another powerful message recalled by George Tarleton,[3] the Doctor predicted that two fundamental questions would have to be answered over the following ten years: 'What is a Christian?' and 'What is the Church? As George commented, he might not have been too happy with the answers some of his students came up with, particularly with respect to the second question.

However, within evangelical circles, Martyn Lloyd-Jones was quite a radical as far as his views on the church were concerned. Until the mid-sixties, evangelicals of different persuasions had generally co-existed and co-operated quite amicably. However, a move by Lloyd-Jones at the preliminary meeting of the National Evangelical Assembly convened by the Evangelical Alliance in October 1966, changed the situation. He made a plea for evangelicals to place fellowship with fellow evangelicals above other church loyalties. This was effectively calling churches to come out of their existing denominations, and was not acceptable to everyone, in particular the Anglican evangelicals such as John Stott. This event triggered a parting of the ways of non-conformist and Anglican evangelicals to some extent. The following year, the first National Evangelical Anglican Congress was held in Keele, confirming that Anglican Evangelicals were still committed to the Church of England, and felt called to change it from within. Meanwhile, Martyn Lloyd-Jones led Westminster Chapel, where he was the minister, out of the Congregational Union and into the Fellowship of Independent Evangelical Churches.

These events are significant, not so much in their results, as a large scale breakaway of evangelicals from their denominations did not occur, but in the underlying principle which triggered them. It demonstrated that the vision for recognition of the true church from amongst the confusion of denominationalism, was on the heart of others than those of the restoration movement.

It was not only for his sermons and writing that Lloyd-Jones is remembered so well; there are many references to the personal conversations he held. He always seemed able to give wise and perceptive advice in answer to the specific questions raised by those who sought his counsel.

To members of the charismatic movement, he remains something of an enigma, in that despite his words of encouragement and support, he has always avoided close involvement with it. Having said that, one wonders whether his faithfulness to a strong evangelical stance has, in hindsight, been proved right, as the centre of gravity of evangelicalism has now clearly moved towards a charismatic position, not by a rapid revolution but by a process of gradual development.

This process of change is no more clearly typified than by events at Westminster Chapel itself following the Doctor's retirement. His successor as leader was R.T. Kendall, who led the church into the charismatic movement[4]. However, the church remained essentially a teaching centre, and RT's autobiography seems tinged with disappointment, that numbers did not increase during his time there. When he retired, the leadership passed on to Greg Haslam, who comes from a restoration background. Had RT seen that the key was not only in good teaching, but also in giving attention to building church? The rest of the story of Westminster Chapel is obviously still to be told. It will be interesting to read that next chapter.

Concluding Remarks

Both the charismatic and restoration movements were radical but natural extensions of evangelicalism. Charismatic developments were the result of evangelical Christians reading the Bible and asking questions on what it had to say about the work of the Holy Spirit. Restoration resulted from evangelical Christians reading the Bible and asking questions on what it had to say about the church.

References

1. Barclay, O., 1997, *Evangelicalism in Britain 1935–1995*, IVP, Leicester.

2. Watson, David, 1978, *I Believe in the Church*, Hodder and Stoughton, London.

3. Tarleton, G., 1993, *Birth of a Christian Anarchist*, Pendragon Press, Lymington.

4. Kendall, R.T., *In Pursuit of His Glory: My 25 Years at Westminster Chapel*, Charisma House.

CHAPTER THREE

RESTORATION ARRIVES . . . AND DIVIDES

The London Brothers[1]

In 1970, Maurice Smith arranged a series of meetings in the Leprosy Mission Hall in London. These acted as a catalyst for a number of house church leaders in the London area to come together. The central leadership consisted of Gerald Coates, George Tarleton, Dave Mansell, Maurice Smith, and John Noble, who became known as the London Brothers. They were involved, the following year, in the Festival of Light organised by Peter Hill, who was also a member of a house group. This was a demonstration by Christians against the 'permissive society', a term used to describe the relaxation in moral standards that had been occurring during the 1960s. Many Christians, both from denominational settings and the new house churches, supported the festival. In addition to conveying its message to the nation of the importance of righteousness in society, it also served to demonstrate the rapidly growing numbers of people who were part of the emerging house church movement.

The London Brothers continued to develop a co-ordinated approach, by moving their meetings to the larger venue of the London School of Economics, where around 500 people would gather together. They experienced the gifts of the Spirit in their meetings, enjoying lively praise and worship, incorporating shouting, leaping and dancing. They also prayed for deliverance of people who were thought to be possessed by demonic spirits. Their ethos was one of friendliness and openness to what God was doing.

They were also asking questions regarding the nature of the Church. They considered the real church was comprised of those who were truly born again. This was distinct from the established church, which consisted of a mixture of true believers and those whose faith was only nominal. The only divisions of the true church were geographical, with the basic unit being the church in the house. Therefore the concept of denominations was seen as wrong, and as something that prevented the church being seen as it truly was. The idea of the church as a body, with each person having their part to play, was also prominent in the teaching. These ideas were presented in a magazine called *Fullness*, which was produced by the London Brothers under the editorship of Graham Perrins.

Restoration Tries to Co-ordinate

Arthur Wallis initiated a significant change in direction of the movement in 1972, by calling a meeting of several leading men associated with church developments outside the denominational framework[2]. This pivotal meeting took place on Thursday February 8 in 1972 in the Forge House in

Talaton, Devon. The purpose of the gathering was originally
to discuss the nature of biblical prophecy. Arthur felt that an
understanding of biblical prophetic teaching, particularly
about the Kingdom of God, was an important key to understanding the significance of the church. Those who came
were Bryn Jones, Peter Lyne, David Mansell, Graham Perrins
and Hugh Thompson. The sense of God's presence was very
real during their time together, and led them to change the
emphasis of their discussions away from the interpretation of
biblical prophecy, to the importance of the prophetic ministry
in the present day. God spoke to them through words of
prophecy, that prophets would emerge to bring God's word
to the church, in vocal presentation, in writing, and through
living out what God was saying. They met twice more
that year, John Noble being added to their number for the
later gatherings. These seven leaders became known light-
heartedly as 'The Magnificent Seven'. The third of the meetings was probably the most significant, in that God spoke to
them about the need to be committed to one other as leaders.
He was not looking for individuals each doing their own
thing, but for them to be functioning together. Their example
of commitment and mutual submission would give them the
ability to teach and lead the church with authority. One of the
prophetic words included the following[3]:

> As you will teach my children by your example of commitment,
> so too will you teach them of submission, for you will teach them
> by your submission to one another. For in this my children you
> have much to learn.

The topics covered at this meeting, including the significance
of the prophetic ministry, commitment and submission, have

been, and still are, key messages of the restoration movement
and are considered in more detail in subsequent chapters.

The agreement of brothers to 'dwell together in unity'
always 'commands a blessing' (Ps 133), and so it proved in
this case. The commitment made by these seven men, who
had the common vision of restoring the church along New
Testament lines, led to the movement rapidly expanding
over the next few years. They felt it would be good to
extend their group to include other leaders of the same
heart, and were joined by George Tarleton, Gerald Coates,
Barney Coombes, Maurice Smith, Ian McCullogh, John
MacLauchlan and Campbell McAlpine. The new group
became known as the 'Fabulous Fourteen'. Although they
didn't continue with the same level of commitment and
unity as the original seven, their discussions began to con-
solidate ideas on the nature of the restored church. They
studied the passage in Ephesians, which lists five key ministries within the church (Eph 4:11-12)

> It was he who gave some to be apostles, some to be prophets,
> some to be evangelists and some to be pastors and teachers, to
> prepare God's people for the works of service, so that the body
> of Christ may be built up.

While pastors, teachers and evangelists were recognised as
valid ministries in the church at the time, where were the
apostles and prophets? Classical evangelical teaching held
that these ministries had died out once the canon of scripture
had been established. The 'Fourteen' considered that there
was no real reason for holding to this tradition, and took the
more straightforward view of scripture that apostles and

prophets were God-ordained ministries relevant for the modern day church. God had already spoken much about the role of prophets and the need of the prophetic ministry in today's church, and so they concentrated on an understanding of the apostolic ministry. They felt that scripture pointed to apostles as being foundational and that they should function in the same way as the New Testament apostles. This led to a discussion on authority in the church, and the concepts of covering and submission. Commitment to the church was seen as an integral part of commitment to Christ, and this was to include submission to the leaders, something that is clearly pointed to in scripture (1 Pet 1:1-5). The leaders were, for their part, to care for their people. This idea of covering was not only to operate within a local church, but was also to extend to leaders of local churches, who should submit to an apostolic covering in return for the wisdom and care imparted by the apostle.

Although God was speaking directly to the 'Fourteen' about the application of these ideas in the United Kingdom, they were undoubtedly influenced strongly by the teaching from Argentina, notably from Juan Carlos Ortiz, and from a group of American leaders known as the 'Fort Lauderdale Five' including, in particular, Ern Baxter.

The joining together of these leading men, and the development of their common vision provided the base from which the restoration movement was able to start rapidly expanding. A key part of this expansion was the promotion of the new ideas about church at large gatherings. The London Brothers were already holding meetings in the capital, and these grew in size and stature until they took over the Albert Hall in 1975, at a meeting attended by 9000 people. It was here that Dave Mansell made his famous remark: 'We've taken the Albert Hall tonight because we couldn't fit you all into our front room'. However, perhaps more significant on a national scale was the development of the Bible Weeks. These started with the Capel Bible Weeks in Surrey in the early 1970s. Although not officially organised by the 'Fourteen', they gave the group a platform to share their new vision, and were to prove a big influence in the rapid growth of restoration during the 1970s and early 1980s.

The difference brought about by the demonstration of the unity of the leadership at these large gatherings was a feeling of confidence. It was difficult for solid feet-on-the-ground Christians who were becoming convinced of the wisdom of this new teaching, to commit themselves to small isolated groups. Now, the teaching was out in the open, it was clear who the leaders of the movement were, and what they were preaching. It was now possible to start a new group in a local-ity, not as an isolated entity, but as one linked to an apostolic covering, who could bring wisdom and direction to the venture. Many such groups began to emerge under the cov-ering of leaders such as Bryn Jones, Gerald Coates and George Tarleton, who were recognised as apostles.

Restoration Divides

Part of the original vision of restoration related to the impor-tance of the local church. This was to be governed locally by a group of elders, linked with other groups but not part of a large denominational structure. It was clear that with the co-ordination of the movement that had occurred in the early 1970s, there was a danger of it developing into a denomination. As if to counteract this possibility, an important word of prophecy came to the 'Fourteen' in 1974, that they were to concentrate less on meeting as a national group, and more on establishing church at a local level. The commitment they had as a group to each other was to remain, but they were encouraged to reproduce the same kind of relationship structure in their locality.

Ideally, this should have happened in the context of a maintained relationship between the brothers, but sadly this did not occur. Instead, a serious division split the 'Fourteen' into two camps. There were two areas of controversy, over the issues of law and grace, and authority.

One of the emphases of the London Brothers was on the grace of God, that in Christ we were no longer under the law. From their viewpoint, this was a restoration of a New Testament truth that had been obscured by unwritten Evangelical rules against such things as drinking, dancing or Sunday activities. They were quite open about their new freedom, for example, making no secret of their liking of alcohol. Although there was no dispute among the 'Fourteen' regarding the principle of not being under law, some were unhappy with the open way that the new freedom was being displayed. The more conservative among the 'Fourteen' preferred to take the line that they should be sensitive to the feelings of other 'weaker' Christians, who might have a conscience on these matters.

The other issue that emerged, related to authority in the church. This had come up for discussion, as it was another area of church life, emphasized in the New Testament, which was perceived to be lacking, particularly in non-conformist Christianity. This had been a key aspect of the teaching brought to them through their contact with Ern Baxter and the 'Fort Lauderdale Five'. During this period they had grown to respect Ern's input. He had spoken at the 1974 Capel Bible Week, where he had been well received by everyone. The American group had already been pioneering in many of the areas that were being considered by the 'Fourteen', and it was natural to look to them as mentors.

The ethos of the 'Fourteen' had always been a gathering of equals. Arthur Wallis, who had originally convened the group, usually chaired the meetings. As the group enlarged, this responsibility was shared by Graham Perrins. However, there was no sense in which there was any additional authority invested in Arthur or Graham; that was simply their function in the gatherings. Ern Baxter was not altogether happy with the ethos of the more radical section of the 'Fourteen'. He also felt that an authority structure was needed among the group, and therefore suggested that Arthur should be recognised as their leader. This did not go down very well generally among the brothers, who did not feel that Arthur was suited to this role, and even Arthur was not sure that this was what God had in mind for him. This became a further source of tension among them.

With these underlying unresolved issues, it was perhaps not surprising that something happened to trigger a major upset. It occurred in 1976 at the South and West Bible Week in Monkton Coombe near Bath. This was organised by Peter Lyne, and supported by others of the 'Fourteen', Graham Perrins, who was leading the worship, John Noble and Arthur Wallis. Ern Baxter had been invited to speak. They were expecting a great time. However, it did not turn out that way. Ern was not at ease during the worship times, and did not have his usual anointing in preaching. In view of the difficulties, Bryn Jones was called to come down to the conference, to see if he could help out. In discussion with Arthur and Bryn, Ern explained that he felt he had been opposed by a spiritual force, when on the platform. Arthur sought God about the matter, and felt that the unease sensed by Ern, resulted from several members of the 'Fourteen' being spiritually deceived in some of their attitudes and beliefs. As Bryn was in America for some while after the Bible Week, they decided that Arthur should write a letter from them both to John Noble and Graham Perrins. This not only highlighted the differences of approach between the two groups, but also brought out the fact that they felt that the more radical brothers had got it wrong, and were not hearing from God on the issues. John Noble, Graham Perrins, and the others who were implicated in the letter, were devastated by its contents; they felt they could no longer continue to work together with Arthur and Bryn. For Arthur who had written the letter, the result was heartbreaking. He had done it as a man of integrity, declaring what he felt God had shown him. He hoped that it would restore good relationships with his brothers, and help them to walk in the light together.

The letter had the effect of separating the Restoration camp into two groups. Although a written message was probably not the best approach to resolving the issues, the lack of determination to address the problem by the more radical wing of the 'Fourteen' also contributed to the division. Arthur's action may have triggered the split, but it only revealed the disunity that was there anyway. It obviously held back the movement, in that there was a lack of coordination in the growth of new churches. In a particular locality, there were often separate groups looking for covering from leaders on either side of the divide. However, in other ways God turned the situation for good. It avoided any danger of the movement developing a hierarchy and pursuing the road to becoming a denomination. This positive outcome of the split has been acknowledged in retrospect by some of the 'Fourteen'.

Such splits have sadly characterised the growth of the church throughout the years. It seems symptomatic of beliefs that are so deeply held. G. K. Chesterton argued that these divisions are in some ways positive, in that they demonstrate the passion and reality of the underlying faith[4]. However, while one can see his point, it is impossible to forget the prayer of Jesus in John 17 that 'his followers would be one as he and the Father were one' (John 17:20-23). There is surely a place where both passion and unity are to be found. I think it is true to say that progress has been made toward this, both in restoration circles and in the church in the UK as a whole, during the years following these events. Although there has continued to be a variety of expressions of the work of God over this period, there has also been a growing sense of mutual respect of the various ways in which God is working amongst different people and different groups. This can only be helpful in our progress together towards unity.

References

1. Walker, Andrew, 1998, *Restoring the Kingdom – the Radical Christianity of the House Church Movement*, Eagle, Guildford, Surrey.

2. Wallis, Jonathan, 1991, *Arthur Wallis: Radical Christian*, Kingsway, Eastbourne (Quotation used by permission of Kingsway Publications, Lottbridge Drove, Eastbourne).
3. *Ibid.*
4. Chesterton, G.K., *Orthodoxy*, Hodder and Stoughton, London, 1996. First published 1908.

CHAPTER FOUR

RESTORATION SPREADS

Apostolic Teams and Resource Churches

The restoration movement was highlighting a number of long-neglected aspects of church life referred to in scripture. Even the serious division that occurred in 1976 could not prevent it from continuing to grow rapidly over the next ten years. The split was however a defining moment, affecting the nature of future developments. There would now be no more co-ordination of the movement at a national level. This had the advantage of avoiding the constraints that would have been imposed by a central organisation, and gave the opportunity for natural growth to occur. It also meant that the word of prophecy that came to the 'Fourteen', encouraging them to concentrate on the local implementation of restoration ideas, could now be carried out.

One of the problems in trying to track the history of the restoration movement is the difficulty of defining what it actually consisted of. The division in 1976 meant that it would never establish an official national identity, and never produce a doctrinal statement. Therefore, it has not been easy to analyse and summarise what has happened.

Andrew Walker has tried to describe the history of the movement following the division, by considering it in terms of two groups, R1 representing the leaders and churches associated with Bryn Jones and Arthur Wallis, and R2 being those associated with the London Brothers[1]. Nigel Scotland in his summary of restoration follows the same nomenclature, but uses a slightly different definition. He refers to all churches not specifically aligned with Bryn Jones as being in R2[2]. This means, for example, that some groups are not clearly classified as being in R1 or R2. Examples are the churches linked to Terry Virgo and Tony Morton. Terry and Tony were leaders who emerged during the 1970s with churches based around Brighton and Southampton respectively. They both had strong links with Bryn, but were both soon recognised as apostles in their own right, independent from Bryn's team. Therefore they fall into R1 according to Andrew Walker's classification, whereas they come under the heading of R2 according to Nigel Scotland. This illustrates that, while there are useful things that can be learnt from this analysis, the complexity of the relationships between restoration leaders means that it is not an entirely satisfactory way to understand the history of the movement. Even Andrew Walker himself admits for example that it is rather difficult to see R2 as an entity.

I think it is somewhat easier to see restoration after 1976 as a collection of essentially independent groups or families of churches, each based around one of the apostolic teams. Several of the leaders who had been part of the 'Fourteen', began to develop teams of workers to help with the establishment and support of churches with whom they were involved. This was based on the pattern of operation of apostles in the New Testament. Paul, for example, was involved in a number of churches, so it was not possible for him to spend sufficient time actually being present in all of them. Therefore he gathered a team of workers around him such as Silas and Timothy. This meant that there were more people, and also a greater variety of people with different strengths and abilities, available to visit the churches. Restorationists, wanting to follow this biblical pattern, developed teams along similar lines. A church that came under the covering of an apostle and his team effectively became part of this family of churches.

Another important concept that emerged was that of a resource church. This idea was modelled on the New Testament picture of the church at Antioch, from which Paul and Barnabas were sent on their apostolic missions. It was considered important for an apostolic team to be supported by a local church, and their base became known as an apostolic or resource church.

While these different families of churches had the common goal of restoring a genuine New Testament mode of church life, there were clearly differences in interpretation of what that biblical pattern actually was. The lack of overall structure and control gave freedom to the individual apostolic teams to follow what they felt was the correct approach. There were also relationships between the different teams, the strength of which depended both on the style of church life preferred by the leadership, and also on personal friendships between the leaders. The history of restoration illustrates many changes of allegiance amongst the leaders, based on both these factors. Andrew Walker's book covers many of these developments in leaders' relationships over the period. It is interesting to reflect on how this parallels the situation in the Acts of the Apostles, where differences in personality and in interpretation of Jesus' teaching, were both clearly problems of the growing New Testament church. The tension between Paul and Peter, for example, was a result of both these factors.

In 1976, the group of leaders known as the 'Fabulous Fourteen' represented the majority of significant developments in restoration at that time, but by no means did they represent all that God was doing. Key people in the movement, not part of that group, were already implementing restoration principles. David Lillie, for example, an important figure in the formative days, was leading a house church in Exeter. He had his own misgivings about being associated with the 'Fourteen', having concern over their interpretation of scripture, particularly regarding their description of the role of apostles. Similarly Roger Forster who had also been around since the beginning, had started the Ichthus Fellowship in 1974, independently of the 'Fourteen'. The combination of these individual groups, added to the fragmentation of the 'Fourteen', meant that by the mid-seventies there was a great diversity within restoration.

What follows is a description of a number of the larger apostolic teams within the Restoration movement.

Bryn Jones and Harvestime

Bryn Jones headed the earliest major example of an apostolic team emerging from the modern day restoration movement in the UK. In many ways it set the scene for much of the subsequent development. Bryn established a church in Bradford during the early 1970s and this provided the base or resource church for the team's development. Bryn also gathered together a group of men with a variety of gifts including Hugh Thompson, a man with teaching ability and Dave Mansell, a prophet. This was developed into an apostolic team, whose primary function was to establish and support churches both in the UK and also abroad.

The team began to develop links in different places around the UK. These were typically with groups of Christians who were responding to the new teaching about church life, and were thinking of starting up a church in their own area along these lines. The group would first approach the team for advice on how to progress with their idea. Members of the team then met with the leaders of the new group to establish the details of who was in the group and their backgrounds. The team then prayed about the situation, asking God for wisdom on how to proceed. They would consider the resources of the group itself, particularly looking for potential leaders. Only when they were happy that a viable group could be formed, and that a mutually agreeable working relationship had been established, was the advice given that people should leave their existing church to form a new fellowship. The degree of covering that could be provided depended on practical geographical considerations, and on the level of independence they felt happy to release to the group. Members of the team visited the new group, and led and spoke at their gatherings, so that all the people could get to know who was providing their covering. They also met with leaders to discuss strategy for the group. Normally these new churches started life as a meeting in someone's home. However, as the church grew and new house groups were added or created, encouragement was given for them to work together under a common leadership, and also to meet together. This usually became the main Sunday gathering, which would typically take place in a hired school hall. When the team felt that the leadership pattern in the church was developed, the new leaders were officially recognised before the congregation. Usually after a further period of evaluation, elders would be appointed, and the church would enjoy a new level of autonomy.

By nature Bryn was a good organiser, and this was reflected in the operation of his apostolic team. This characteristic, coupled with a desire to implement the teaching on authority and submission, which was an important emphasis of restoration teaching in these early days, meant that there tended to be a good degree of order within the family of churches that emerged. However, to think of the churches under Bryn operating under an overbearing rule is misleading. I was part of one of the groups from which Southampton Community church emerged and was involved in the preparatory meetings with Bryn and Dave Mansell. The early development followed quite closely to the pattern I have described above. Initially we looked to Bryn and his team for apostolic covering. His input to us was always full of care and wisdom. He was a positive leader, but as a church consisting primarily of young Christians, we needed that kind of help. The concept of recognising the authority of leaders and of submitting to them, was part of the teaching and culture in the church. However, this rarely strayed into undue authoritarianism. Within a few years, elders were appointed in the church, and after a further few years, Bryn was happy to recognise one of our leaders, Tony Morton, as an apostle in his own right. A fuller version of this story will be covered in the next chapter.

A number of important developments took place within Bryn's apostolic team, which would become commonplace in other teams that emerged subsequently. The resource church needed to be large and therefore ideally required a building. This could also provide the offices for full time team members. The Bradford church accordingly purchased Church House in the centre of Bradford in 1977. It also developed commercially, acquiring the name Harvestime. While the main aim of all aspects of the work was the promotion of the gospel, several of the projects initiated by Harvestime also helped to support the growing team financially. For example, the coffee shop gave rise to evangelistic opportunities but also made money. Training of new leaders was seen as a very important aspect of the work, and a correspondence course called School of the Word was produced. This was followed by the establishment of Riddlesden College near Keighley not far from Bradford, which provided a residential leadership training programme.

Bryn's team also began to move into the international arena. From the beginning, opportunities had arisen for them to go on overseas visits, where they began to extend their apostolic church-planting ministry in other countries. This consisted mainly of short-term trips to speak at churches and to meet with leaders to offer advice. In some cases however, the visits were much longer, and the team member would move home and family to the new location for a period of a couple of years or even longer. Peter Parris and Bryn himself went on extended visits to the USA to help the development of churches in the 1970s. This was to set a pattern, which was followed by the other apostolic teams that emerged.

In many ways these can be seen as natural developments of a group hoping to carry out the function of an apostolic team in the twentieth century. However, they also served to change the face of restoration quite dramatically, from the simple concept of Christians meeting together in homes for fellowship and encouragement, to the formation of multi-million pound business ventures and large citywide churches. Several other teams began to emerge starting from the mid 1970s, most significantly those led by Gerald Coates and Terry Virgo. While all the teams have their own distinct flavour, many aspects of their basic mode of operation owe much to Bryn's example. Bryn sadly died in 2003, but his significant contribution to the development of restoration ideas both in the UK and on the international scene will long be remembered.

Pioneer

Gerald Coates from Cobham emerged as the leader of another of the early apostolic teams. He was originally part of a Brethren assembly, but after being baptised in the Holy Spirit in the late 1960s, he began to meet with a few like-minded Christians in his front room. The group grew under Gerald's guidance to the extent that his leadership qualities were recognised on a wider scale, and he became one of the 'London Brothers'. At this stage in the development of restoration, there was an emphasis on understanding the

New Testament teaching on the Kingdom of God. This was seen as being outworked in an 'alternative society', which would consist of committed relationships, community and discipleship. In recognition of this aim, Gerald's group in Cobham was first named Kingdom Life. He was one of the 'Fabulous Fourteen' that met together in the early to mid 1970s to consider how the new truths that God was bringing to the church should be implemented. Among the variety of viewpoints represented in that group, Gerald was clearly part of its radical wing. He was strong on teaching about the grace of God, and that we were no longer under the Law.

After the 'Fourteen' split up, Gerald continued to be a significant voice, influencing the direction in which restorationism developed. He advocated an increased emphasis on the church being outgoing, both in its relationships with other Christians, and in evangelism. He put less stress on authority and submission in the relationship between himself as the apostle and the churches he covered. In order to reflect these changing values, his growing apostolic team was renamed Pioneer. The new name was in many ways prophetic, as the changes instituted in Gerald's team typified what was happening elsewhere in the restoration movement. During the 1980s, many restoration churches followed Gerald's lead, with less emphasis on internal church matters, and considerably more on outreach and mission. Some observers, such as Andrew Walker, have described these developments in terms of the emergence of new churches, as distinct from the earlier restoration churches. Using this analysis it is not unreasonable to think of Gerald as the founder of the new church concept. It seems to me, however, that most of the things that Gerald introduced were not radically new concepts, but a different emphasis. He built on what was already established, but added a balance that had been lacking in the early days of restoration.

The home page of the Pioneer web-site does not mention the word restoration, but it does mention church-planting, cell churches and discipleship, all central themes of restoration[3]. It comments that much of Pioneer's work happens at a local level and is resourced by individual churches, again reflecting the heart of the restoration message. Pioneer is still actively involved in caring for and establishing new churches around the UK and elsewhere in the world. There is also a clear emphasis on reaching out, which includes a commitment to social action, as well as just sharing the good news of the gospel. Pioneer also describes itself as an association of ministries, leaders and initiators, providing a home for individuals with national and international ministries. This emphasis on support as opposed to government is now common among apostolic teams around the UK. Again Pioneer does not use the term apostolic in its description but that is clearly what it is.

New Frontiers International

If ever there was a story of a local boy who made good, then Terry Virgo's is that story. The full version, which makes an excellent read, is found in *No well worn paths*[4]. Terry was brought up in Brighton and is still based there today despite his international ministry.

He became a Christian in his teens, and initially went to a local Baptist church. He had a slow start to his Christian life, continuing for a while with his old life of drinking and parties. However, one day he made a clear decision to change direction in his life. He got involved in church life, and started to read the Bible and other Christian books as he commuted to work in London. He began to hear about the baptism in the Holy Spirit, but like many in the church at that time, was confused by the different viewpoints. However, while praying with some other young people from a Pentecostal church, he experienced a touch from God, which convinced him of its relevance to Christians today. It was at this time that Terry's ministry began to emerge. He shared his experience in the small group with whom he had been meeting, and very soon they had all been baptised in the Holy Spirit. As he became more involved in church life, he began to feel that God was calling him to leave his employment. In June 1963 he resigned from his job.

This started a period of 'living by faith', which he spent mainly in evangelism in the Brighton area. It was also a time for him to learn some practical lessons of the Christian life in preparation for what lay ahead. In 1965, this preparation entered a new phase, when he felt God lead him to sign up for three years training at the London Bible College. The time proved beneficial, not only in what he learned about the Bible, but also because whilst there, he met and then married Wendy. He also had his first encounter with restoration. He was invited to a house church that met near to the college in Buckingham Street. The sense of God's presence and the friendliness of these meetings made such an impact on Terry, that he determined that he would not settle for the well-worn path of a traditional church life.

At the end of their time at LBC, Terry and Wendy were invited to take on the leadership of an evangelical free church in Seaford, a few miles outside Brighton. At that time, it was not a charismatic church, but even though Terry explained his stance on the baptism and gifts of the Holy Spirit, they still wanted him to come. God blessed their time at the church, although it was certainly not all plain sailing. In common with what was happening in many churches around the country at that time, there was tension between those who were coming into a charismatic experience and those who felt this was not of God. Over a period of several years, God used Terry to transform this traditional evangelical church into one that was not only charismatic, but also moving in restoration principles. He was developing into a strong leader, but combined this with an understanding of human nature, which allowed people time to catch his vision and come with him. This powerful combination has continued to prove the basis for developing what has become the largest of the apostolic teams in the UK.

During his time at Seaford, two other significant developments occurred, which set the scene for the expansion of Terry's influence. Whenever he got the chance, Terry went to the meetings that were being organised by the emerging group of restoration leaders in the 1970s. These meetings envisioned him with the new concepts of church life that God was revealing at that time. Terry invited several of them back to Seaford, and they had a significant impact on the church. The second new development was that Terry began to receive invitations from other churches and groups in the Sussex area, to help them in their development. In this way, Terry's apostolic ministry slowly but naturally began to emerge. Terry was not officially part of the 'Fabulous Fourteen' leaders that met during the early 1970s, but he was

invited to some of their meetings just prior to the group splitting up. After the division occurred, he felt more aligned to
Arthur Wallis and Bryn Jones, and continued to meet mainly
with them, although he still saw Gerald Coates from time to
time at Capel advisers meetings. When the Capel Bible Week
closed down in the mid 1970s, Bryn commenced the Dales
Bible Week and Terry shared in its leadership.

Events now began to gather momentum rapidly. Terry
had always felt God calling him to the Brighton area, and
sensed that it would be more strategic for him to be based in
Brighton itself rather than in Seaford, which was outside the
main centre. The opportunity arose to lead a group of
Christians who were considering splitting off from their
Baptist church in Hove over the charismatic issue. They had
asked Terry for help, and he felt he should take on the leadership of the group. His family moved from Seaford to Hove
in 1978, leaving the thriving church that had been established. Another development that occurred around this
time, was Bryn Jones' encouragement to Terry to gather a
team around him, to help serve the growing number of
churches that were looking to him for support. He followed
this advice, and the team of leaders that developed was
given the name of Coastlands. Developments then followed
the pattern pioneered by Bryn Jones and Harvestime. The
church in Hove acquired a building and grew rapidly,
becoming a resource church and providing a good base for
the growing apostolic team. In 1979 they held the first
Downs Bible Week at Plumpton Race Course in Sussex.

Up until this time, Terry had been happy that he and his
team were able to provide help to churches that sought his
assistance. He had never seen them as being joined together

in a more formal way; he did not consider them as Coastlands churches. In fact he had resisted the idea that they should be. However, God began speaking through a series of prophetic words. These focused on the need for change in order to accommodate the growing work, and in particular, on the strength that would come from working more closely together. As a result of considering these words, he felt that it was right to move on to a new phase in their development; the apostolic team was to become a family of churches. When the move was shared with the leaders, it was received well and all the churches that had been helped by the team were happy to relate to them on the new basis. This development, however, was quite significant from a theological point of view. It can be argued that it was moving away from the picture of an apostolic team portrayed in Acts, to a mode of operation more like a denomination. The move was marked by a change of name from Coastlands to New Frontiers. Churches that were with Terry were now firmly New Frontiers churches. As Terry's ministry extended overseas, the name was changed again to New Frontiers International (NFI).

Whatever the scriptural validity of the concept of a family of churches, Terry's strategy was to prove extremely successful. He had built slowly at the beginning, but had laid down a solid foundation, which was able to receive the remarkable growth that was to follow. Church leaders wanting to make the transition of their church to a New Testament pattern were naturally drawn to Terry and New Frontiers International. Terry was a solid man of God, clearly biblically based, sensible, and with a balance of strength and humility. NFI reflected all these values and represented a secure base to which they could transfer their allegiance to escape the limitations of their existing denomination. It is not difficult to see the reasons for the success of NFI.

More expansion ensued on both a local and a national scale. The Hove church soon outgrew its building. It then divided into small congregations covering the Brighton and Hove area, before coming together again in a new much larger building in Brighton. Up to the end of the 1980s, Terry's vision had been primarily to support churches in the South of England. However at the beginning of the 1990s, he felt God speak to him about expanding across the nation, and set out to establish a number of churches across the country, particularly in the Midlands. In keeping with this more national emphasis, the Downs Bible Week was closed down, to be replaced in 1991 by the Stoneleigh Bible Week. This was held on the National Agricultural Showground near Coventry, and had considerably better facilities than the Plumpton Racecourse. The week expanded to two weeks in 1995, by which time the event was attracting around 20,000 people.

The success of Terry and NFI in the UK inevitably made an impact on the international scene. He became a regular traveller to many countries, both speaking at conferences, and being asked to give support and advice to churches. At one stage, between 1993 and 1995 he moved with his family to America, in order to spend two years helping out a church in Columbia, Missouri. However, as time progressed, NFI became uncomfortable with the 'international' label in their title and, in 2003, reverted back to their old name, but now written as 'Newfrontiers'.

Terry is genuinely a modern day apostle, and his story is not yet fully written. The Stoneleigh Bible Week closed down, not because it has been unsuccessful, but because God guided them to do it. This perhaps points to one of the main reasons that Terry has been successful. He has been willing to hear God, and be obedient to that voice. It will be interesting to follow the next chapter in his exciting saga.

Salt and Light Ministries

The three teams that we have considered in some detail, have had perhaps the largest influence on a national scale. They also represent the spectrum of operational styles within what one might call the mainstream developments of restoration. They do however, only represent part of the story. One of a number of other significant teams is Salt and Light ministries, which emerged from the work of Barney Coombes. His involvement in Restoration began when he successfully led the transition of Basingstoke Baptist Church in Hampshire from being a traditional evangelical church, to one operating on restoration principles. He also built a team around him that became known as Salt and Light Ministries. On their website the team is described as 'an international family of leaders and churches who have been drawn together by a common desire to see the Body of Christ grow to be all God wants it to be'[5]. Barney himself is referred to as someone 'widely received for his apostolic ministry and as a pastor of pastors.' Their ethos is somewhat similar to that of New Frontiers. Their mission statement emphasises the Kingdom of God and the church more than evangelism and outreach. This does not mean they are not active these areas as they have a range of outreach projects. However, they do seem to have stayed closer to the original vision of the priority being the establishment of the Kingdom of God.

Ground Level

Another important apostolic team is Ground Level led by Stuart Bell. Stuart started a house group mainly of young people in the early 1970s in Lincoln, which grew to become the Lincoln New Life church. The apostolic team developed in the late seventies when leaders began to gather regularly from around Lincolnshire, Humberside and Norfolk for times of sharing and prayer. It became officially known as the Ground Level Ministry team under the leadership of Stuart in 1987. It has now grown from concentrating specifically on the 'Humber to Wash' region, to serving other areas of the UK and overseas[6]. The team vision emphasises the fivefold ministry of apostles, prophets, pastors, teachers and evangelists mentioned in Ephesians 4. They do have a list of churches, which are part of their network, but the emphasis is on being in partnership with the churches rather than having a ruling role. They offer support and care to church leaders and aim to help equip them to fulfil their calling. This is fulfilled in part by monthly leaders days, and also through the annual Grapevine 'bible weekend' held at the Lincolnshire Showground over the August Bank Holiday.

Cornerstone (c-net)

Cornerstone developed under Tony Morton, based around the Community Church in Southampton[7]. The church started in the mid seventies when several groups around the city, which had a common vision for the establishment of a New Testament church, agreed to join together. Initially they looked for apostolic help to Bryn Jones. The church grew rapidly and Tony emerged as the principal leader. Bryn continued to have some input to the church for a few years during which Tony's apostolic calling was demonstrated, as several churches around the Southampton area were established. Tony was officially recognised in his apostolic role in 1981. Since then the network expanded and acquired its up-to-date name of c-net. As with the other teams, there was an initial concentration on the local area, which subsequently grew to be nationwide and international. Sadly Tony left the ministry in 2004 and the c-net network disbanded. All the churches and projects that were part of the network continued, but they were simply no longer joined under the same grouping. I have been involved with the Southampton church from the beginning and more detail on its development is given in the next chapter.

Ichthus

Ichthus Christian Fellowship and its associated apostolic team are led by Roger Forster. Roger obtained a degree in Maths and Theology at Cambridge, and after a period in the Royal Air Force, became an itinerant evangelist. Ichthus started in 1974 with 14 people. Their aim was to plant churches. They developed rapidly, first in London and the surrounding counties, subsequently expanding across the UK and to other nations. Their emphases are on love for God and each other, humility and openness to the Holy Spirit and evangelism. The strong focus on evangelism perhaps marks them out as a little different from some of the other restoration groups. Indeed, although Roger attended some of the very early meetings of the restoration movement in the late 1950s and early 1960s, he does not appear to have associated very closely with its rapid phase of development in the 1970s when restoration leaders were coming together. However, Ichthus believes that evangelisation is to be carried out by 'planting, growing and linking churches in which every member will be taking an active part'[8]. Thus their ethos and operational style are very similar to those of other restoration teams. Another feature of Roger Forster and Ichthus is that they have stayed somewhat closer to the mainstream of UK Christianity than many of the other restoration groups. ICF is not only a member of Evangelical Alliance but also of Churches Together in England. Roger and his wife Faith have been prominent in the evangelical Spring Harvest Bible weeks.

Vineyard

The Vineyard group of churches was founded in the United States but has transferred very successfully across to the UK. It is almost synonymous with the legendary John Wimber, although interestingly he did not found it. John Wimber was raised in California and on leaving school became a professional musician where his claim to fame was involvement in promoting the internationally successful duo, the Righteous Brothers. He and his wife, Carol, became Christians in 1963 and joined an independent Quaker community at Yorba Linda. He gradually moved away from the music business, and in 1970 signed up for a course in Biblical Studies at

Azusa Pacific College, graduating in 1973. During this time
he served as co-pastor of the Quaker group. However, in
1975 he ended his pastorate, and became involved with
Peter Wagner in the Fuller School of World Mission in
Pasadena. Around this time, his wife Carol became filled
with the Spirit, and started to organise a meeting in their
home. The Quaker community did not accept the charismatic leanings of this new group, and they left to become a
separate fellowship. John became the leader in 1977. He was
initially still uncertain about the place of the supernatural in
the Christian life. However, God spoke to him very clearly
over the issue of healing, and he introduced praying for
healing into their meetings. Progress was initially slow – it
took ten months of prayer to see their first healing! However,
it eventually came, and John learned a lot through the
process[9].

The church grew rapidly, reaching around 5000 members
in 1983, by which time they had moved their meetings to a
warehouse complex in Anaheim, still in the Los Angeles
area. The congregation joined a small group of six other
churches called Vineyards led by Ken Gullicksen. This grew
with the addition of the charismatic Wimber, who took over
the leadership of the group in due course.

Around this time, John Wimber was already becoming
known internationally. He was arousing interest with his
teaching on the miraculous gifts of the Spirit. He majored on
how God's people could be equipped for the work of the
ministry, and on the value of the miraculous in evangelism.
His introduction to the UK came when he met David Watson
at the Fuller Seminary in 1981. He initially visited David
Watson in York and David Pytches at another renewed

Anglican congregation, St Andrews in Chorleywood. This led to a large conference being held at Westminster Central Hall in October 1984. This was followed up over the next few years with further large-scale events at different locations around the UK. The conferences were characterised by the distinctive worship style. There tended to be fewer of the noisy, lively songs, that were normally an important part of charismatic worship. Instead, there was more emphasis on drawing close to God, and encountering his presence, and this was reflected in the quieter, soft rock style of the music. There is no doubt that he had a great influence on the UK church scene, particularly on the renewal movement, which he gave a much-needed boost during the 1980s.

He also had an influence on restoration churches, primarily through his friendship with Terry Virgo. They first met at the 1984 conference in Westminster Central Hall, and became good friends. John invited Terry to visit him in California, and also asked him, in view of his experience with Bible week organisation, if he would be willing to administer a conference for him. Terry was pleased to do this, and over the next few years, five conferences were held in Brighton. These conferences not only gave further opportunity for people in the UK to hear John Wimber's message of encouragement, but also helped the process of reconciliation between renewal and restoration that was taking place during the 1980s. John Wimber was well accepted in renewal circles, particularly by charismatic Anglicans. They now saw him working together with a restorationist, whom they had previously held at arms length. As they observed Terry at these conferences and heard him speak, they realised that their previous worries were quite unfounded. The barriers were beginning to be broken down. Terry was now invited to speak at Spring Harvest and write articles for denominational magazines. He was also a significant influence on John Wimber himself, through his powerful teaching on the grace of God.

However, perhaps John Wimber's most important contribution to the UK church scene, was in the establishment of the Vineyard churches. In 2005, 70 churches were listed as being part of the Association of Vineyard Churches in this country[10]. Vineyard represents an interesting variant of new church operation. The style and ethos of the churches are very similar to restoration and other new churches. However, they unashamedly describe themselves as a denomination, with an extensive set of by-laws. John Wimber felt that this regulated approach was the most responsible way to care for churches that came within his sphere. Restorationists and indeed most evangelical Christians would go along with most of what is covered in the by-laws in terms of the basic beliefs. The emphasis on pastoral care and accountability has strong echoes of the restoration message. Where many restorationists would differ is in the very prescriptive ordering of church life that is presented. One interesting aspect of the by-laws, is that it is the church pastors that are linked to Vineyard; the churches are considered part of the association by virtue of the pastor's commitment. Like NFI, the rapid numerical growth seems to be associated with the security offered by a well-structured organisation. The approach of the Vineyard in this respect has similarities to several of the other large new apostolic churches that have developed in the United States[11]. However it is the only one to have had a significant impact in the UK.

John Wimber's ministry has been described as being part of a 'third wave' of the move of the Holy Spirit, the first two being the Pentecostal and Charismatic movements. In retrospect, this is perhaps going a little too far – if it was a new wave, then it was certainly far smaller than the first two. He did not introduce any new concepts to Christian thinking. The signs and wonders ministry, which was a central part of his message, had also been an important component in both of the other movements. The importance of equipping all Christians for ministry was also already part of the restoration message. What John Wimber brought were ways of accessing and making real the supernatural aspects of the Holy Spirit. He was able to communicate faith to people, so that they could not only receive the benefits of these gifts from God themselves, but also learn to use them for the benefit of others. His teaching has certainly helped encourage many, particularly in the renewal movement, to believe that God still intends these gifts to be used in the Church today. However, while expectation of the miraculous is now much more widespread among evangelical Christians, we are still seeing much less of it in UK churches than in many other parts of the world. The style of worship and indeed many of the actual songs emerging from Vineyard, have also been widely adopted. However, John's most lasting contribution to the UK church is in the establishment of the Vineyard churches. These are growing both in number and in size, and therefore in their influence on the UK Christian scene. While clearly a separate denomination, they are very open to local inter-church initiatives, and have a strong commitment to reaching out.

The Jesus Fellowship Church (Jesus Army)

The Jesus Fellowship Church is a unique branch of the restoration movement. Its lifestyle incorporates not only the aspects of New Testament church life recovered by other restoration churches, but also the aspect of community living. Other restoration and renewal churches have experimented in this area, but have generally found it a difficult road. David Watson, for example, gives us the benefit of his experience in *I Believe in the Church*[12]. Although feeling that this was part of New Testament Christianity, he found it very difficult to implement. The Jesus Fellowship Church has shown that it is possible in modern day western society to operate a Christian community lifestyle.

The church started when renewal hit the Baptist Chapel at Bugbrooke in Northamptonshire in the 1970s. Like many of the similar groups that emerged at that time, they were full of love for one another and had a desire to take a fresh look at the way the New Testament described church life. To quote from their web-site[13]:

> Around 1973 some families took in a single or two and started living in 'extended families'. Someone had the idea of buying food in bulk at the cash and carry, then sharing it around the church, as a way of living more simply and leaving more money for God's work. There was a notice board in chapel where people could pin notes: 'Sheila needs a sofa', 'Fred has time to mow lawns on Fridays', 'Barry has a carpet to give away'. We were starting to share what we had (Heb 13:16).
>
> Suddenly Acts 2 and 4 came alive! The first Christians had shared everything in common. The love of Jesus had abolished the social injustice of 'haves' and 'have-nots'. Here was a new

culture, a 'city on a hill', a 'Zion of God', where brotherhood and equality reigned. We were already half way there, so shared community living was the next logical step. So as God provided the funds, we bought one or two larger properties, and folk sold up their own homes and moved in.

That was in 1974, since then we have grown to the point where there are around 80 community houses, large and small spread over much of the UK. The road hasn't been easy, but it has certainly been blessed by God.

The community is known as the New Creation Christian Community. It exists as part of the overall Jesus Fellowship Church. Members of the church may opt to live in one of the community houses, but do not have to. There are around 2,500 members in the overall church, of whom around 700 are also part of the Community. Their statement of faith is that of a bible-believing, evangelical and charismatic church. They belong to the Evangelical Alliance. They have developed a sound financial basis for operating as community, which allows people to choose whether to join, and also the opportunity to leave if they wish to. Members have also created a number of small businesses, which have helped to give people employment. One interesting aspect of the Jesus Army is that they do not give great prominence to a single leader. They clearly must have gifted leaders, who have both radical vision and the ability to build church, but the focus of their message is not on them, but on Jesus and on the church that has developed. That seems very healthy to me.

The alternative society that they have pioneered, has captured an aspect of New Testament church, which has eluded other restoration groups. Initially, the radical nature of the Jesus Army was even viewed with some scepticism by other restorationists. However, they have passed the test of time. Whether it is possible and right for the whole church to live is this style is still debatable, but they have certainly presented us with a challenge; we cannot simply write off the present-day possibility of 'holding all things in common' as in the early church.

Concluding Remarks

The split early on in the history of restoration did not prevent the development of strong churches over the following 20 years. There are clearly a variety of styles of implementation of the restoration message, and emphases have changed as the movement has progressed, but it has certainly made its mark on the UK church scene. To gain some more insight on its impact at a personal level, the next chapter describes my own journey through this period, and in particular, the development of the Community Church in Southampton, which I have been part of since it began.

References

1. Walker, Andrew, 1998, *Restoring the Kingdom – the Radical Christianity of the House Church Movement*, Eagle, Guildford, Surrey.
2. Scotland, N., 2000, *Charismatics and the New Millennium: the Impact of Charismatic Christianity from 1960 into the New Millennium*, Eagle, Guildford, Surrey.
3. Pioneer web site <www.pioneer.org.uk>.
4. Virgo, Terry, 2001, *No Well-Worn Paths*, Kingsway Publications, Eastbourne.

5. Salt and Light web site <www.saltandlight.u-net.com>.

6. Ground Level web site <www.groundlevel.org.uk>.

7. Southampton Community Church web site <www. newcommunity.org.uk>.

8. Ichthus web site <www.ichthus.org.uk>.

9. Wimber, John, and Springer, Kevin, 1986, *Power Healing*, Hodder and Stoughton, London.

10. Vineyard web site <www.vineyardchurchesuk.com>.

11. Wagner, C. Peter, 1998, *The New Apostolic Churches*, Regal Books, Gospel Light, Ventura, California.

12. Watson, David, 1978, *I Believe in the Church*, Hodder and Stoughton, London.

13. Jesus Army web site <www.jesus.org.uk> (Permission to use quotation from website given by Jesus Fellowship Church).

CHAPTER FIVE

A TALE OF THREE CHURCHES

This chapter is the story of my own journey through the years in which the restoration movement was developing. It helps to show how the movement affected a typical individual at the time it was happening.

The 'Cong'

I wouldn't say that I am an emotional person by nature, but whenever someone mentions Chingford, or I revisit the town, my heart skips a little beat. Chingford is an unremarkable London suburb, but it's where I grew up, and will always be special to me for the happy memories of my youth. It is located on the north-east edge of London's suburban sprawl. To the south is continuous settlement right to the centre of the city, while to the north is Epping Forest. There is actually a clearly defined row of houses that mark the edge of London. Chingford thus has the advantages of being close to the life and culture of one of the largest and most interesting cities in the world, and to some very beautiful forest land. Like any town, it has its claim to fame and infamy. Norman Tebitt was its MP for many years, and it is the family home of the Kray twins – the family grave is in Chingford cemetery. More recently, there have been two television documentaries on the town, one covering its general history, and one on David Beckham, the Manchester United and England footballer who spent his formative years in the town. It was also one of the first places in the country to be impacted by the restoration movement.

My family moved to Chingford when I was five and soon after, started attending South Chingford Congregational Church. My parents were Baptist by background, but the 'Cong' was only two minutes walk from our house, it was evangelical and had good youth organisations. At a very early age, I was therefore introduced to the concept that the denomination of a church was less important than being with God's people in one's locality. The church building provided a modern, pleasant setting for the main meetings, but the part of the site with the fondest memories for me was the green corrugated-iron church hall at the back. There were events happening in that hall every day of the week and, during my teenage years, I spent a good proportion of my evenings there. Though only having a membership of around 100, the church ran a Sunday School from ages 5–16, Boys Brigade, Girl Guides and Young People's Fellowship (YPF). They also visited hospitals and old people's homes on a regular basis, as well as supporting several missionaries.

Every Sunday we went to Sunday School, which I was never very keen on. The alternative of playing football seemed much more attractive. However, it gave me a good basis of biblical knowledge, which has been of great benefit in my Christian life. I joined the Lifeboys (the junior version of the Boy's Brigade) at the age of eight and stayed with the BB until I went away to university at 18. Even then I used to go away with them to summer camp, until I finally moved away from Chingford in 1971. Looking back, I am extremely grateful to the many people who worked so hard to run the BB company, the 28th Waltham Forest. They gave us so much practical help and fun, as well as introducing us to the gospel. The downside for most of us was wearing uniforms and doing drill parade, but by belonging I learnt to play the drum, about nature in a wayfaring class, first aid, and gymnastics. Then of course, most importantly, there was the football; we had a game on most Saturdays during the season.

The stated aim of the Boys Brigade was the advancement of Christ's kingdom among boys, and in our company that aim was on the hearts of all the leaders. We heard the gospel clearly in our bible class on a Sunday, and by being in the BB, we were part of the church environment, and many of us became Christians. Although this type of organisation does still exist today, they don't really have the same role in society. There are now specialist groups outside the church for those interested in gymnastics and football, and it's all done more professionally than most churches could or should try to do. Even in the 1960s, the cultural relevance of the BB and similar organisations was diminishing. However, I can only testify that it was good for me, and has left me with a profound sense of well being about my upbringing in the church.

There was also the Young People's Fellowship (YPF). This was particularly appealing for me, attending an all boys senior school, because it gave me the opportunity to meet those ethereal beings of the opposite sex. Important though this was, the most significant thing I can recall about these sessions was that it was where the 'rubber hit the road' in terms of applying all the things we had heard about Christianity. I began to understand that it meant a personal commitment of my life to God. It was also the convention that you couldn't do this quietly by yourself, you had to respond to an appeal at one of the Youth for Christ or National Young Life Campaign rallies that were held regularly in Chingford at that time on Saturday evenings. Eventually, I plucked up the courage to 'go forward', and on November 20th 1962, I officially committed my life to God, although I'd actually decided to do so some time earlier. One thing I recall about this decision was the feeling that I would have to give up any thought of being a 'pop star', something that appealed to my imagination at that time with all the excitement of sixties music. As it happened, later on God did give me the opportunity to express my musical interest in being part of several Christian singing groups.

The 'Cong' was probably typical of many evangelical churches of that time. A lot of good work was being done, and people were becoming Christians. For young people there were many things going on, both in individual churches, and in inter-church activities such as Youth for Christ. Equally, there were also many churches where the gospel was not clearly preached, and where very little was happening from a young person's perspective.

The minister of the church at the time was a godly gentleman named Lance Vinall. As he was coming up to retirement age, it was time for a new minister to be appointed. The process of choosing the replacement was typical of the non-conformist church approach. Various prospective candidates came to 'preach with a view' to being appointed, and the members decided by a majority vote the one they thought was the most suitable. I can only remember one visitor, a young man named George Tarleton who looked rather like James Dean. He was lively, interesting and funny. To the delight of the young people, the church members liked him too, and he was duly voted in. I can vividly remember his ordination; we were honoured by a visit from the legendary Dr Martyn Lloyd-Jones, one of the best known evangelical leaders in the country at that time. George had been at London Bible College, where 'the Doctor' had been one of the tutors. However, it wasn't the good Doctor that I can remember particularly, but the fact that the church was packed, and being late, I had to stand at the back throughout the lengthy proceedings.

The young people's group was delighted to have a young and energetic minister. We used to go round to the manse with George and his delightful wife Dorothy after the Sunday meetings, where we had both fun and a good challenge to our growing Christian lives. The group grew as people started becoming Christians in a number of the different secondary schools in the Chingford and Walthamstow area. At the end of my GCE year, 1965, I started playing the guitar. Not long after, we started a Christian group, the Gospeltones, which played at Christian events around the area for a couple of years. We were never going to hit the big time, but one of our claims to fame was an appearance in Trafalgar Square at a Christian event in 1967. It was freezing cold and my hands were so numb I could barely form the chords to play.

The other thing that happened over these years of the mid-sixties, was that we began to hear about the baptism of the Holy Spirit. I didn't take much convincing that, if these things such as speaking in tongues were in the Bible, then surely they were for Christians in the present day as well. They just seemed rather scary at the time. However, one weekend when we were away with the Gospeltones, the issue of the Baptism of the Spirit came up, and I asked Ken Terhovan, who was leading the weekend, to pray that I would receive it. I didn't speak in tongues at the time, but I did experience a new sense of the presence of God with me. Ken also prophesied over me that I would have the opportunity to present the gospel to many people in a foreign country. Little did he know that the Gospeltones had been invited by British Youth for Christ to go to Finland, and that we would end up appearing on Finnish television. This was an impressive introduction for me to the encouragement provided through the gift of prophecy. The night after being prayed for to receive the Holy Spirit, the group were playing at a local church, and I was asked to give my testimony. Speaking in public was something that didn't come naturally to me as a teenager, but that night I really sensed the power of God in me as I spoke. I later realised that power for witnessing was actually one of the main reasons for the baptism of the Spirit (Acts 1:8). Speaking in tongues came later, quietly one day when I was praying.

George was himself baptised in the Spirit, and although the subject was never specifically preached, many of the other leaders around the country who were also baptised, came and spoke at the church. I can remember John Noble, Campbell McAlpine, David Lillie and Arthur Wallis at various different church events. George was also becoming quite a celebrity. He was generally quite outspoken, and he took a particular stand against the craze for Ouija boards that was going around at the time, pointing out the spiritual dangers of the occult. He wrote a booklet about this, and also appeared on television. As young people it felt like we were part of a really exciting move of God. However, what we didn't know was that there was a lot of opposition mounting against George amongst some of the older members of the congregation.

Soon after that, in 1967, I went off to university at Southampton to study physics. The 'things of the Spirit' were a taboo subject within the University Christian Union at this time, and also in most of the churches in Southampton. However, God provided for me in that situation. Despite the rarity of our breed, on my physics course was another spirit-filled Christian, Steve Matheson from Penarth in Wales. We enjoyed a great friendship for the three years we were there. In our third year, the move of the Spirit was spreading, and we had a small informal Sunday afternoon prayer meeting where we got together with other like-minded Christians.

I really looked forward to my holidays from university to get back to the warm fellowship and presence of God at the 'Cong', where things continued to progress well. I had a further reason to want to go back to Chingford in my final year. I had started going out with Jean Wakerly, one of the youth group. She had been brought up in a Strict Baptist church. She was also studying the Acts at school in RI (Religious Instruction as it was called then), and, when she read about believers receiving the Spirit as a separate experience after they had become Christians, was keen to seek this herself. She asked her Baptist minister about it and he gave her the usual evangelical line that you received all of the Holy Spirit when you first became a Christian. She wasn't convinced and, when she heard about what was happening at the 'Cong', came along and joined our young people's group, even though it meant a long bus journey from where she lived.

When I finished at university I returned to Chingford. Jean and I got engaged, and signed up as official members of the 'Cong'. Our first members' meeting turned out to be our last, and was an event we will never forget. George had produced a leaflet discussing his vision for the way forward for the church (It is reproduced as an Appendix). The paper was entitled 'Glory in the Church' and highlighted three areas in which George felt we should develop: the gifts of the Spirit, the body of Christ, and worshipping the Father. It was really an excellent summary of what God was saying to the church as a whole at the time. We were really excited by this, and expected an enthusiastic response. What actually happened was the voicing of quite antagonistic views. I can't now remember what the specific criticisms were, but I remember feeling they didn't seem to have any real foundation. Sadly George couldn't take these criticisms and made a dramatic exit from the meeting. Shortly afterwards, he resigned from his position as pastor. We felt at the time it was a shame he didn't hold on for a bit longer to win the opposition round, but that wasn't to be. The bubble of the last few exciting years had burst.

Our own stay at 'the Cong' after all this was not very long, but this was not caused by the events in the church. While at university I had felt God speak very clearly that I should go into medical physics as a career. I had applied for the two jobs that had come up in London hospitals at that time, as I would have been able to commute to them while living in Chingford. However, I didn't get either of them and began to think about the possibility of going somewhere else in the country. About that time a job came up back in Southampton. I applied for it and got it. I started in February 1971, leaving Jean still in Chingford. We married in July of that year. George came back to the 'Cong' to take the service, as that had been agreed before all the trouble. It was the last wedding he took at the church.

George was a very gifted man. He had been involved in acting and was a captivating speaker. He also had a tremendous vision of what God was doing in the early days of the restoration movement, and possessed a great ability to communicate that clearly and with passion. He had a very positive influence on me as a young person in his church, and helped to set my path on the Christian life, which I have continued to follow.

On leaving the 'Cong', he set up a Christian Fellowship in Chingford. Some of the folk from the church joined him in this venture. He later linked up with other Christians from the area, including Dave Mansell, to form the North London Community Church. He was also one of the 'London Brothers' who got together in the early 1970s to discuss the restoration concepts they felt God was highlighting. George was a radical, and was in his element envisioning new ways of being church. He made a great contribution to the growing vision of those early days. Unfortunately it was all too short lived. His radical nature was probably a bit extreme for some, and the challenges he brought inevitably resulted in conflict with those who disagreed with him. He became a member of the 'Fabulous Fourteen' and was therefore intimately involved with the split that occurred in the restoration movement. As with the situation at the 'Cong', George did not react well to conflict and sadly, after a few years, he left the ministry. He returned to working with people with hearing difficulties, his profession before he went to Bible college. He has written his story in *Birth of a Christian Anarchist*[1]. He still has a belief in God but has embraced Gnosticism, one of the deviations from Christianity in the early church. For those of us who are still seeking to follow through George's original vision, and particularly for me being so encouraged by George as a young man, the book makes sad reading. We have kept in touch with George and Dorothy, as they don't live far from Southampton. They are still lovely people, but just view Christianity differently from most of the rest of us in the church.

Kendal Avenue Pentecostal

From February to July 1971, I was in Southampton during the week and going back to Chingford at the weekends. During that time we had to make a decision about which church we would join when we settled in Southampton after we were married. While I had been at university, I had gone to many different churches but never really settled into one. I didn't feel the need to. I had my roots back at Chingford and there was good fellowship in the Christian Union, even if most weren't charismatic. However, now we were settling in Southampton, we had to find a church. This presented a problem, as there were no 'renewed' churches that I was aware of. I had previously had some contact with Kendal Avenue Pentecostal church. This was situated on the edge of the big Millbrook housing estate, although only a few of the congregation actually lived on the estate. While at university, I had been in charge of the Christian Union 'Team Visits'. We sent out groups of students to different churches in order to contribute to meetings or take young people's groups, and a team had gone to Kendal Avenue on a couple of occasions. I thought it would be worth finding out what it was like. At that time there was a certain wariness about Pentecostal denominational churches, even among charismatics, so we were somewhat apprehensive. We did find the meetings a bit unusual, but received such a warm welcome from Tony and Sheila Stone, who were leading the church, that we felt right about going along. The church believed in the baptism and gifts of the Spirit, but did not have a vision for the church similar to the one that had been emerging at Chingford. We never felt quite at home there, and never joined the church as members, but we did make some good friends, and I joined another singing group with the slightly better name of His Folk.

The great significance of us going there was in the contacts we made. One of the couples who became our close friends were Ron and Evelyn Rothery. They had been involved in setting up the church, and Ron was one of the elders. They had a welcoming heart and were very encouraging. After we had been at Kendal Avenue for about a year, some of the university students started coming along to the

church. There was now a growing charismatic group at
the university know as *Agapé* (the Greek word for love used
in the New Testament). They met separately from the
Christian Union and several of them had adopted Kendal
Avenue as the church to go along to on a Sunday. I enjoyed
meeting up with some of the folk I knew at the university,
such as Tony Morton, Adrian Thomas and Martyn
Dunsford.

At that time, a number of folk from Bitterne Park Baptist
Church also started to come along, particularly Roy and
Gillian Pearson and Rodney and Edna Martin. They had
experienced the baptism of the Spirit and were seeking to
move on in the Spirit, but this was being opposed by the
church and they felt they had to move. A number of young
people from the Bitterne Park church also came with them.
We got to know them really well. Rodney played the
guitar and joined His Folk. Roy and Gillian were very
enthusiastic about the things of God, and were full of fun
and life.

In these years of the early 1970s, we were beginning to
hear about the things God was doing in the restoration
movement elsewhere in the UK. Some folk had visited the
Capel Bible Weeks, and Jean and I were still in touch with
George and others in the North London Community
Church. We heard about the prophetic nature of the church,
the importance of house groups, the idea of everyone having
a part to play and the emergence of apostles.

Ron was invited to attend a meeting in Paignton in
Devon where he met Bryn Jones and heard more about
these ideas. When Tony Stone left Kendal Avenue to go into
full-time evangelism, Ron and Evelyn felt it would be good

to continue the meeting for young people after the Sunday evening service, which Tony and Sheila had previously hosted in the manse next to the church. They opened their home for the gathering. Ron also got to know a number of the students who were coming along to the church, and some were beginning to look to him as a father figure. Meanwhile, Rodney and Edna along with Jean and I, started meeting up at the Pearson's home for informal meetings, which were great fun. One evening we just sat there laughing all evening – 20 years before the Toronto Blessing when 'laughing in the Spirit' became commonplace.

The Southampton Community Church

The Early Years

Early in 1975, things began to come to a head. Some of the elders at Kendal Avenue were not happy about Ron's home meetings or his restoration ideas. He was asked to stop the meetings in his home. Several of us had been keen to see how the house group ideas would have developed within the context of Kendal Avenue, but it now looked as though this could not happen. After much heart searching Ron resigned as an elder on January 31st. He and Evelyn had been part of the church for many years. It was a very hard decision. Both Roy and Ron had been in contact with Bryn Jones, whom we all respected as an apostolic figure and were happy to look to for guidance. Bryn came down with Dave Mansell to meet with us on February 9th 1975.

The meeting was held at Rodney's house. Roy, Ron and I were present along with Tony Morton and Julian Boden from the university. Bryn explained that he had been aware of developments in Southampton, and that he now felt it was the right time for us to begin to join together. He suggested we should meet in small groups midweek, Ron and I on the west side of town, and Roy and Rodney on the east with Tony and Julian focusing on the university group. We should then all come together on each Sunday. He was seeing Ron as the leader for the present, and also wanted to bring in Ian McCullough to be working closely with us. Ian ran a house fellowship in his home in nearby Emsworth, and was an experienced restoration church leader, one of the 'Fabulous Fourteen'. He felt that we should support Ian financially as our leader and also welcome in other ministries such as himself, Dave Mansell and Barney Coombes. He wasn't planning to appoint elders at this stage, but wanted to see how things progressed before doing that officially. We decided to call ourselves Southampton Christian Fellowship. After a further local leadership meeting, we had our first Sunday gathering on March 2nd at the Social Centre for the Blind. About 60 people attended. The meeting was led by Ron, and Ian spoke. We were under way!

We met at the Blind Centre for only a few weeks and on May 25th, we moved to Gregg's School. In the early days we were mainly a young church. There were very few families or older folk. The number expanded quite rapidly, mainly through the addition of new students. We were very keen. The meetings started at around 3.30 in the afternoon and then at about 5.00 we broke to share tea together. After that, we moved on into the evening meeting, which sometimes went on till 9 o'clock. We arranged the chairs in a large circle, and during the worship time the meeting was open for people to contribute. Ian took most of the teaching, although others of us got some opportunity to share as well. His theme was one I'll never forget. He wanted to lay a foundation for the church on the love of God. Several of us wanted to get into the gifts of the Spirit, but his idea of basing us firmly on God's love was most helpful and demonstrated the wisdom of Bryn in asking Ian to lead us at the beginning.

Despite the excitement of these early days, tensions began to emerge. We were a young church, mostly below thirty. There was also a high percentage of students. Some dissatisfaction grew with the leadership style of Ian and Ron who were quite a bit older. Ian also brought over from Argentina some brothers he knew well to lead our meetings. We thought we were radical, but these chaps were in a different league, and many in the fellowship found it difficult to relate to this aspect of the direction we seemed to be moving in. Bryn sensed this, and so after about a year made a change in the leadership arrangement. About 15 of us, who were a kind of unofficial leadership group gathered at Tony's flat, and Bryn shared with us the changes he felt should occur. Ian would no longer provide our 'covering'. This would come from Bryn himself. Bryn also invited Ron and Evelyn up to Bradford where he was keen for Ron to be involved in the Church House refurbishment project they had just started. Ron and Evelyn were not only an excellent, encouraging couple, but Ron was also a very experienced plumber by trade, and Bryn felt this was a strategic move. They would not only be a useful addition to his team in Bradford but Ron could also help practically in the work of Church House. It was clear that all of us in the leadership group were happy for Tony to take on the central leadership role in the church. Tony had a more intellectual style of preaching, better suited to the predominantly student population of the church. He was also much more their age, and had the confidence and support of the people.

For Jean and me, it was the first of many upheavals that would characterise life in a church that was, to borrow the title of Terry Virgo's book, walking 'no well-worn paths'. During the first months of the Fellowship, we had been leading one of the house groups in our area, and I had been meeting as part of a central leadership team with Tony, Roy and Ron. With the changes, this was all disbanded and we found ourselves on the outside of the leadership, not leading a house group. However, even in these disappointments God has a way of having his hand on things. We joined a house group led by David and Ruth Spencer who became our lifelong friends. Within another year or so, we were leading a house group again, which grew to over thirty people at one stage. We had found our ministry in the church. We continue to lead a small group some thirty years on. We were also sad to lose Ian, and particularly Ron and Evelyn, who had been so kind and supportive to us as we took our first steps into house group leadership. In retrospect, I think we lost a lot with their going. We kept in good touch with Ron and Evelyn as they moved around the country, and eventually returned to Southampton.

Probably the most remarkable happening in the first years of the church was the healing of Elzunia Ashe. Zunie had been at Kendall Avenue and was in our group at the start of the church. Although only in her twenties, she developed ovarian cancer. After initial treatment, the tumour re-grew quickly and her prognosis was very poor. We prayed and fasted and cried out to God for healing. The whole church was together. Miraculously Zunie was healed from that cancer and is still alive and well thirty years later. During her time in the hospital Zunie had been to my department for a scan, and I was therefore aware the medical details of her case. There is no doubt in my mind that this was a medically attested healing. We were all delighted, and this gave hope and expectation for further healings. However, we were to find later over the years, that even when you pray and have all the faith you can muster, people do not always get healed. We have learnt to be thankful when they do, and to weep with those who weep when they don't.

One of the things that characterised the early days of our church, as in other similar restoration churches, was the vibrance of the worship. We were excited about what God was doing with us as individuals, and in drawing us together as his people. We really enjoyed praising God. We sang, clapped, raised our hands and danced. We were also blessed with several creative people, who wrote many new songs, some of which became part of Christian songbooks used nationally and internationally. Probably the best known is 'Be still' by Dave Evans, but there were a number of others by Pete and Dilly Fung, Cary Govier, Wendy Churchill, and Sue Hutchinson.

The church began to grow rapidly, and we moved to a larger school building in Bitterne Park, much to Roy's delight, as it was just down the road from his house. We also joined up with West End Evangelical Church to become Southampton Community Church. They were a group of 50–60 people from the West End area, ironically on the east side of Southampton. Many of them had received the baptism of the Holy Spirit, and were keen to start developing restoration ideas in their church. They had asked Arthur Wallis to provide their 'covering'. As Bryn and Arthur were working together, they felt that it made sense for West End to join with us, in 1977. Tony and Bob Hall from West End were prayed in as the joint leaders. West End church owned a building, and although we didn't use it initially as a meeting place, it was a useful resource, which became the church junior school. Also, around this time Bryn appointed the first official elders in the church, Tony, Geoff Wright, Pete Light and Roger Popplestone.

The late 1970s were a time of great development. The church grew rapidly to number several hundred people. Most of those who joined us were already Christians, either students or people from other churches, who had caught the vision of what God was doing in restoring his church. At that stage we were focussing on building the church, rather than on reaching out in evangelism. We became large enough to support several full time employees including Tony, Pete and Roger. The leadership also felt that it would be good to split down into smaller groups meeting in local areas. We met in schools, community halls and even hotels.

The church was flexible enough to cope with these changes, as the house groups were still the basic unit of belonging. Alterations to the outer structure of meetings could be made without disturbing the strong relationships in the house groups. One of Tony's visions was for us to become a city-wide church, and so from time to time, we would start meeting in a particular area where there were no people in the church. Once a house-group had been established in that area, we would move on to the next one. It certainly felt unsettling, but we did manage to spread across Southampton reasonably effectively.

Naturally we were not always popular with Christians from other churches. Some ridiculed us, while others sat back taking the advice of Gamaliel, that if what we were doing was from man, it would fail, and if from God, they should not fight against it (Acts 5:34-40). The most serious accusation was that of sheep-stealing. While we didn't go out of our way to persuade people from other churches to join us, we were very pleased when they did. One of the visions of the restoration movement was that denominational barriers would be broken down, and that all Christians in an area would all be able to be together in a new type of church structure, based on the picture of church found in the New Testament. I don't think many of us had a clear idea of how exactly this was to be achieved. One possible way it could happen was that people would join us, and we would become the focal point of Christians in Southampton coming together. Therefore it seemed good when people left churches where there was little spiritual life, to join us. Surely it was better for them to join a church where God was present and they would be encouraged to grow spiritually, than to remain where they were? A phrase coined by Arthur Wallis that was often used was: 'Come with us and we will do you good.'

It was almost inevitable that people would come to join us. God's hand was clearly on us and Christians were keen to become part of what he was doing at that time. One can obviously empathise with faithful pastors who were losing the folk in their church. However, as with other moves of God that led to breakaway groups, the effect on the rest of the church was to act as a wake-up call. There are now many churches in Southampton, as elsewhere in the UK, that embrace the gifts of the Spirit, have house-groups and enjoy lively worship.

In parallel with the emergence of the Community Church, God was moving in another group of young Christians in Southampton at Swaythling Methodist Church. They also felt that they should become an independent group. Calling themselves the Lighthouse Fellowship, they sought apostolic advice from Gerald Coates. This led to Southampton being impacted by the national split among restoration leaders. As Bryn was on one side of the divide and Gerald on the other, there was sadly no co-ordination between our two fellowships in Southampton despite the similarity of vision. The Lighthouse Fellowship has changed its name several times down through the years, but it has also acted as a catalyst for churches in Southampton to adopt many of the restoration principles. Over the time between the late 1970s and the beginning of the twenty-first century, many of the rifts between churches caused by the splits have been healed, and there are now generally good relations between churches in Southampton, probably better than they have ever been. There is quite a level of the unity of the Spirit, and even a number of initiatives involving churches working together. However, we are still a long way off a full unity of the faith and a genuine walking together. While certain aspects of the restoration vision have been realised, there is still much work to do.

During the years of the late 1970s Bryn Jones was still our covering apostle and we attended en masse the Dales Bible Weeks, which were organised by the Bradford Church.

These were times of great inspiration and encouragement and also valuable for consolidating relationships. The teaching included emphasis on the importance of pastoral care and of the need of submission to those in authority in the church. This influenced the nature of the house groups and the role of the house group leader. The responsibility of the leader was not only to organise the weekly meetings, but also to care for those in his group. We were trying to work out the idea of shepherding quite rigorously. The aim was to meet with everyone in the group reasonably regularly on an individual basis to see how they were getting on in their Christian lives. At one stage, we had the infamous 'green forms', which covered a series of questions on people's relationship with God, their quiet times, their family life, work life and church ministry. It was too intense really, but no one could claim they were not being cared for!

The teaching on shepherding and submission in the early days of the restoration movement has come in for quite a lot of criticism. The concepts of shepherding and submission are clearly scriptural. 1 Peter 5:1-5 provides an explanation of the nature of spiritual leadership. Shepherds of the flock are to consider themselves servants, not lording it over those people for whom they were responsible, but being examples. Hebrews 13:17 encourages believers to submit to those in authority over them in the church. The combination of these two passages paints a picture of a beautiful relationship between people willingly submitting to a caring, non-authoritarian leadership. People in the church could submit to this kind of leadership without having their lives dominated. I think what happened in the early days of the restoration movement, was that the teaching of these biblical concepts was not always conveyed in a balanced way. There tended to be more emphasis on submission of believers than on the responsibilities of the leader. The potential dangers were of leaders assuming control of people's lives, and of individuals becoming afraid to make their own decisions, feeling they had to 'submit' things they were planning to do to their leader for his approval. In retrospect, most of us would agree that we were somewhat unbalanced in the way we implemented these ideas. We did sometimes try to interfere rather too much with people's decisions. However, in most cases this was out of a genuine love and concern for the individual involved. In my experience in the Southampton Church, examples of leaders abusing their authority by trying to control people were quite rare.

We also had weekly meetings of house group leaders. Although it was another evening of the week with a meeting, they were times of great encouragement. The task of looking after around twenty or so people in a group could be quite draining. Most of us had little training or previous experience with pastoral work, and there were inevitably one or two folk in the group with difficult problems in their lives. Caring for them tended to take up a lot of time and energy. Coming together with fellow leaders to encourage each another and to pray for those in our care was very helpful. For those of us in full time jobs, all these activities meant that we were busy most nights of the week. As happened in the very early days of the New Testament church, we were meeting almost daily. However, many of us, including Jean and I, now had young families and this level of commitment was having an impact on family life. We were encouraged to devote one night per week to our families. On reflection, this balance seems considerably over-the-top, and our families did suffer to some degree. (When my son read this, his comment was 'no lasting damage done!'. I think that would be true of most of our families.)

Tony's vision for growth started to develop beyond the confines of the Southampton church. We already had folk from nearby Totton, Romsey and Winchester with us in the church, and Tony was looking for the right time to plant these new believers back in their own town as soon as he felt a viable group had emerged. Roger and Pat Bellis and Colin and Ruth Little from Romsey joined us while we were in David and Ruth Spencer's group. Every now and then, the whole church would descend on Romsey to hold a meeting there to spread the word about the restoration movement. Soon a group of a dozen or so had gathered who were keen to meet together. The Romsey church was then ready to start on its own, but still getting strong support from Southampton in the early days. A similar thing happened in Winchester. Some folk from the Southampton church who worked in Winchester, moved house, and joined the people who were already there, to help them become established.

The vision of reaching out overseas also began to emerge, and Tony took a few others with him on an exploratory visit to France. Pete Light admits in retrospect, that they had rather more faith than apostolic wisdom, but nevertheless relationships began to emerge with folk in other countries.

We also began to think about the education of our children. Was it right that we should send our children in their vulnerable early years to a school environment, which was at the least humanist, and at worst quite hostile to the gospel? Some phrased the question: 'Would the Israelites have sent their children down the road to the local Egyptian school?' There were a number of schoolteachers in the church and the real possibility of setting up our own school began to be considered. We were still thinking of ourselves as setting up an alternative society. This might start as a school providing a Christian education for our own children, but once it was going could provide an excellent education in a Christian environment for others in society as well.

It was decided to set up the school in the old West End Evangelical Church building with Geoff Wright as its first headmaster. Of course money was a big issue. The initial idea was that people in the church would pay what they could afford for their children's education, even if this was much less than the actual cost. The church would make up the rest of the cost from central funds. It began as a primary school, but it grew quite quickly, and within a few years there were both junior and senior schools with numbers of around 120 and 80 pupils respectively. The senior school was based at the beautiful Fisher's Court building in Fair Oak.

As we were part of Bryn Jones' Harvestime church family, we had supported the Dales Bible Week up to 1978. When Terry Virgo started the first of the Downs weeks at Plumpton Racecourse in the South, we joined him there in 1979. However, Tony had visions for having one of our own, and started up the New Forest Bible week in 1980. At first it was a relatively small affair with numbers in the hundreds rather than thousands. The initial idea was to provide a time of teaching and envisioning for the Southampton church. Nevertheless, it demonstrated that we had the administrative capability of running a Bible week, and provided valuable experience for planning larger events in the future.

A Resource Church

The remarkable development over the first few years of the life of the church was enabled by the vision and energy of Tony. Bryn could see that here was a man with an apostolic anointing, and in 1981, Tony was officially recognised and 'prayed in' as an apostle. The following year saw the commencement of Cornerstone, as the apostolic arm of the Southampton Community Church, which was now clearly functioning as a resource church, providing advice and support to other churches.

Cornerstone initially consisted of Tony, David Damp, Pete Light and Arthur Wallis. Arthur had recently joined the church along with his son Jonathan and family. It was a real privilege to have Arthur and Eileen with us. They were people of great wisdom, and provided a good balance to a church that was essentially made up of young enthusiasts. Mission into other countries continued to develop into Europe, and then into Asia and Africa. Pete Light felt called to the work in Asia, and this grew into a project in its own right called Impact Asia. Many visits took place, particularly to India and Nepal. Churches were planted and grown, leaders were taught, and all this was accompanied by outstanding miracles, including instances of people being raised from the dead.

On the home front too, things were expanding. Churches from all around the south of England were seeking apostolic covering from Tony, and in some cases, leaders from Southampton were planted out to support churches further afield. Roger and Christine Popplestone went to lead a church in Teddington, and Ken and Heather Ford to

Bridgewater. Tony was always clear that his input into other churches was to be impartational rather than governmental. He wanted to help churches grow, but he didn't want to develop a hierarchical structure of churches with all the leaders accountable to him. However, he did want to provide a framework where not only church leaders would be encouraged in gatherings of their peers, but where all the folk in the churches could come together and be envisioned. The site where we had the New Forest Bible weeks wasn't big enough to accommodate all the folk in the growing family of churches, and hence came the idea for the South and West Bible Week at the Bath and West showground in Shepton Mallet in Somerset. This ran for several years during the mid 1980s. We had up to 3000 people attending those weeks. It was very hard work, but they were times of great encouragement.

Even in a resource church, or maybe, particularly in a resource church, there needs to be a focus on preserving a healthy local body of Christians where people have a place of belonging and an opportunity to grow. Several new full time staff were taken on including Phil Orchard, Dave Adcock and Adrian Thomas. Dave and Phil took on pastoral and teaching roles while Adrian, who had been in banking, took on the finances. To cope with the growing staff, we purchased a building in the Shirley area of town. This had previously served as a Police Station and a Library, and now became King's House. It provided office accommodation, and also had a room large enough for meetings of up to about 50 people. To provide more of a sense of belonging, the church divided first into a few congregations of about 150, and then into about nine area groups of about 50 people.

For us this was a significant time. It meant we could finally meet in our own local area of Shirley, after helping establish groups in several other different areas of town. In 1984, Jean and I were prayed in as elders to lead this congregation. It was very exciting, but a lot of hard work, being responsible for the Sunday meetings, children's work, and also the overall pastoral care of the folk in the congregation. Given that we had three children and I had a demanding job, this was not easy. Fortunately we had good people to lead house groups in the area, and plenty of folk to share leading and speaking at meetings. Now that we were meeting locally, and also had a good sense of togetherness among ourselves, we felt that it would be an opportune time to reach out to the local community. We dropped hundreds of tracts around the area with information about our meeting. However, hardly anyone new came along.

Then we had a devastating event. Arthur and Eileen's son, Jonathan, and his wife Sylvia, along with their two daughters, Katrina and Fiona, were living in Shirley and were part of our area. They were gifted and very encouraging, being a great asset to our church. Suddenly, out of the blue, Katrina, who was fourteen at the time, developed appendicitis and died. We were all devastated. She was a beautiful girl, so full of life and had loved dancing. We couldn't believe she was gone. However, while we were only a small group in Shirley, we were still part of the larger community, and help came for Jonathan and Sylvia from across the church.

Tony was always keen for growth, and had begun getting a vision for a centralised city church. So, after just a year, we were merged with the Freemantle and Hollybrook areas to become a 'Westside' gathering of around 150 people. We still met in Bellemoor School where we had been as the Shirley area, but the feel was very different. I can remember feeling very disappointed by this, as our role co-ordinating our little area church had disappeared. We were still to be pastorally responsible for the house groups in the area, but now suddenly a big part of what we had been doing was gone. It did, however, have a good side. The larger setting for Sunday meetings meant that the pressure on people to run meetings, lead worship and organise the children's work was much reduced. These larger area groups did not last very long either. After another year or so, we all started to meet together on a Sunday as a city-wide church in the very plush main lecture theatre of the Boldrewood Building at the University of Southampton. We had met there for special gatherings over the years, but it now became our regular Sunday meeting place.

In 1984, when we were prayed in as elders, there were twelve couples in eldership. Some were full time employees of the church and others, like me, had secular jobs. We met either as men, or together with our wives, to discuss where the church was headed. It was not a decision making body, as we only met about monthly, and decisions had to be made much more frequently. As non full time elders, we had some say in the way the church was going, but the full time folk ran the church on a day-to-day basis, and made the final decisions on issues that came up. Tony's role in the church was interesting. Although he was leading a growing apostolic team and was very often away from Southampton, he still continued in the role of senior pastor within the Community Church, having a very strong influence in all major decisions. He carried on doing both jobs up until 2001, when he decided to focus on the apostolic role. In retrospect, he probably stayed too long trying to do both things. Even Paul never tried to run a local church as well as being an apostle.

Being part of a pioneering non-denominational church gave the freedom to shape things as closely as possible to scriptural principles. However, there were downsides. As there was no infrastructure, everything had to be started from scratch. At the 'Cong', we not only had the Sunday School, but also organisations such as the Boys Brigade and Girl Guides, which gave children and young people a good place to belong. At this stage, there were not all that many teenagers in the Community Church. Our own children were around that awkward age of about 12. They did not always enjoy church meetings. These consisted of about an hour of worship followed by a 40-minute talk. The worship was lively and great for adults, but was rather unstructured, and the talk was not really geared to children. The children's work covered primary school age, but after that they were expected to stay in the main meeting. The girls often enjoyed helping look after the babies in the crèche, but the boys were bored. I remembered how much I had enjoyed Bible class in the Boy's Brigade, which went on in parallel to the sermon, and was targeted to our age. So Jean and I set up an alternative scheme where, three weeks out of four, the boys would have their own session that was geared to early teenage boys. On the fourth week they stayed in the main meeting to help them get a feel for the adult teaching. This seemed appropriate, as they were in that intermediate stage of becoming an adult. We tried to ensure that these weeks happened when the speaker in the main meeting was 'teenage-friendly'.

The small number of teenagers also meant that there was not very much organised for them in the way of social life. To help with this, we joined the team of people who were looking after the youth work and opened our house as a place where the young people could meet for fellowship. This later became a kind of young people's house group. This seemed a logical step. As we were into house groups as adults, wouldn't this also be a good model for the children as well? It was a small start at that stage, but house groups have since become an integral part of the much larger youth work we now have in the church.

As a church we began to sense God was encouraging us to have a positive impact on social issues of the day. The first of these was over the issue of abortion. Abortions had been legal in the UK since the late 1960s, and like many Christians, we felt it was clear from the Bible that this was not right. We heard about pregnancy crisis centres being set up in the US, and approached some of the people who had been involved for advice. Phil Clarke, who had already established a Christian GP practice in Southampton, and was one of the elders in the church, took on the leadership of the project. It became known as Firgrove after the name of a road near King's House. Some time later, a house in this road was purchased to act as a centre for counselling girls who had either an unplanned pregnancy or who had previously had an abortion. Over the years, many thousands of people have been helped, and the ministry has extended to include a program of teaching in schools called 'Choices'. This encourages young people with the message that Christian morality is still a valid option for life in the present day. Although a relatively small group, they have been very influential in helping the establishment of many other similar centres, both in this country and abroad. Phil has recently written a book entitled *A Heart of Compassion* which includes the story of Firgrove[2].

Colin and Brenda Henderson joined the church after being with Bryn Jones in Bradford. Colin was a remarkable man who had retired from the Air Force. He had the energy and personality to establish new initiatives and to implement them with a military precision. One of his early projects was Crossroads. This was a group led by Richard and Judith Willcox together with David and Ruth Spencer. It aimed to provide practical help to people who were finding things difficult. Referrals came from various places including Social Services. They set up a telephone help-line at King's House, which was at one stage manned both during the daytime and evenings.

Central Hall

We had been looking for a building that was larger than King's House for some years, and many alternatives had been investigated. Finally, Central Hall came on the market. Situated in the centre of Southampton, it was originally a Methodist Central Hall, built in the 1920s as part of the Methodist Church programme to commemorate the centenary of Wesley's death. A central hall was to be built in every major town. It was an impressive construction with a large main auditorium holding around 1000 people, and a range of other rooms surrounding it. It had hosted revival meetings with the Jeffries brothers in the early days of the Pentecostal movement, and also proudly boasts to be the first place where Billy Graham preached in the UK after he arrived in Southampton from the United States. Many older Christians in Southampton have very fond memories of the lively meetings held in the building.

Sadly the church that met in Central Hall declined during the 1960s, as people moved away from the city centre, and it was eventually sold to the local education authority. They used it for examinations, and had converted some of the complex into small rooms for vocational training such as painting and decorating. The building had got into a poor state of repair, and the education authority now wanted to sell it. We expressed an interest, but for some reason there was quite a lot of opposition in the Council to a Christian group taking it over. However, God has a way of overcoming the 'schemes of men', and in 1991, we were able to purchase it. We agreed that the education authority could continue to use the building for examinations. This was useful to them, and also to us, as it generated some income.

Paul Gander was responsible for supervising the restoration work on the building. He had a big job on his hands, including getting rid of the many pigeons, which had made their home in the loft! We all helped out with the cleaning, and eventually it was ready for our first meeting on 7 April 1991. The acoustics of the main hall were very poor. There was a large wooden central floor area, surrounded by tiered seating built on a concrete base. It was very echoy. However, it was great to know that Central Hall was again being used for its original purpose to glorify God. Gradually, with carpets, curtains and a good PA system, things were improved. The other rooms were also prepared, and became useful on Sundays for children's work. The partitions that had been constructed for the vocational training area were knocked down to leave the original 'small hall', which can comfortably accommodate meetings of around 150 people.

Purchasing Central Hall ushered in a new phase for the church. Owning a building meant that every meeting wasn't a major logistical exercise of setting up the musicians' gear and the PA system. Most of the seating was permanently in position, so the task of arranging chairs was considerably easier. Colin Henderson had a great vision for the building. He wanted to see a range of meetings on a Sunday and then a variety of activities during the rest of the week. It was all rather different to the original ideas we had set out with, of sharing fellowship in simple meetings in homes, but there were clear advantages of owning a building.

Gradually the building was improved, and it began to be used for the variety of events Colin had envisioned. One, which we became involved in, was Sunday Afternoon at Central Hall. This was a meeting for older folk. It had a more conventional hymn-prayer sandwich structure, but also often included some sort of entertainment, such as a music group. We always had tea and biscuits, sometimes putting on a special meal. The meetings were really enjoyable and the old folk loved them. They did, however, require a lot of organisation, particularly the transport to and from the building.

Some of our midweek meetings also began to be focused on Central Hall. There were equipping meetings, which covered different aspects of the Christian life. Then once a month, instead of house groups, we would all meet together for prayer together at Central Hall. It also became the venue for specialised groups within the church to meet. The musicians, for example, used it for practice and to store their PA equipment. It was also great for larger organised events.

Tony began to host conferences in Central Hall. Flying High became an annual event geared mainly at leaders in Cornerstone churches.

The purchase of the building coincided with there being a rapid increase in the number of teenagers in the church. This was very handy, as we could now look to develop youth events based around Central Hall. Billy Kennedy was appointed as the youth pastor. The smaller youth groups, like the one we had been involved with in Shirley, were now replaced by a central organisation. Saturday evening was the time of the main event for teenagers. This became known as Sublime. It includes a lively and loud worship time. The leadership style is quite 'hands off' and the young people themselves both lead and speak at the meetings. During the week they meet in home groups, also led by folk from the youth congregation. Occurring about once a month, the Big Story is a larger event, aimed at being open to Christians from other churches and also non-Christians. The nationally known Christian rock band, Delirious, made some of their early steps towards fame in concerts organised at Central Hall. Later, Billy took on a wider leadership responsibility within the church, and Dave Boniface was appointed to look after the youth work.

The youth group is also very mission-oriented. Regular short-term visits are made by the young people to various projects across the world. The whole ethos is one of enthusiastic worship and vibrant Christian life. The group has been very successful and attracted a lot of young people. However, this 'high-octane' style of Christianity was a bit too much for some of the young folk in the church, who preferred the rather calmer approach at Highfield Church, one of the local Anglican churches, which also runs a successful youth programme.

Despite the excitement of getting our own building, the years of the early nineties seemed to be characterised by a diminishing of the initial sense of enthusiasm in the church. We had been going for nearly twenty years, changing form and developing new projects. Many of us were also not as young as we used to be. I think we had become a little weary in doing good (Gal 6:9). For me there was certainly a warning. In 1989 I became ill with an undiagnosed condition put down to a virus. I was off work for 6 weeks and then not back to normal strength for around 6 months. I had definitely been doing too much. In addition to all our efforts in the church, I was really trying to do two jobs at work, manage the Nuclear Medicine Department, and also run a research team at the same time. I needed the enforced rest to regain strength and also to stop and hear God.

The spiritual wake-up call to the church came in 1994 with the Toronto Blessing, the rather unusual movement that has influenced churches across the world. It seemed bizarre at the time, and still does in retrospect, but it was just what our church needed. The fruit that it bore gave clear evidence that it was from God. First, just one or two were touched, but it spread quickly around the church and we were soon having special Sunday evening meetings where we waited on God, prayed for one another, and laid hands on each other for God's anointing. We laughed, cried, fell on the floor and lay on the carpet. We were spiritually renewed. Many of the young people in the church were touched as well, and the joining of all ages in these evening meetings in praying for each other was a great encouragement. Many people's lives were changed, and had their spiritual batteries recharged. The meetings went on for several months, but the effect on the church for good lasted much longer.

The centralisation of the church on Central Hall had a definite impact on the role of house groups. From being the foundation of the church in the early days, they had gradually become an optional extra. People were busy in all the centralised activities of the church, and many felt they didn't have time or the need for being part of a house group. Although we still had house groups, the ethos of the church had changed. We have never had an official membership, but in the early days everyone was in a house group, and most people were strongly committed to the church. It was clear whether or not you belonged. The move to Central Hall changed this. It was now possible to just come along on a Sunday and enjoy the worship, without necessarily feeling a very committed part of the church.

Around this time, teaching on cell church started to become quite popular. For those of us who had been in the church from the beginning, it was difficult to see what was new about this. It seemed to be promoting small home groups as the basis of the church, suggesting that they should be considered as the fundamental place of belonging to the church. The structure of cell group supervisors and area elders was a little more prescriptive than our arrangement, but the principle was very similar. The leadership decided to try to implement the idea. All small groups including the existing house groups were to come up with a mission statement summarising the aims of the group. This was meant to include an outreach aim. Several new groups began focusing on different themes. There was a folk music group that met in pubs, with the aim of reaching out to the people that they met there. One of the more successful ones, dubbed the 'prison cell', was based around the aim of visiting inmates, and reaching them with the good news about Christ. Some good outreach was done, but we didn't manage to change the culture of the church to become focused on cells, and thus didn't really become a cell church.

The most significant development in the area of evangelism was the Alpha course. Phil Orchard took over the responsibility for this in our church soon after it was first introduced in the mid 1990s, and has been running a course once a term ever since. They are usually based at Central Hall, although some happen in people's homes. Generally there are at least twenty or thirty people on each course, sometimes as many as eighty. Many people have become Christians, and several have been added to the church. The format, based around faithful exposition of the scriptures, the warmth of being part a small group, and of course the meal, has proved to be a real winner when it comes to introducing folk to the gospel. Being a big church has helped a lot with Alpha. There have always been enough people inviting their friends along to make a viable course, and also to cover the practical requirements of preparing the meal, leading the groups, and speaking. In addition, having a full time person to provide excellence in organisation, has been a major factor in its success.

Another great success in evangelism has been the work on the Flower estate, where road names like Honeysuckle, Primrose and Bluebell suggest little of the problems that exist there. Conventional family life has largely broken down, and there is a high level of unemployment. The young people have little hope for the future, and drugs are very much part of the culture. The church in Southampton was making little impact on the estate. Enter Bob and Colette Light. Bob had been brought up on the estate and became addicted to drugs. He moved down to Cornwall where he was befriended by a Christian who led him to Christ. His eyes were opened to a whole new view on life. He was so grateful for his salvation that he began to feel God call him to go back to the area where he had been brought up, and share the good news with the folk there. Who was better equipped for the task than someone who'd been there himself? Bob came to our church and started to work in the estate, initially with children, setting up Club Zion. Young people and students from the church helped him organise the lively event, which attracted good numbers of young-sters. Some of them became Christians, and the Light house-hold was always full of visitors. Soon adults were impacted as well, and several came to Christ. At this stage, Bob was still working full time, and the combination of this and the growing move of God in his area, was becoming too much. The church agreed to employ Bob and support him in the work. They continue to make a big impact on the estate. Every year there is a special event in the summer, called 'Daisy Dip' week, the name of the park at the bottom of Daisy Road. The project is another example of what can be achieved with God's anointing coupled with the support of a large church.

During the 1990s, the popularity of counselling began to increase. Developments in psychology had led to a better understanding of what 'made people tick' and counselling enabled this knowledge to help individuals 'find themselves'

and make sense of life. Helping people to live happy and fulfilled lives has always been a key aim of the church. This was
traditionally achieved through pastoral care, both through
leaders with a responsibility for caring and through people
generally having a loving heart for each other. This had
proved helpful to many, but some people with particular
psychological difficulties had been beyond the usual experience of house group leaders or other untrained pastoral
workers. It was hoped that a better understanding of behaviour and its influencing factors through counselling, could
help people who were in this situation to overcome their
problems. For Christians it was important that such counselling was based on a biblical framework, and took into
account the spiritual aspects of a person's being. Hence
Norma Parrack, who was a social worker, was employed part
time by the church to set up a counselling service. A number
of courses have subsequently been established, which have
been helpful to many people in the church. Some of these
have gone on to be used by other churches. Many people
have also been helped through individual counselling, and
the experience gained has meant that we have been able to
establish courses to train counsellors. These developments
have also been very helpful to house group leaders. We have
been able to get help for people with long standing problems,
who need more specialist support than is available in the
average house group setting.

One of the excellent things that developed over this latter
phase of our church life, was that we were welcomed back
into the fold of the other churches in Southampton. We
hadn't been a flash in the pan. God was with us. Many of the
other churches were now practising the things that we had

pioneered, such as the gifts of the Spirit and house groups. Also, as we were the largest church in Southampton with around 1000 people meeting each week, we couldn't really be ignored. We became part of the Evangelical Alliance and sometimes one of our full time leaders would be appointed a chairman of the local EA group. We also became part of various other groups of church leaders that met together across the city. Citywide prayer meetings and other gatherings were organised often using Central Hall as the venue. It has been great to see the hall full of worshipping Christians from across the city, recalling the old days soon after the building was constructed. At one of these Streams in the City gatherings it was encouraging to hear Ron Rothery and Don Cox from Millbrook Christian Centre recalling the exciting times they remembered from the early days in Central Hall.

The coming together of churches and church leaders has gradually begun to have more tangible effects. One memorable gathering was the meeting at Whitsun in the Millennium year when Christians from across the city met together in Mayflower Park. For the following three years we had a summer programme of events called Hi-Life. These focussed on reaching out to the city, either in evangelism or in social action. A wide range of churches got involved. I remember some particularly enjoyable afternoons in the first year of Hi-Life, when a team of us went up to the Flower Estate. Bob Light had a long list of people who were struggling with gardening, painting and other household chores. It was great to be able to demonstrate the love of God by helping these folk in practical ways. Unfortunately, like a number of the inter-church initiatives it didn't become a permanent feature. While there is a good sense of unity amongst

Christians in Southampton, it feels to me that we still have some way to go to achieve the oneness that Jesus wants, and that is still very much my prayer for the church.

There were also some good prayer initiatives. One of these was Nehemiah Walls, organised by Hannah Morton. Individuals across different churches agreed to take a specific hour each week to pray for the city. There weren't quite enough of us to cover each hour of day and night but nevertheless there was regular prayer for Southampton and it was a good example of Christians across the city working together. Every month Hannah would produce a list of items for prayer. These were mainly for the projects in which the different churches were involved. I found it really encouraging to learn about the excellent work that was being done by Christians across the city. I was beginning to feel part of the real city-wide church. Unfortunately, this was another of the inter-church projects that didn't last. Is it just coincidence that Southampton Football Club was relegated from the Premier League the year after Nehemiah Walls stopped?

Speaking of football, for some of us this has been an important part of church life. My dad was an excellent footballer and so are both of my sons. Somehow, in my case, it seems to have skipped a generation, but I was nevertheless keen and took part in the football activities of the church. My five-goal match is part of the church football legend, mostly due to the surprise factor that I could possibly have done it! Geoff Scutt has organised Friday night football for more years than I care to remember. I played until I was 54 when my body told me enough was enough. The church also has a team playing in the local church league and often winning it – another advantage of being a large church. This and other sporting involvement has been a valuable part of being community and a great way bridging the generation gap.

The strength of the leadership team in Southampton meant that people in various ministries were attracted to join us. Graham Cooke, who was originally based with the Citygate church in Southampton, had developed a strong prophetic ministry. When that church underwent a split, he and his wife Heather, along with a number of others, decided to join us. He developed a School of Prophecy, which reached out nationally and internationally. Many of the teaching sessions and conferences were based at Central Hall. Peter and Irene Butt from the London area also joined us. Pete was a gifted Bible teacher and together with Phil Orchard started up a number of teaching courses in the church. Another addition to the team was Steve Lee who has a great heart for evangelism. His forte was preaching on the streets. He learnt how to escape from a straightjacket and would do this very theatrically to draw a crowd of onlookers. He then used the opportunity to relate what they had seen to the freedom from sin that Christ wanted to bring to their lives. He is a man of great energy with a vision to bring the gospel to people where they are. He developed his evangelistic efforts into a project called Miracle Street, which purchased several large vehicles, in which they travel round the country carrying out missions. Another of his acquisitions is an enormous tent, which can hold several hundred people.

There were also growing developments overseas. Pete Butt and others began visiting some African countries to run Bible teaching programmes. We retained our contacts with India, Nepal and other Asian countries through Impact Asia with Peter Light. Dave Adcock felt a particular burden for

France. He made good contacts with a variety of Christians and regularly takes groups of people from the church on visits. To assist in this he arranged for the church to purchase a property in Normandy, which acts as a base for visitors.

Towards the end of the 1990s, Tony was beginning to feel the strain of effectively having two jobs, running an apostolic team and a large local church. In addition, he had developed cancer, and although he thankfully recovered from this, he felt it was time to make a change. He decided to continue with the work of c-net, but to hand over the reins of leading the Community Church to Billy Kennedy. Billy had been in leadership for a number of years. Therefore he knew and was part of the ethos of the church, and was known and respected by the people. The official ceremony happened in January 2002, and although there was inevitable sadness about losing Tony's involvement after 25 years, the move was generally felt to be good. It certainly seemed like the transfer of leadership had followed a biblical pattern. Billy had been trained under Tony's leadership, and was being passed on the baton to train others (2 Tim 2:2). There were prophetic words about Billy's task being to work across the generations in the church. The handover happened without any major traumas and everyone was pretty optimistic about the future.

However, although things were going well with the church, developments with c-net came to a halt. In June 2004, it was announced that Tony was standing down from leadership due to personal issues in his life. This came as a great shock to the church and the implications are still being worked out. However, God gave me a word of encouragement in the situation. This one act did not destroy or nullify all the good work that had been done over the years. Tony had built well. He was not building his own empire. He had worked along with others to build the Church of Christ and this will stand. The action of one person, however sad, will not get in the way of God's overall purpose. After much deliberation about the future, it was decided to close down c-net, and in October of the same year, a conference was arranged to mark the closure. Although c-net finished as an organisation, all the projects that came under that umbrella were still to continue. While there were to be no more meetings of the whole c-net group, individual relationships would continue on a more local level. For the Southampton church, Allan Cox was to take over responsibility for outside missions.

Other projects originating from the Community Church have sought to address different topical issues. Over recent years we have seen several married couples in the church separate, something that was almost unheard of in the early days. John Deagle, along with folk from other churches, has established the 'twobecomeone' programme, which seeks to bring teaching for couples at all stages from marriage prepa- ration to 'MOTs' for those married for a while. Groundswell, another inter-church initiative started by Colin Henderson, aims to help people with AIDS. It is not primarily evangelis- tic, but just seeks to demonstrate God's love by getting alongside folk with this terrible disease.

This brings us up to date with the story of the churches with which I have been involved. I'm privileged to have been part of some great moves of God. There have obviously been ups and downs, as in anyone's life, but I think we have seen the church move on in some significant ways, and much good had been done to many people both within and outside the church.

Concluding Remarks

What God has done through the Community Church has resulted from being a large group of Christians committed to each other, working together and able to pool its resources. Given that we are still only a part of the whole church in Southampton, it is interesting to consider how much more might be achieved across the town, if all God's people were to work together with the same level of co-ordination and commitment. Despite the successes, we are clearly not the perfect church. Centralisation has had its disadvantages as well as its advantages. Having large central meetings and being involved in so many different projects, we have certainly lost something of the warmth of fellowship we knew in the early days. How can a large resource church still be a place of warm fellowship? I think this is one of the important issues that large restoration churches like ours need to address. We will think about this along with other key challenges to the church in general in the last section of the book. Jesus is still preparing his church to be his bride. It's important we understand where we are as a church in the process of preparation, and the steps that will now take us closer to this union with God, and with one another.

References

1. Tarleton, G., 1993, *Birth of a Christian Anarchist*, Pendragon Press, Lymington.
2. Clarke, P., 2006, *A Heart of Compassion*, Authentic Media, Milton Keynes.

CHAPTER SIX

THE SHAPING OF RESTORATION

Having looked at the major apostolic teams that have emerged as part of the restoration movement and the detailed history of one of them, we now consider some of the influencing factors on the movement from both within and without.

Bible Weeks

One of the most effective ways of spreading the message of restoration was through the Bible Weeks. They had been a vital part of the emergence of restoration in the early 1970s, and continued to have a significant role through to at least the year 2000. Bryn Jones' team again led the way with the Dales Bible Week, which ran very successfully between 1976 and the mid eighties. It was held at the Great Yorkshire Showground in Harrogate, which made modifications to their arena, allowing up to about 8000 people to gather. These were always memorable events, despite the practical difficulties of accommodating large numbers of people in tents and caravans. I remember particularly Dales '78. As a family, we had all the usual problems of looking after two under-twos in a tent, while trying to get to as much of the busy programme of meetings as possible. To add to this, it rained almost every day, making life extra difficult for the campers. I can still remember people queuing at the local launderette to dry their clothes and camping gear. The owners eventually put up a notice 'no drying only' to keep away the hoards of sodden campers who were making life difficult for their regular customers. Despite all this, it was a wonderful time of encouragement to see God stirring so many people with excitement about what he was doing around the country.

Bible Weeks provided an excellent opportunity for people interested in restoration ideas to learn in depth about them, and to see their outworking in the lives of people at first hand. Many people who joined restoration churches were convinced that this was where God was leading them through coming to a Bible Week. Living in close proximity with one another afforded the opportunity to develop relationships, and also the time to talk through pastoral problems, that was much more difficult to find in the hustle and bustle of normal daily life. I remember one of the elders of our church commenting that he was able to achieve as much pastorally during a Bible Week, as in several months back in the local church setting!

The concept of a Bible Week was not new. The Keswick convention had been running since 1875. However, the success of the early restoration Bible Weeks was obviously noted in evangelical circles, resulting in the emergence of Spring Harvest and New Wine. These are run along similar lines, and have been a great blessing to the church in the UK as a whole. At the time of writing, several apostolic teams have stopped organising their Bible Weeks, including Newfrontiers' Stoneleigh event. The ones that are still operating are generally on a rather smaller scale.

Disillusionment

The early days of restoration were ones of great hope and excitement. God had given his people a glimpse of the glory of his kingdom. We had a new vision of what our relationship with God could be like, and what church could be like. It was a taste of new wine. I have tried to argue in this review that the movement has had a very positive impact on church life in the UK. Despite that, its influence has fallen well short of the expectations of the early pioneers. They had hoped that the vision of vitality of our individual life with God, and of our lives together as the church would rapidly impact the whole church. This would then be followed by a revival, with many people becoming Christians, drawn by the attractiveness of being part of the alternative society.

There are several reasons for things not working out quite in this way. One contribution was the lack of clarity in the theology behind the movement. Its origin was based around the idea of restoring the church along New Testament lines. The principles were well defined in the first meetings in the early 1960s. However, as the movement developed, the vision broadened and became blurred. The desire to interpret scripture afresh gave an ethos of experimentation. People were open to new ideas, without always the wisdom to distinguish the good from the bad. The overstatement of the ideas of shepherding and submission is an example of this. A scriptural concept was misinterpreted, resulting in instances of abuse of authority. Another area of difficulty was in the diversity of ideas about how the vision of restoration should be brought about. In church history, movements like restoration have often started with the hope of uniting the church with a fresh vision, but have ended up being in division themselves through lack of agreement about the way ahead. Sadly, restoration has not been immune from this, and there have been a number of deep personal divisions between brothers who had set out at the beginning to walk so closely together.

For some people these difficulties have proved too much. Some members of restoration churches, including several prominent leaders of the early days, have left the faith altogether, while others have returned to established churches. The stability of many traditional churches, combined with their spiritual renewal has proved an attractive alternative to some Christians not always convinced with the way their restoration church was going.

My own view is that our disillusionment has resulted at least partly from a lack of determination to keep the vision in line with God's word. No move of God in the church to date has managed to get everything right, and restoration is no exception. I feel it is important that the church does not to write off the whole movement because of the difficulties. The right response is surely to celebrate the good that has been achieved, learn what we can from the mistakes, and seek God afresh for where he wants to take us from here.

The Changing Face of Evangelical Christianity

Alongside the developments in restoration ideas, the rest of evangelical Christianity has also undergone major changes in the last quarter of the twentieth century. The rapid development of the renewal movement experienced in the Anglican and Catholic churches in the 1960s and early 1970s, did not continue at the same rate in subsequent years. In the Church of England, however, there has continued to be a growth in renewal, with its evangelical and charismatic wing having an increasing influence. Two developments are particularly noteworthy.

The New Wine Bible Weeks, held annually at the Bath and West Showground in Shepton Mallet in Somerset since 1989, attract increasing numbers of Christians. They were started by leaders from the Anglican church of St Andrew's at Chorleywood. New Wine is charismatic in style and teaching, and promotes the renewal movement among UK churches. It has not only effectively brought charismatic teaching to Anglicans, but has also been valuable in bridging the gap between the renewal and restoration movements. Many folk from restoration churches attend and enjoy New Wine. More recently they have established a vision for New Wine Networks, which aims to establish churches across the denominations founded on the same values of worship, teaching and ministry in the Holy Spirit as expressed at the New Wine summer festivals. This interesting development indicates that this part of the renewal movement is actually adopting some of the restoration emphasis on the importance of church structure. It is encouraging to see the reason for this move is a desire to see churches and church leaders identifying with each other and working together more closely than they have done in the past.

The second influential development emerging from the Anglican charismatic movement is the Alpha course. This was developed by Nicky Gumbel of the Holy Trinity Brompton Church in London as a means of explaining Christianity to people outside the church. It has proved an extremely effective way of sharing the good news of the Christian message, and has been taken up by churches of all types from Catholic to new church. Its presentation of the gospel includes teaching on the baptism and gifts of the Holy Spirit. It is interesting that the leaders of both St Andrew's and Holy Trinity were influenced by John Wimber.

There are still a relatively small number of strongly charismatic churches within the Church of England, but their influence is steadily growing. There is also a growing number of Church of England ministers, who are charismatic. They are often able to influence the churches for which they have responsibility, bringing teaching on the Holy Spirit and new life into the congregation. However, the transitory nature of their ministry means that sometimes a good work that is started is not sustained, because they move to a different church. If their successor does not share the same vision then the renewal can be lost.

The renewal in the Catholic Church has not experienced the growth of that among Anglicans. There is still a faithful minority of Catholics, who continue to hold to charismatic teaching and practice. However, there are very few priests who are likeminded, so that charismatic renewal is rarely a central feature of a local church. The more usual situation is for charismatic activity to be confined to the margins of church life.

The renewal movement within the non-conformist churches followed a quite different pattern. Initially, most churches fought hard against the charismatic movement. Indeed the majority of folk who left churches in the 1970s to establish restoration or new churches, came from non-conformist fellowships that refused to accept charismatic teaching. That situation has changed relatively slowly but significantly between 1970 and 2000. Gradually, faithful Christians in such churches began to see that being charismatic did not mean that people became strange, or went off the rails in their Christian life. They also began to see that the teaching on the baptism and gifts of the Holy Spirit really was a very reasonable interpretation of scripture. Charismatic and restoration churches in their locality were not an overnight wonder, they consisted of other faithful Christians and what's more, they were growing. They could see that this was not something of the devil, as had been suggested by some in the early days, but something that God was clearly blessing.

A growing number of leaders within non-conformist churches began to be filled with the Spirit, and this inevitably led to a change in the stance of their churches. Even national leadership positions of several of the different denominations were being filled by those who were openly charismatic in their belief. Perhaps the largest influence on a national scale has been the Evangelical Alliance. Since 1983 its director has been a charismatic, and this has impacted the acceptance of the teaching in evangelical churches. The very successful Spring Harvest Bible Weeks have also been influential. Though not as radically different in their style as many of the restoration Bible Weeks, they are clearly charismatic in ethos, and have helped enormously in the raising the credibility of teaching about the role of the Holy Spirit and the gifts of the Spirit in the church today.

In the local context, the process of change resulting from the acceptance of charismatic teaching has often been gradual. Operation of the gifts of the Spirit is usually first confined to fringe meetings of the church, with little effect on the main congregational gatherings. The extent to which a change in practice occurs, varies considerably from church to church. Some have moved away from the traditional hymn-sandwich style of meeting, led very strongly from the front, to one where there is more freedom for participation. This is usually accompanied by the worship becoming expressive, and a growing sense of the reality of God's presence in the congregation. Operation of the vocal gifts of the Spirit such as tongues and prophecy usually happen to a limited extent in main meetings, although times of prayer for healing are more common. Outside of the main meeting, the concept of house groups has been taken up by many churches of all denominations. Many are still going through such changes, and are managing the transition at their own pace. Undoubtedly the changes in most 'renewed' churches are modest compared to those in restoration or new churches, but there is a growing similarity in style. One interesting development is that some churches are now developing a dual allegiance. They are opting to stay within their denomination, while at the same time seeking input and direction from one of the restoration apostolic teams.

It is clear that the spread of the renewal movement into non-conformist churches on a reasonably wide scale, has stemmed the flow of people into restoration churches. Christians who felt that the baptism of the Spirit and gifts of the Spirit were intended for today's church, or who realised the importance of genuine fellowship in small groups, or who were seeking to grow in their area of ministry, could now find the opportunity for these things within their own church. There was no need to move to a restoration church, or to create one if there was none in the locality. These New Testament principles of church life were operating on a much wider scale amongst churches in the UK. Although this might be seen as a failure of the restoration movement (even the end of restoration has been pronounced by some), I think it is part of the success story. Restoration ideas have now spread across the whole church much more effectively than would have occurred if it had relied on people leaving their churches. Restoration never had a vision of setting up a separatist movement. It always wanted to see the whole church restored to New Testament principles[1].

During the last two decades of the twentieth century, Christians in the United Kingdom from across the denominations, have come closer, both in their beliefs and in the way their churches worship. This has led to an increasing unity among evangelical Christians, which is making a significant impact on the church. Christians are becoming more and more captivated by a vision of a unified church. This is relatively easy to accept in principle, but the practicalities of coming together are quite considerable. It is encouraging that discussion of ways in which we can work together as Christians is coming higher on the agenda of more and more church leaders. On a national scale, the work of the Evangelical Alliance and gatherings such as Spring Harvest are evidence of this increasing desire to work together. Also, in many areas around the country, Christians are beginning to come together and work together as the whole local church. It's probably true to say that at no time since the days of the New Testament church, has there been such a sense of the unity in the Body of Christ.

However, a word of caution is necessary. Having commented on the far-reaching changes that have occurred in the non-conformist church scene in the UK, it needs to be stressed that the teaching on the baptism and gifts of the Spirit is by no means universally accepted. There are still a good number of individuals and churches, who feel that these do not apply to the church today.

The Toronto Blessing[2]

Starting in 1993, an unusual phenomenon impacted the church worldwide, which also had a significant effect in the UK. Rodney Howard-Browne, a preacher from South Africa, had been conducting a series of meetings in America in which some of the audience became subject to powerful experiences of the Holy Spirit. Whole sections of the congregation would fall to the ground as a result of Rodney blowing on them, and people would find themselves laughing uncontrollably. He was invited to the Airport Vineyard Church in Toronto for a conference from January 20-23rd 1994, where similar events occurred. Such was the impact of God's hand upon the church during the conference, that they decided to continue having meetings, six nights per week every week from that time and into the foreseeable future. At first, thousands of people from across the world would come every night to experience being touched by the Holy Spirit. As the years went by, the numbers went from thousands to hundreds per night, but the presence of God still continued to flow. Many individuals who received a touch of God went back to their own churches bringing the same anointing to the people there. The level of consistent commitment to ministry at this church over a number of years is quite remarkable. God had found a group of people, who were not only open to receive an unusual move of the Holy Spirit, but who were also willing to sacrifice the time and effort to serve the rest of the church, by faithfully ministering it to them.

Similar events started to happen across the United Kingdom from the middle of 1994. Naturally it was renewal and restoration churches that were most receptive to God moving in this way. A common occurrence was for people to fall over under the overwhelming presence of the Holy Spirit when they were being prayed for. This was known as being 'slain in the Spirit'. Catchers would be appointed to ensure that physical injury did not occur when they fell. They would then lie on the floor, often for a considerable period, doing 'carpet time', while the Holy Spirit brought encouragement and healing to them. Other manifestations of the work of God were uncontrollable laughter and roaring. These experiences were not new among charismatic Christians, but it was their frequency that dramatically increased. Many churches organised extra meetings where people would pray for each other to receive God's blessing. People were encouraged by the physical manifestations and the exciting sense of God's presence. However, there was also a lot of emphasis on allowing these experiences to be the means of us moving into a deeper walk with God.

Inevitably, the bizarre nature of the events caused a negative reaction in some. Even those who were open to be touched by the Holy Spirit and were encouraged by the movement, questioned why God would do things in this way. It was certainly a surprising development, and particularly surprising that the UK church should be so receptive of it, given our natural reserve in showing emotion. The frequency of the physical phenomena gradually reduced, and churches continued to hold their extra meetings until they felt that God had ceased to move specifically in this way. However, even when the physical experiences became less apparent, it was clear that many individual Christians and many churches had been permanently touched by this move of God. There was a new level of the reality of the Holy Spirit in people's lives. It renewed vitality in many churches that had lost the sense of his presence. It brought people of all ages together as a result of their shared experiences. Sadly too it alienated some, who did not feel that the move was from God. However, overall there was a significant positive impact on the churches and Christians who received the events from God.

Cell Church Concept

The cell church concept began to be discussed in the UK during the late 1980s. Since the 1970s, a number of different churches around the world had begun to experience remarkable growth by basing their operation on small group gatherings. The best known of these is the Yoido Full Gospel Church in Seoul, South Korea led by Yonggi Cho, which has numbers in the hundreds of thousands. The principles of cell church have been described in a series of books by Ralph Neighbour[3]. He argues that most churches currently have a 'programme-based' design. They have a number of programmes such as children's work, youth work, worship or administration. Gifted people tend to specialise in one of these areas. He is critical of this type of structure, in that it under-utilises the gifts of many church members, who find they do not have a role to play. Much of the ministry is focused around a single pastor, who has to manage all the different programmes, and therefore doesn't have the time to get to know people as individuals. He will also typically not spend much time in one place. Many move from church to church every few years, leaving a new leader the task of trying to pick up the running of the church where the previous one left off. 'Programme-based' churches usually own a building, which is also under-utilised, and consumes a large amount of resource, both in manpower and finance. They also often fail to foster a genuine sense of community, which is at the centre of God's heart for the church.

He contrasts this with the New Testament picture of church, which was based around small meetings in homes. He argues for a church structure centred around small groups, which he refers to as cells. These cells should be the focus of church life. Everyone in the church should be in a cell, and that is their basic point of contact in the church. Attending the cell gatherings is a priority. Community is developed through the relationships within these cell groups. The whole church is made up of a number of groups, managed by a hierarchy of cell supervisors and pastors. Church growth can be seen in terms of the cell structure, using an analogy with biological systems, where healthy cells successively grow and then divide, resulting in growth of the organism. In the same way, growth and subsequent division of cell groups leads to church growth. A strong co-ordination of the groups is required to manage the cell division process, and this characterises the life of many of these churches. An important feature of cell church is that cells are the central focus of the church. This contrasts with churches, which have optional small groups as part of their operation, but are still essentially 'programme-based'.

The relationship between cell church ideas and the restoration movement is an interesting one. The growth of restoration churches has generally been similar to the pattern prescribed for cell church. They nearly always started as a group of Christians meeting in a home, seeking to live out the Christian life together as God's people, and reach out through the group to the local community. As people were added to the group, it became too large to meet in a single home, and divided to become two new groups. In the typical structure that eventually emerged, everyone was part of a local house group, and the house group leaders were responsible to a church elder. Therefore, when the cell church concept was introduced in the UK in the early 1990s, restoration Christians quite reasonably found it difficult to see what was new about it.

Despite the similarities, I think that there are some subtle differences in philosophy. Restoration churches had a broad aim of recovering the heart and practice of church life of the New Testament. Meeting in small groups in homes was very much a part of this, as this was how Christians met in the early church. However, it was never considered to be a prescriptive part of church life in the way that cell church is described. As restoration churches developed, many of them had periods when house groups were suspended for the church to concentrate on other things for a time, such as prayer or a particular teaching programme.

As restoration developed, the difference between its practice and that of cell-church has increased. Many restoration churches expanded quite rapidly and often purchased buildings, both of which added to the effort required in management. There were of course organisational advantages in the greater efficiency of centralisation. However, the result was that these churches changed from being based around small groups to become essentially 'programme-based', with house groups forming only part of the structure. In such churches, a good proportion of members are not part of a small group. Therefore in many cases, restoration churches are now quite a long way from the cell church concept.

There is a feeling among many restorationists that these changes have resulted in a loss of the sense of community that characterised the early days of the movement. They have sensed the need to recover this ethos, but have found it difficult to reconcile this with all the other demands of being a large church. Some restoration churches investigated the cell-church concept in the early 1990s, but relatively few found it possible to make the transition. If people's primary commitment was to the cell group, where would they find manpower to run the Sunday School, lead the worship, or be involved in the various community activities and missions? A few churches in the UK have successfully implemented the cell church concept and are experiencing growth[4]. The Ichthus churches in London represent an example of a restoration church, which is essentially operating the cell system. However, in general, cell church does not seem to have provided the answer to this difficulty in the UK.

David Lillie

David Lillie and Arthur Wallis in the 1950s and '60s sowed the seeds of the restoration movement. David Lillie brought to this partnership the radical vision of the church, and in many ways we might describe him as being the father of restoration. However, while Arthur still remained heavily involved in the development of the main stream of the movement, David began to fade from the visible leadership at the beginning of the 1970s. He became unhappy with several of the changes that were taking place in the restoration churches. He had been captivated by what he felt was a very clear vision of a New Testament style church, and he continued to be faithful to the vision, in spite of the changes that were occurring in the movement. His picture of the local church was of small groups meeting in homes, hiring local halls for larger gatherings when necessary. Local churches might be established by apostles and have ongoing visits from them, but should be run by the local eldership. The church would be characterised by strength of relationships and by everybody contributing to its life. David has explained his ideas in a number of books and pamphlets. *Beyond Charisma*[5], in particular, contains a very well argued study on what we can learn about the principles of church life from the account of the early church in the New Testament.

A reflection on these original principles makes it clear how much the movement has changed from its roots. David was particularly unhappy with the development of the role of apostles, which changed from the original vision of being church planters to become people with pastoral responsibility for large numbers of churches. In this way the church was losing its God centredness and becoming man centred following the pattern of similar developments throughout church history.

David continued to hold these views as he moved into his nineties, and until recently with failing health, had been circulating his thoughts and vision for a quiet revolution in the church in the form of a newsletter entitled *Church Matters*. He also continued to receive visits at his home near Exeter from national church leaders seeking his wisdom on issues that they faced. While having quite a specific view of what the church should look like, one senses this vision is quite close to what God wants and shows good consistency with what the New Testament teaches.

Changing Philosophy

'Constant change is here to stay' is a phrase we have often heard quoted in restoration church circles, and certainly reflects the situation both in the church, and in life generally in the latter half of the twentieth century. The Church has always had to adapt to changes in the social and cultural environment. While the scriptural principles on which it is based remain constant, it has to respond by applying these principles to the new questions that result from changes in society. The years 1950–2000 have seen a rapid rate of change in most areas of life in the United Kingdom. Technological developments have changed our day-to-day living, and medical advances mean that we can enjoy life for longer and in better health. However, it is in the area of morality where arguably the most fundamental changes in society have occurred. For example, in the middle of the twentieth century, life was clearly based around the nuclear family. It was the expectation of most people to marry, and for children to be brought up by two parents. A very dim view was taken of a girl becoming pregnant outside of marriage. While people were certainly not angels, society in general held to certain standards. In the last days of the twentieth century, the biblical concept of sex being expressed only within marriage has been rejected by society with disastrous results: the break up of family life and the resulting increase in insecurity of our children, the dramatic rise in the number of abortions, the acceptance of homosexuality, and the spread of AIDS. While it is debatable whether Britain (or anywhere else) has ever been a truly Christian country, there is no doubt that biblical principles have had a significant role in influencing its laws and government in the past. However, it is clear now that morality in our society is not based on the solid rock of what the Bible says, but on the sinking sand of what the majority feel is acceptable. The church has had to come to terms with these fundamental changes, and has had the challenge of discovering which of its doctrines are clearly biblical, and distinguishing them from those that are merely the traditions of men.

The rapid changes in society were reflected in the ethos of the 1960s of 'doing one's own thing'. The thinking was to break free from the traditions of the past, to go back to first principles, and take a fresh look at the meaning of life. This meant becoming radical, and opening up the possibilities of all existing and new philosophies in the search for reality. There were many healthy aspects of such an approach, but the removal of all baselines, in particular the word of God, led to the deterioration in moral values we have seen over the last 50 years. The philosophy of life over this period is often described as changing from a modern to a post-modern viewpoint. Modern philosophy describes the view that there is an underlying order to everything. All the questions of life have an answer that can be addressed through improvements in our knowledge. The developments in science and technology are part of this philosophy. It is also reflected in hierarchical forms of management and administration in organisations. The idea is that with a well reasoned structure the organisation is bound to be successful. By contrast, post-modern thinking is based on the idea that there is no underlying order or certainty in life. Morality is now defined by what seems right to the majority, and is worked out in the concept of political correctness. The downside of this philosophy, is that because there is no certainty or purpose, there is a sense of hopelessness; there is no answer to the central question about the purpose in life.

Postmodernist philosophy is a mixed blessing for Christians. The idea that there is no absolute truth is something that we conclusively reject; we believe that the truth is found in Jesus. However, a post-modern approach may be able to help us with the seeming paradoxes in Christianity. We have long battled with debates over the dual nature of Jesus, predestination versus free will and most recently, a loving God versus an angry God. Postmodernism allows us to live with seeming paradoxes in tension. For example, in the latest debate, it's wonderful to know that God loves us so much, but it's also quite reasonable for him to be angry about sin. A postmodern approach lets us rejoice in all God's truth without having to necessarily tie it all up in a systematic theology. It has also led us to look at our faith in radical new ways. By doing this within the constraints of God's word, this has become a healthy questioning of all aspects of Christian life, including our understanding of Church. While there is no doubt that the move of God in the Church over this period has been one originated by the Holy Spirit, it also seems reasonable that its timing, occurring alongside these fundamental changes in attitude in society, is not mere coincidence. The postmodern culture has provided an environment where people have been open to new approaches to church life.

Emerging Church

This is a relatively new concept that describes some of the latest and more radical developments within churches[6]. Emerging churches are exploring new forms of church structure in an attempt to be relevant to the culture of today's society. It is the response of God's people to the rapidly changing environment of the later years of the twentieth century. Proponents of emerging church argue that, because society is changing, the church has to change to be relevant to the new culture. Many such churches now exist, and they are doing good work in reaching out, particularly to young people who are part of the 'club culture'.

The emerging church approach is experimental. New ideas about how church should be structured are tried, and if successful they are continued and developed. A large part of the motivation for deciding what works, is what is successful in attracting non-Christians to come along. A whole variety of things have been tried. One idea, which has been used in some large churches, is to divide the church down into separate congregations. These might be geographically based or culturally based. A youth congregation, for example, can concentrate on having meetings that appeal to younger people, without the need to compromise the style of worship that would be needed to accommodate a broad range of ages. Another more radical approach has been to cut down dramatically the number of whole church meetings to just a few per year. The purpose of this is to allow people more time to develop friendships with neighbours, and to work in the community as local councillors or school governors.

There are similarities between restoration ideas and those of emerging church, in that there is the same radical openness to change in the way church is organised. However, there is a fundamental difference in philosophy. Restorationism is based on looking at scriptural patterns of church, and seeing how these apply to the modern day, whereas emerging church is much freer to experiment with different church models. These models do not necessarily have to have any base in the biblical description of church; they are rather judged on how successful they are. This lack of scriptural reference is a concern to evangelical restorationists like me. I believe that if we aim to become the church that Jesus wants, we have to be based on scriptural principles. These principles have not changed because of the post-modern spirit of the current age.

Contemplative Christianity

One aspect of the developing post-modern philosophy has been a generally increased interest in spirituality. The New Age movement is one example of this trend. In the church there has also been a move towards understanding and experiencing the spiritual side of the Christian life. This has always been part of our faith, right from the early days of the church. However, with the advent of modern rational thought, it lost some of its prominence in Christian teaching. The focus on the work of the Holy Spirit in the charismatic movement had the effect of Christians thinking more about the spiritual side of their lives. Encouragement to make spiritual intimacy with God a priority in our lives, has become a feature of evangelical preaching and writing. In the busyness of modern day living, devoting time to being quiet before God, is seen as a very important practice. There are also retreats organised, where groups of people go to a quiet place to meet with God themselves, while also sensing the support of being together with other Christians seeking to be with him as well.

Restorationists have readily taken up contemplative teaching, seeing it as yet another scriptural aspect of church life that has needed restoring. This move has interestingly been a means of joining the hearts of Christians in restoration churches with those in the Catholic Church, for whom the practice of contemplation is a central part of their lives as Christians.

The Faith Movement

The faith movement is a development of Pentecostal and charismatic teaching. It follows basic evangelical Christian beliefs, but adds some new interpretations on the meaning and practice of faith, some of which are quite controversial.

One of the principal ideas is the belief that God wants his people to be living in prosperity. This is, of course, consistent with the many scriptures that speak of the blessings of following Christ (Matt 5:1-12). The movement specifies that this applies to every area of life, including health and material blessings. Believers are encouraged to pray in faith for health and material prosperity. Then, based on the promise spoken by Jesus that 'whatever we ask in his name we will receive' (Mark 11:22-24), they are to hold on to that faith until they receive their request.

Another aspect of the teaching and practice in the faith movement, is the position of leaders. Great honour is bestowed on the 'man of God', and blessings to believers are related to their willingness to support their leader financially. The leaders must be examples to their flock in demonstrating God's blessing on their lives. Therefore they often tend to live ostentatiously, dressing sharply and driving expensive cars.

The faith movement is enormously popular in the USA and in developing countries. Its influence has spread through large crusades and more recently by satellite television, where a good proportion of the channels promote the teaching of the movement.

This approach to Christianity has received a mixed response in evangelical circles in the UK. The Evangelical

Alliance commissioned a book on the subject to help Christians think through the implications of these new ideas[7]. Although this is a balanced evaluation of the movement, it is essentially negative about much of its teaching. Not surprisingly, many Bible-believing Christians question the emphasis on material prosperity. Jesus spoke clearly about the dangers of riches (Matt 19:16-30). Most evangelicals would understand the primary meaning of the scriptural promises of prosperity to relate to our spiritual lives. While we believe that our natural lives are in God's hands, we balance the promises of prosperity with other verses on the dangers associated with the love of money, and on being called to share the sufferings of Christ. Many would also be very concerned with what seems almost like worship of the senior leaders, which seems a long way from the humility of character required by leaders which is described in the Bible (1 Pet 5:1-5).

The relationship between the faith movement and restoration is quite interesting. Recovery of the miraculous gifts of the Spirit was clearly part of both the restoration movement, and of the charismatic movement as a whole. This aspect of faith teaching was quite prominent in the early days of restoration. Very often, restoration churches would reach out in faith to pray for one of their number who was seriously ill. Members were urged to be in faith that the person would recover. Faith was often encouraged by words of prophecy, or words of knowledge being spoken about what God wanted to do in the life of the person. When God had spoken a specific word about someone, then faith in this word would ensure that it would happen. A few remarkable healings have certainly taken place as a result of such prayer, but equally, we have to be honest and say that many times when people have prayed with as great a faith as they could find, the specific requests did not actually happen. The result is that the very dogmatic teaching that all we have to do to get prayers answered, is pray in the name of Jesus and believe, is not heard very often in restoration churches. While most Christians believe that God answers prayer, and does miraculously heal people in the present day, this is not something we can just pray in faith about and expect to happen, like putting a coin in a slot machine.

This whole area of the miraculous is a very difficult one for Christians who really want to believe the Bible, but also face honestly what happens in the real world. I think most of us have to say that we don't quite understand the apparent discrepancy between what Jesus said about us receiving things asked in His name, and the fact that this doesn't always happen in reality. I cannot easily identify with the resolute faith of those in the faith movement. However, I certainly view their stand with a measure of admiration.

One key issue regarding the faith movement, is its impact on progress towards church unity. While old barriers between different groups of Christians are steadily being broken down, this is a new one that is being erected. Amongst Christians in general today, it is often easy to sense the unity of spirit that we have, even when we don't agree on all points of doctrine. However, the preaching of the faith movement is so passionate, and the centrality of the faith teaching so marked, it is sometimes quite difficult for those of us who are not sure about it, to sense that same oneness with its proponents. This could be a potentially damaging issue for the church. However, as with most differences, I believe it can be solved with an attitude of humility on both sides of the fence, and a genuine willingness to learn from one another.

The Colour Divide

The word racism means quite different things to different people. My own view is that there is currently little evidence of discrimination against people in the church in the UK because of their colour. Many black people quite happily integrate within churches of all denominations. As evidence of their acceptance, one of their number is the current Director General of the Evangelical Alliance. The fact that his colour is hardly ever mentioned, demonstrates that everyone naturally accepts that he is the best person for the job. However, there is still an enormous colour divide in the church. Many black Christians choose to worship in what are known as 'Black Majority Churches' (BMC). My own view is that this is primarily an issue of culture. Some black Christians do, no doubt, find it difficult to find a place of acceptance in predominantly white churches (but then so do some white people!). It is unlikely that skin colour is a major issue in this respect. When one visits BMCs or sees them on television, the reason for the divide becomes apparent. The style of their meetings is very different. Lively worship is very much a part of charismatic church meetings and indeed of some other evangelical churches, but Afro-Caribbean churches reach a different level and style of liveliness. The passion in the preaching is rarely matched in predominantly white churches. The teaching of the faith movement has also been more influential in black churches. All these factors combine to create quite a different ethos from most white churches. This ethos reflects the culture of the members, and black Christians who are part of them seem generally content to meet separately. Relatively few white Christians are motivated by the difference in style to join them.

In my experience, black churches do not tend to get very involved in inter-church initiatives. There is also very little interaction between restoration churches and black churches despite areas of similarity. This issue is another that needs to be addressed if we are to achieve the unity that Jesus prayed for amongst his family.

Integration of Streams

A very important and influential prophetic word that has come in different forms over recent years, describes a picture of the church as being composed of a number of different streams. As these streams flow on, they merge with each other to become larger rivers. Eventually they all join up to become one huge river flowing to the sea. Richard Foster has written a very interesting book trying to identify these different streams[8]. Instead of seeing the streams as being the different denominations, which are perhaps the most obvious sub-divisions of the church, he sees them as different traditions that are found across the church. He lists these as

1. *contemplative* – the prayer filled life
2. *holiness* – the virtuous life
3. *charismatic* – the Spirit empowered life
4. *social justice* – the compassionate life

5. *evangelical* – the word centred life
6. *incarnational* – the sacramental life (using physical items and ceremonies to encourage contemplation on God)

His argument is that these streams are flowing in the life of the church. Certain individuals and churches have emphasized perhaps one or a few of these aspects of life. Each has been valuable as a means of people touching God. As the streams come to flow together, the strength of joining our resources into one mighty river will be enormous. The prospect of this word coming to fruition is tremendously exciting and is deeply at the centre of my heart.

Concluding Remarks

The development of the restoration movement has been affected by many factors both from within and outside the church. Generally, these have caused restoration churches themselves to develop a more balanced church life, adding outreach to the initial emphasis on building church. However, some aspects of the original vision have begun to fade from view. The formation of large churches, for example, has tended to result in a loss of the warm fellowship that was characteristic of the early days of restoration.

The most positive outcome of the restoration movement is the way in which its ideas have been incorporated into other parts of the church in the UK. Lively worship, the gifts of the spirit and house groups are now an integral part of many evangelical churches. This has resulted in a greater level of unity across the denominations. David Pawson has suggested that now is the time for what he describes as the fourth wave of church history[9]. The first three were Catholicism, Evangelicalism and Pentecostalism/charismatic movement (Note that Christians are very fond of wave terminology. The waves described by David are different from the wave theory mentioned earlier, where the three waves are Pentecostalism, the charismatic movement and the signs and wonders movement instigated by John Wimber). David Pawson's fourth wave is the coming together of the evangelicals and charismatics. He argues that the philosophies of both groups have become considerably closer of late. The barriers between them are much smaller than in the past and it seems clearly feasible that they could be broken down altogether. Having seen the demolition of the barriers of Soviet communism and South African apartheid over recent years, is this too much to ask?

We will finish our overview of the place of the restoration movement in church history on this optimistic note. The church is surely on the brink of exciting possibilities. To be in the best position to go forward, we need to have a good appreciation of our scriptural foundations. In the next part of the book, we will look in more detail at the philosophy of restoration, and how it fits into the picture of the church we have in the Bible.

References

1. Jones, B., 1999, *The Radical Church: Restoring the Apostolic Edge*, Destiny Image Publishers Inc, Shippensburg, PA.
2. Roberts, D., 1994, *The Toronto Blessing*, Kingsway, Eastbourne.

3. Neighbour, R.W., 1990, *Where do we go from here? A guide-book for the cell group church*, Touch Publications Inc, Houston, TX.
4. Astin, H., 1998, *Body and Cell: Making the transition to Cell church: a first-hand account*, Monarch Books, Crowborough, East Sussex.
5. Lillie, David, 1981, *Beyond Charisma*, Paternoster Press, Exeter.
6. Gibbs, E. and Bolger, R.K., 2006, *Emerging Churches: Creating Christian Community in Postmodern Cultures*, SPCK.
7. Perriman, A. (editor), 2003, *Faith, Health and Prosperity, A report on 'Word of Faith' and 'Positive Confession' Theologies by the Evangelical Alliance(UK) Commission on Unity and Truth among Evangelicals*, Paternoster Press, Cumbria.
8. Foster, R., 1998, *Streams of Living Water. Celebrating the great traditions of Christian faith*, Harper Collins, London.
9. Pawson, D., 1993, *Fourth Wave Charismatic and evangelicals: are we ready to come together?*, Hodder and Stoughton, London.

Part 2
What is the Church?

The underlying theme of the restoration movement was a desire to restore a genuinely New Testament form of church life. This applies both in the recovery of a biblical church structure and perhaps, more importantly, of the real sense of God's presence that clearly characterised the lives of the first believers. The thinking and doctrine of restorationists, like other evangelical Christians, is firmly based on the Bible as the plumb-line for God's truth. What then is the biblical view of the Church, or perhaps, to rephrase the question more poignantly, what is the sort of church that Jesus wants? This part of the book aims to address these questions.

I am attempting to discuss the issue directly from a biblical perspective, rather than ask what restorationists believe, for two reasons. First, a biblical understanding of church is the key issue to be addressed. Second, there is quite a range of views on church among those in restoration or new churches. This diversity has served to blur the vision of the early restorationists. My hope is to encourage us to get back to biblical basics in our understanding of church.

The chapters in this part of the book can be considered in three sections. First, we will look at the teaching given on the Alpha Course[1]. This gives a biblically based description, which reflects the 'centre of gravity' of current evangelical views on the subject. Then we will consider in some detail the biblical principles of how the early church operated. Finally, there will be a description of a model of the church originally presented by David Lillie in his book *Beyond Charisma*[2]. This is an attempt to encapsulate what the Bible teaches about church structure.

References

1. Gumbel, Nicky, 1993, *Questions of Life. A Practical Introduction to the Christian Faith*, Kingsway Publications, Eastbourne, UK.
2. Lillie, David, 1981, *Beyond Charisma*, Paternoster Press, Exeter.

CHAPTER SEVEN

THE ALPHA COURSE DESCRIPTION
OF THE CHURCH

The Alpha Course introduced by Nicky Gumbel during the 1990s has made an outstanding contribution to today's church, both in the UK and throughout the world. It is primarily an excellent means of sharing the gospel with non-Christians. However, it also has another less obvious, but nevertheless very important role. It has put together a simple and very understandable statement of what evangelical Christians believe. Most would sign up to the majority of teaching proposed in the Alpha course[1]. Significantly, it includes teaching on the baptism and gifts of the Holy Spirit, which is now acceptable to most, though certainly not all, evangelical Christians.

Nicky includes a summary of what the Bible teaches about church. His main message is that the church is essentially a group of people. It consists of all those who are Christians, in the evangelical sense of the word. This means those who have turned from their sin, trusted in Christ for forgiveness, and committed their lives to him. He points out that this is actually quite different from many people's understanding of the word 'church'. It would often be seen as a building, a career or a denomination. Other authors have also discussed the inadequacy of the word 'church'. In a radical book on the subject, John Metcalfe[2] argues that the English word 'church' is a poor translation of the Greek word 'ecclesia', which is used to describe the church in the New Testament. This is best defined as a people called out to be together. When we are called by God to become Christians, we find that we are actually called out to be joined in a special relationship with a lot of other people, who have also been called by him. The debate about whether 'church' is the right word will, no doubt, go on. However, the important thing is that we understand how God wants us to be together as his people.

Nicky Gumbel gives a good scriptural description of church by considering the various pictures that are given in the Bible to portray its nature.

God's people

The church is described first and foremost as being a group of people. When we become Christians, we become part of God's people – his church. It's part of the package. In the act of being baptised to identify our individual commitment to Christ, we are identifying with his people as well (1 Cor 12:13). This means we are joined together with people who, like us, have had the wonderful experience of coming to Christ. Surely a church made up of such people would be a fantastic group to be part of. It is! It's an amazing privilege to be part of God's people. I can remember one summer holiday in my teens, being on a National Young Life Campaign holiday at Witherslack Hall in the Lake District.

We had a mixture of Bible teaching, prayer, sport and walking in the beautiful countryside, all in the context of being a group of Christians together. I remember thinking this must be a little taste of heaven.

The trouble is, of course, that church life is not always like that. The church is composed of imperfect people, and the idyllic life we might imagine is not quite realised in practice. For many non-Christians this is a problem. John Lennon is famously quoted as saying that he thought Jesus was OK, but that his disciples were thick. One of the most common objections when presenting the Christian message is the poor example of the church, and particularly its lack of unity.

In any group of people, or indeed any human relationship, tension will arise because of different outlooks and personal interests. To be successful, all inter-personal relationships have to be carefully nurtured through good communication and understanding. In principle, the church has the potential of being a loving caring community, that is not only looking after its own, but is also looking to help those outside and welcoming them in. The picture we have of the church in scripture is truly wonderful. It is surely a vision to pursue, even if we are a group of imperfect people. As we aspire to the vision and nurture our relationships, much good will be realised.

God's Kingdom

God's people are also described as being a nation (1 Pet 2:9), and there are a lot of references, particularly in the teaching of Jesus himself, about being part of the Kingdom of God. The picture here is of the world consisting of two kingdoms, the Kingdom of God where God rules, and the Kingdom of Darkness where Satan rules. People either belong to one or the other. Before we become Christians we are part of the Kingdom of Darkness. When we commit our lives to Christ we transfer allegiance to the Kingdom of God and come under his rule. We become part of the holy nation spoken of in the Bible (1 Pet 2:9). The question of the complete meaning of the Kingdom of God in scripture is a big one, about which whole books have been written[3]. However, in simple terms, being in the church is like being in a kingdom where we are under the rule of God.

God's Family

The next picture of the church is that of being a family. When we become Christians we become sons of God, and therefore brothers and sisters to each other. This is probably the picture of the church that is closest to God's heart. He is, by nature, a father, and a father's priority is his family. There is a television advert for a pasta sauce depicting an extended Italian family enjoying a meal together. The grannies are sitting and laughing together while the children are running around playing. It is a scene that pictures how I think God loves to see his family enjoying life together. Rick Warren's excellent book, *The Purpose Driven Life*[4] describes one of the central purposes of our lives as being 'formed for God's family'.

The sense of being part of the family of God wherever one goes is very precious. In my job I am lucky enough to have the opportunity to travel to scientific meetings in different parts of the world. In 1984, I attended the annual meeting of the Society of Nuclear Medicine in Los Angeles, and had arranged to stay over the following week to visit some hospitals in California, who were doing similar work to me. I thought that over the weekend, it would be nice to meet up with some Christians. Through the leader of our church, Tony Morton, I was put in touch with a church that had just started up in the Los Angeles area called the Pasadena Christian Community. This was a small group of no more than twenty believers, who had recently moved from the eastern United States to set up a church in the area. I wrote to them to find out where they met. To my delight they not only gave me details of their church, but they offered to put me up for the weekend. I arrived at the house of Lou Engel on the Friday night and joined the group for a barbecue and an informal meeting. They asked me what I would like to do for the weekend. Whilst travelling to Pasadena on the bus, I had seen the San Gabriel mountains in the distance, and said I would be keen to go there. I am also very keen on sport, and so added that I'd love to get along to a baseball game. On the Saturday morning they arranged a trip to the hills where we had a picnic. In the afternoon they were holding an evangelistic event in a local park. They were all involved in taking part and really wanted a video record of the events. I was given the job. I had never touched a video camera before, but fortunately I managed OK, and the recording came out surprisingly well. On the Sunday, one of the church members took me to watch the Los Angeles Dodgers baseball team, taking time to answer all my questions on the intricacies of the game. We all joined together for the church meeting on the Sunday evening before my host, Lou, drove me back into Los Angeles where I was due to catch the Greyhound bus. I was absolutely overwhelmed by the hospitality of this group. They had never met me before. They only knew that I was a Christian and, on the strength of that, accepted me as a member of their church family. It was one of the most moving experiences of my life. It serves to illustrate the wonderful privilege we have to be part of God's family, and the potential for the quality of extended family life that we can enjoy, if we are prepared to be giving in our attitude.

God is the Father of this family. Father Cantalamesa, a leading figure of the Roman Catholic Church, has commented that the answer to all the whys of the Bible is the love of the Father[5]. He considers that: 'If the written word of the Bible could become a single voice, this voice more powerful than the roaring sea would ring: THE FATHER LOVES YOU'.

The nature of God's creation ensures that each person belongs to a family. These are generally not large groups of people. They are small enough that, in a properly functioning family, each person is loved and made to feel an important part of the group.

The early believers adopted the concept of family, by meeting in small groups in homes. I believe that God intended this pattern for the church, because he wanted to have family-like groupings, where everyone is loved, and everyone is important. God loves us individually. We are very special to him. Through small groups he can express his love in tangible terms through the love and concern of other people.

The Body of Christ

The body of Christ is another powerful picture of the church. It is described in some detail in 1 Cor 12, but the concept is referred to throughout the New Testament (e.g. Eph 1:23, Eph 4:25, Col 1:24). Christ is seen as the head of the body, controlling all the other organs. Each person in the church is one of the body parts. From this picture one can understand a number of key aspects of church life.

For organs of the body to function correctly they must be connected to the head. Nerves send messages both from the head to the organ and from the organ back to the head. Communication in both directions is important to the proper running of the body. Similarly we must be in direct contact with Christ, sending prayer messages to him and listening out to what he has to say to us.

As each organ has a useful part to play in the functioning of a body, so each Christian has a valuable contribution to make in the church. Each of us is made in the image of God. We reflect something of him in our lives through both our personality and our actions. None of us provides a complete reflection of God ourselves as an individual. We all have failings and areas where we don't reflect God's nature. This is where we need to be complemented by each other. Together we can really be the body of Christ. Paul put it this way when writing to the Ephesian church (Eph 3:10):

> God's intent was that now, through the church, the manifold wisdom of God should be made known to the rulers and authorities in the heavenly realms, according to his eternal purpose which he accomplished in Jesus Christ our Lord.

There are some verses in scripture, including several in Ephesians, which are so big that my reaction is just to say 'Wow!' This is one of those verses. When we realise that the church is only made up of ordinary people like us, this seems impossible. Together, however, as the body of Christ properly functioning, one can imagine this might be feasible. It does not seem realistic with the church as it is at present, being so fragmented in different groups. However, if we think about how it could be if we were all pulling together, then this amazing statement could become reality.

If we, as the body of Christ, are to work towards this vision, there needs to be good co-ordination. This is again well illustrated by the picture of a body. The organs of the body do not work in isolation. For the whole body to function correctly, each organ needs to bring its contribution at the right time, taking note of what is happening elsewhere in the body. I am currently getting into golf. I think nearly everyone who has taken up the sport realises that it not easy to hit a golf ball well and reliably. To do so, requires a great level of co-ordination between several parts of the body. Like a good golf swing, achieving this level of co-ordination within the church is going to take a lot of work. We will need to understand that we are mutually dependent on each other. We must recognise the value of all the different sorts of people to the operation of the body, and our need of each of them.

God's Temple

Another quite different picture of the church is that of being a temple (Eph 2:19-22, 1 Pet 2: 4-8). This picture would have been particularly applicable to the Jews at the time when the New Testament was written. Under the Old Covenant that

God made with the Jews, access to his presence was limited. The temple was the place where God specially met with his people. Under the New Covenant, God's presence is in each believer all the time through the Holy Spirit. Therefore the temple of the Old Covenant, as the place of God's presence, has become the church in the New. It is composed of people who are seen as living stones built together to form a strong structure. It is based on the firm foundation of the teaching of the early apostles and prophets, which is recorded in scripture. Each stone in the building is correctly aligned by reference with the cornerstone, who is Christ.

The Bride

The final picture referred to in the Alpha book is of the church being the bride of Christ. There are several references, which make analogies between the love of a husband for his wife and that of Christ for his church. Ephesians 5:25-27 is a good example:

> Husbands love your wives just as Christ loved the church and gave himself up for her to make her holy, cleansing her by the washing with water through the word, and to present her to himself as a radiant church without stain or wrinkle or any other blemish but holy and blameless.

This picture illustrates, first of all, the love of Christ for the church as a bridegroom for his bride. We often think of Christ's love to us as individuals, which is of course incredibly precious. But Christ also loves us a group of people. He is very interested in how we get on together. In his prayer recorded in John (John 17:20-23), Jesus prays with great passion for his disciples and all those that believe in him because of them.

> My prayer is not for them alone (the disciples), I pray also for those who will believe in me through their message, that all of them may be one, Father, just as you are in me and I am in you. May they also be in us so that the world may believe that you sent me. I have given them the glory that you gave me, that they may be one as we are one: I in them and you in me. May they be brought to complete unity to let the world know that you sent me and have loved them even as you have loved me.

His deep desire is that we get on together really well, in fact with the same sort of oneness that is shared in the Godhead! This is another of those 'wow' verses. Jesus heart for his church, as a group together, is enormous. The picture of the church as a bride illustrates his deep desire for his people. In human terms, the love of a bridegroom for his bride is one of the strongest human emotions. Of all the people in the world, the groom has chosen this particular person, and how proud he feels on that day of their wedding when she looks so wonderful. All my three children have been married recently so the excitement is fresh in my memory. What a lot of preparation goes into getting the bride to look her best. And what a joy it is to see her looking so beautiful. The wedding day is very important – it marks a completely new path of life for both partners. Although the build-up and preparation take a lot of work, they seem appropriate to mark such an important occasion.

In Revelation, John has a vision of the 'new Jerusalem',

which is generally taken to be another biblical picture of the church. It is pictured as a bride coming from heaven 'beautifully dressed for her husband' (Rev 21:1-4).

I'm sure when Paul and John wrote these words on the beauty of the church, they must have had some difficulty to relate it to the imperfect nature of things in the church at that time. The picture of the bride without spot or blemish, beautifully dressed was a vision for the future. Today, 2000 years later, there is still a gulf between this picture and reality, and it still speaks of the future. The bride is not yet fully ready for the wedding day, but Jesus is working to prepare her for it. This seems such an impossible goal, but it is nevertheless what we are encouraged to set our sights on. In our individual lives, the possibility of being sinless seems remote, but we can sin less and less. Similarly, in the church, this goal of purity should be one to which we can be moving, even if its realisation seems a long way off. The beauty of the picture is surely enough to inspire us to seek it with all our hearts – to encourage us to ask how we can prepare ourselves to become the church that Jesus wants us to be.

References

1. Gumbel, Nicky, 1993, *Questions of Life. A Practical Introduction to the Christian Faith*, Kingsway Publications, Eastbourne, UK.
2. Metcalfe, John, 1990, *The Church: What is it? The Apostolic Foundation of the Christian Church*, The Publishing Trust, Buckinghamshire.
3. Ladd, G.E., 2002, *The Gospel of the Kingdom – Scriptural*

studies on the Kingdom of God, W.B. Eerdmans Publishing Company, Grand Rapids, Michigan.

4. Warren, Rick, 2002, *The Purpose Driven Life*, Zondervan, Grand Rapids, Michigan.

5. Martin, R., 1994, *The Catholic Church at the end of an Age – What is the Spirit Saying?*, Ignatius Press, San Francisco, CA (Quotation used by permission of Ignatius Press).

CHAPTER EIGHT

CHURCH PRINCIPLES FROM THE OLD TESTAMENT

For those of us living under the teaching of the New Testament, interpretation of the Old Testament is not always very straightforward. Fortunately, Jesus gives us some important tips. He explains that the principles of life he is presenting as the new covenant, are the same as those on which the old covenant is based (Matt 5:17).

'Do not think I have come to abolish the Law or the Prophets; I have not come to abolish them but to fulfil them'

Jesus came to bring a more excellent way of working out those principles. For example regarding the old covenant teaching on 'an eye for an eye' Jesus says

You have heard that it was said 'Eye for eye and tooth for tooth'. But I tell you, Do not resist an evil person. If someone strikes you on the right cheek, turn to him the other also. And if someone wants to sue you and take your tunic, let him have your cloak as well. (Matt 5:38-40)

This rule from the Old Testament was to do with interpersonal relationships. God's heart under both the old and new covenants was that people would get on well together. The old law gave a practical rule that was fair, but Jesus' way was even better. This new way is possible for us because we have new hearts through the presence of the Holy Spirit.

How can we apply these ideas to the church? Under the old covenant, God's people were the Jews. He was keen to have a relationship with man, and chose Abraham and his descendants as the people with whom he was to have this special affinity. Under the New Covenant, God's special people are the church. Therefore, there are obvious parallels between Israel and the church. What principles can we learn about God's heart for Israel, that might give us understanding about church?

The first and most obvious one, is that God loved his people, and was totally committed to them. The picture of God being the husband of the church applied to his relationship with Israel. When they were unfaithful to him, he likened it to committing adultery. God cared passionately about his relationship with Israel, just as he does with the church.

It is also interesting to look at the way things were organised in Israel. God worked in this case through families. The nation was founded on Abraham's family, and as they grew in number, they were subdivided into groups according to their families. God had arranged this natural subdivision into small groups where everyone had an identity and was linked together in close relationship with others. Another example of the use of small groups, was when the people were in transition between Egypt and Palestine. Moses was having difficulty in carrying out his leadership role over the nation, and his father-in-law, Jethro, came up with the idea of splitting the people up into small manageable units (Ex 18). This allowed many disputes to be addressed locally, so that Moses only had to deal personally with a much smaller number of cases, to which he could apply his full attention. This principle was carried through into the New Covenant. Both Jesus and Paul stressed the importance of loving one another. This was worked out in practice by arranging people in small groups. Jesus focused much of his teaching on a small group of disciples, and the early church was based around small meetings in homes.

Another principle relevant to the organisation of church life can be seen in the history of the national leadership of Israel during the Old Covenant period. As the Jews settled into their promised land around 1400 BC, a system of government based on local tribes emerged. There was no central focus of organisation and this allowed gifted individuals like Gideon and Samson to emerge from time to time, to help the Jews against their enemies. This arrangement did not guarantee that the Jewish people would be faithful and remain close to God, but it did provide a framework where it could be acknowledged that God was the king of his people. There was no earthly king to take the place of God, and he seems to have been happy with this arrangement from an organisational point of view.

This situation remained until about 1100 BC. At this stage, the leadership of the people was provided by priests, such as Eli and Samuel. Both had been good leaders, but problems arose when they passed on the role to their sons, who were unfortunately not suited to the task. Towards the end of

Samuel's life, when he was in the process of passing on the leadership, the people of Israel became dissatisfied. The elders of Israel arranged a meeting with Samuel, and asked him to appoint a king for them. They wanted to be like the other nations around them, who all had kings (1 Sam 8-9).

Samuel was not happy with this request, and decided to pray about it. God spoke to him explaining that he was not happy about it either. The people of Israel were essentially rejecting God as their king. He told Samuel to warn the people about all the disadvantages of having an earthly king, particularly about all the demands he would put upon them. However, when they were still determined to go down this route, he told Samuel to let the people have their own way. Samuel appointed Saul as the first king.

Having a king certainly didn't solve the problems of Israel. When there were good kings who followed God's ways, the nation prospered, but many of the kings were not godly, and this brought God's judgement on them. Kings ruled over Israel for around 500 years until it was defeated by the Babylonians, and for a time ceased to be an independent nation. The remarkable thing about the Jews is that although they lost their land and never again had a king, they retained their identity as a people. After seventy years in captivity, they were restored to the land of Israel where they stayed until they were driven out by the Romans in the first century AD. This forced them to spread out to many different countries all over the world. However, they retained their customs and that special sense of being God's people. They suffered severe opposition over the years, but God's hand has still been on them, and they have survived. Even more remarkably, in recent times they have been re-established as a nation in the land that God had promised them all that time ago. Their story is indeed unique in human history, but it is also entirely consistent with the writings of the prophets of the Old Testament, who predicted this course of events.

Concluding Remarks

Under the Old Covenant, God wanted his people to recognise that he was their king. He was not happy with the people having one of their number as a king, although he did allow them to have kings for a season. The New Testament seems to echo this same heart of God in its teaching on the church. He is not looking for a hierarchical organisation focused on individual people in prominent positions. He is rather looking for a people arranged in small groups or families that love each other and who acknowledge that he is their king and lord.

CHAPTER NINE

JESUS ON THE CHURCH

The Old Testament gives us some insight into God's heart for his people, but to look in more detail at how the church was meant to operate, we need to turn to the New Testament. What are the biblical principles of church life? One way of looking at scripture is to take an overview from a particular point of view. In this case, we read through the New Testament with just one question in mind – what is it saying about church? The Bible is not written as a textbook, so we can't go to the section on church and just read that in isolation. It is also not prescriptive about many aspects of life. We usually have to search the scriptures, not to get a list of rules, but to understand what the principles are.

My hypothesis is that we can learn more from scripture than from any other source about the shape of church that Jesus wants for the twenty-first century. Christians are very worried by the falling numbers of people attending church, and there is much talk about how we can adapt to make the church more attractive to those outside. While it is important that we consider such issues, we must surely give more weight to understanding the sort of church that Jesus wants, the sort of church that is outlined in scripture.

The Words of Jesus

One thing, on which the Bible is very clear, is that Jesus is the head of the church. Therefore what Jesus has to say about the Church is of paramount importance. He is recorded in the Bible using the word 'church' only twice. However, there are many occasions where he refers to the relationships between his followers, which obviously represent a vital aspect of church life. I want to consider some of Jesus' key words relating to the church. These deal with the principle of its foundation, its unity and its function.

The Foundation

One of Jesus' direct references to church has been the cause of great debate over the years. The verses are found in Matt 16:13-18:

> When Jesus came to the region of Caesarea Phillippi, he asked his disciples, 'Who do people say the Son of man is?' They replied, 'Some say John the Baptist; others say Elijah; and still others, Jeremiah or one of the prophets.' 'But what about you?' he asked. 'Who do you say that I am?' Simon Peter answered, 'You are Christ, the Son of the living God.' Jesus replied, 'Blessed are you, Simon son of Jonah, for this was not revealed to you by man, but by my father in heaven. And I tell you that you are Peter, and on this rock I will build my church, and the gates of Hades will not overcome it.'

The traditional Roman Catholic interpretation of these verses is that Jesus was saying that the church was going to be built around Peter. The passage is used to justify the importance of Peter and his successors, the popes, in the leadership of the Roman Catholic Church. Indeed, if one takes these verses at face value, this does not seem an unreasonable interpretation. However, there are two problems with this view of the passage. The first is that it seems totally out of context with the rest of scripture. If this really were the case, then it would be of enormous significance to the development of the church, and surely of utmost importance to reinforce and expand the teaching elsewhere. This does not happen. There is no suggestion that Peter is to be the basis on which the church is to be built. In fact the rest of scripture is very clear that the foundation of the church is Christ himself. 1 Cor 3:11 states, for example, 'For no one can lay any foundation other than the one already laid, which is Christ Jesus'.

The second problem with the Roman Catholic interpretation is found from consideration of the original Greek text. The name Peter in Greek is 'Petros' meaning 'little rock', whereas the word Jesus uses for the rock on which he is to build the church is 'petra' meaning 'big rock'. This suggests quite strongly that Jesus was not implying that Peter himself was the rock. So what was the 'big rock' that Jesus was referring to? The most reasonable explanation is that he was saying that it is the confession of Jesus as the Messiah that is the basis of the church. Everyone who is called out from the world to come into the church enters on this confession. This surely gives an explanation, which is much more in accord with the rest of the New Testament. Jesus probably used the play on words based on the meaning of Peter's name as a rock to emphasize this significance.

It is also no doubt significant that it was Peter who played a key role in this vitally important scenario. Peter was often the leading spokesman of the disciples, and by making this confession, he was effectively the first official member of the church. Peter was also to have a special role in developing the church. Jesus had a personal discussion with Peter in which he encouraged him to care for God's people (John 21:15-22). We do not have any record of Jesus speaking in this personal way to any of the other disciples. In Acts, Peter goes on to have a leading role among the apostles in the early church. However, he did not function in a unique leadership role superior to all the others. The teaching on Peter's primacy among the apostles was not introduced until several hundred years after the events described in scripture. In retrospect, it does not seem consistent with a simple interpretation of what we read in the New Testament.

Unity

When asked what was the greatest commandment, Jesus replied:

> Love the Lord your God with all your heart and with all your soul and with all your mind. This is the first and greatest commandment. And the second is like it: love you neighbour as yourself. All the Law and Prophets hang on these two commandments. (Matt 22:37-40)

Elsewhere, Jesus explained what he meant by our neighbours. These are the people we come into contact with during the normal course of life. We are to show love to them. He also applied this specifically to the relationships between his disciples. In the context of his last supper with them he spoke these words:

> A new command I give you: love one another. As I have loved you, so you must love one another. By this all men will know that you are my disciples, if you love one another. (John 13:34-35)

While he wanted his disciples to love all people as their neighbours, he intended them to have a special relationship with each other. This was to be such a feature of their life together that other people outside would notice. This heart for love between his disciples is seen again in the prayer we have already considered in John 17. Jesus prayed passionately that those who followed him would be one as He and the Father were one.

Christians over the years have struggled to understand the concept of the Trinity. However, while we do not fully understand it, we can muse on the wonder and beauty of this picture of perfect harmony between the different aspects of God's being. In the church, we too have different roles to play, each of us demonstrating a small part of the 'manifold wisdom of God' (Eph 3:10). This analogy with the Godhead gives us a vision of what Jesus has in mind for His church. It is a wonderful vision; one that is worth working towards with all our hearts as God's people. Our love for one another in the church and our complete unity is something obviously very close to the heart of Jesus.

Commissioning Words

After the resurrection, Jesus spoke some very significant commissioning words to his disciples, words which still echo down to us in the church in the twenty first century. Matthew 28:18-20 reads:

> Then Jesus came to them and said, 'All authority in heaven and on earth is given to me. Therefore go and make disciples of all nations, baptising them in the name of the Father and of the Son and of the Holy Spirit, and teaching them to obey everything I have commanded you. And surely I am with you always to the very end of the age.

Shortly after, in Acts 1:8, there is a follow up to this. Jesus told his disciples to wait in Jerusalem until they received what he referred to as the baptism of the Holy Spirit.

> But you will receive power when the Holy Spirit comes on you; and you will be my witnesses in Jerusalem, and in all Judea and Samaria and to the ends of the earth.

Pretty well everything that Jesus spoke about the church was mind-blowing. Here Jesus is talking about his vision for the worldwide church. I wonder how the disciples felt about being told that their mission was to go to the ends of the earth with the good news about Jesus. They had been with him for three years. They had seen the most incredible things. Of late they had been witnesses to the resurrection. However, even with this build up, these words must have seemed daunting to a handful of men and women, not natural high-fliers by the standards of the world, especially now that Jesus was about to leave them. Yet things worked out exactly as Jesus had said. The disciples did share the gospel in Jerusalem, then Judea and then did go off to other parts of the world. The sense of vision given by Jesus and the empowerment of the Holy Spirit combined to enable the disciples to make excellent progress with the task. However, the job was not finished in their generation. The baton has been taken up by successive generations of Christians. It is still in the process of being fulfilled 2000 years later in the early twenty-first century. The Christian message has now spread almost everywhere in the world, but there are still some people who have never heard it. God is still calling his church to go across borders into those areas where the gospel is not known, and where it is opposed. There are still remarkable stories today of courageous Christians, willing to give their lives for the sake of spreading the gospel.

Other words of Jesus

Overall Jesus does not appear to have taught much specifically about the church. However, it is worth noting that at the end of John's gospel, he comments that there were many other things about Jesus that he had not recorded. Jesus almost certainly did say other things about church, which are not included in the gospels. In Acts 1, for example, we read that 'Jesus appeared to them over a period of forty days and spoke about the Kingdom of God' (Acts 1:3).

These things about the kingdom are not recorded, but all that Jesus said, would have been fresh in the disciples' minds and hearts, and would have directed the way they set about the task of building the church. We have to imply that what the apostles did in the very early days of the church reflected closely this teaching that Jesus had given them only days before.

The Example of Jesus

We learn from Jesus, not only from his words, but also from his lifestyle. He gave us the perfect example of how to live. So what does his lifestyle tell us about the way his people should come together in the church? What stands out here is the way Jesus related with his followers primarily through a small group. He was first and foremost a small group leader. He also preached to crowds, teaching them and healing many people, but for a lot of his time he focused on his immediate group of disciples. He wanted them to grow spiritually and be filled with his life and wisdom. This depth of ministry could not be achieved with the crowds, who only heard his teaching on occasions. To get through to his disciples, he shared his whole life with them. He spent time teaching them the message of the gospel, but he also spent time with them doing normal things, eating together, walking together and just enjoying life together. What he taught them had the opportunity to get built in to their lives and change them.

We can also look at what Jesus didn't do. He never tried to establish any structure amongst his disciples. When they tried to argue about who should be the greatest among them, he rebuked them for it. He had no official hierarchy amongst the disciples, although he did acknowledge that some, notably Peter, James and John had natural leadership qualities, and he tried to nurture that. He was also short on ceremony. We only read of him being involved in baptism, marriage and breaking of bread. His lifestyle with his disciples was rather characterised by its informality.

The wisdom of this approach to passing on his message was proved by its results. At times it must have seemed unpromising, as the disciples asked naïve questions and then, when the crunch came at the arrest of Jesus, they deserted him. However, the end result is, as we say, history. From this group of rather uneducated men, sprung a religion that has transformed the world. Their ability to do this had been nurtured during the three years they spent as part of Jesus' small group.

Concluding Remarks

Although Jesus only rarely mentioned the word 'church', he gave key directions about its foundation, its internal relationships and its mission to the world. He had also lived closely with his disciples and given them a model of how to live together. As Barry McGuire once said 'Jesus laid it down so heavy that there ain't never been anyone able to pick it up since'[1]. Jesus' challenges to the church are great. We haven't got there yet, but this tremendous vision is what has got the church as far as it has. We need to press on to see the ultimate fulfilment of his prophetic words.

Reference

1. McGuire, B., Personal communication.

CHAPTER TEN

THE BIRTH OF THE CHURCH

The words of Jesus give us vitally important understanding on fundamental aspects of the church, but it is in the Acts that we see the church in practice. What can we learn from the way the early church operated, that can help us understand God's heart for the church today? Here were people who had been close to Jesus himself, and understood his heart. They had only recently come from being with him; they were fresh from an intensive teaching course on all that related to living a Christian life, including all Jesus thoughts about his church. Surely there is much to learn. J.B. Phillips puts this thought most succinctly[1]. Referring to his reading of the Acts he says

Yet we cannot help feeling disturbed as well as moved, for this surely is the church as it was meant to be. It was vigorous and flexible, for these are the days before it ever became fat and short of breath through prosperity, or muscle-bound by over–organisation. These men did not make 'acts of faith' they believed; they did not 'say their prayers' they really prayed. They did not hold conferences on psychosomatic medicine; they simply healed the sick. But if they were uncomplicated and naïve by modern standards we have ruefully to admit that they were open on the God-ward side in a way that is almost unknown today.

Having emphasized the importance of studying early church developments, we need to be careful when interpreting the writings in the Acts and the Epistles. The apostles were very much on a learning curve. The Bible clearly shows that there were differences of opinion between them. They no doubt made mistakes. This has to be considered in our interpretation.

The Early Days in Jerusalem

Immediately after Jesus ascended to heaven, there appear to have been about one hundred and twenty believers. They went to Jerusalem where Jesus had instructed them to wait until they were 'clothed with power from on high'. The apostles themselves lodged together in a house in the city (Acts 1:12-13), but they also met with the larger group of 120, probably at the temple; Luke 24:53 records that when they returned to Jerusalem they stayed continually in the temple, worshipping God. It seems a little strange that they should meet at the temple, as that was the centre of worship for the people who had recently rejected the teaching of Jesus, and had him killed. However, the temple at that time had a large number of rooms, which were used for public gatherings, and it is quite possible that the disciples used one of these rooms to meet together. They spent most of the ten days between the ascension and the Day of

Pentecost together, waiting for God to move. Having witnessed the resurrection and the ascension, and heard Jesus' commission, they were filled with great expectation. This was a complete change from the despondency they had felt following Jesus' death on the cross. Now they were constant in prayer and in praise to God. During this time, Peter took the lead in directing the selection of Matthias as the replacement for Judas within the group of twelve central apostles. It is interesting to note the style of his leadership was in no way authoritarian; it was consensus among the apostles that decided the process of selection (Acts 1:15-26).

On the day of Pentecost itself, when all the believers were gathered together, probably in the temple precincts, the most remarkable events took place.

> Suddenly a sound like the blowing of a violent wind came from heaven and filled the whole house where they were sitting. They saw what seemed to be tongues of fire that separated and came to rest on each of them. All of them were filled with the Holy Spirit and began to speak with other tongues as the Spirit enabled them. (Acts 2:2-4)

What Jesus had promised had now come. The baptism of the Holy Spirit (Acts 1:5), the baptism of fire (Luke 3:16) and speaking in tongues (Mark 16:17), had all appeared almost in an instant. It is not hard to imagine the excitement of the moment, and not surprising that they made a lot of noise. This made an impact on people in the vicinity. People in Jerusalem at that time came from a variety of countries, and recognised the languages the disciples were speaking in.

They couldn't understand how Galileans were suddenly speaking about the greatness of God in many different tongues. They wondered what this all meant.

This gave the apostles their first evangelistic opportunity, and what followed was in many ways no less remarkable than what had already occurred. Peter stood up and spontaneously spoke to the crowd that had gathered with outstanding clarity. He put the Christian message in the context of the Jewish faith, exactly what the group of people gathered at that time would have needed. He also explained in a nutshell how to become a Christian; his words are still regularly quoted when we describe the steps people need to take to come to Christ. I can imagine some of the other apostles scratching their heads saying 'Where did that come from?' Peter was a simple fisherman with no formal education. He, along with the other apostles, had struggled to understand many of the things Jesus had been teaching them. Yet here, in an instant, he had managed to put all the pieces together and present a superb, erudite explanation of the gospel message. I expect it did not take them long to remember Jesus words:

> But the Counsellor, the Holy Spirit, whom the Father will send in my name, will teach you all things and will remind you of everything I have said to you. (John 14:26)

The combined effect of the baptism of the Holy Spirit with the accompanying sign of speaking in tongues, and Peter's presentation of the gospel, meant that three thousand people were added to the church on that day. Suddenly the apostles had started something. Jesus had said they'd be his witnesses in Jerusalem – they were able to tick that off very quickly. But how were they to deal with all these people becoming Christians?

They continued to meet in the temple courts, but also got together in their homes. They were full of the new life that the Holy Spirit had breathed into them.

They devoted themselves to the apostles teaching, to fellowship, to breaking of bread and to prayer. Everyone was filled with awe and many wonders and miraculous signs were done by the apostles. All the believers had everything in common. Selling their possessions and goods they gave to anyone who had need. Every day they continued to meet together in the temple courts. They broke bread in their homes and ate together with glad and sincere hearts praising God and enjoying the favour of the people. And the Lord added to their number daily those who were being saved. (Acts 2:42-47)

There is much to be learned from looking at this passage. It gives us a clear picture of life at the very beginning of the church. The picture is one of great excitement, of great hope, of joy and optimism. There appears to have been relatively little official organisation, but people wanted to be wholeheartedly committed to being part of the church. Belonging came from the strong sense of the unity of the Holy Spirit that all the new Christians felt. They shared meals with one another and were keen to study doctrine and pray. Not only did they meet together, they were also willing to sell their possessions, and hand over the proceeds to the apostles, whom they trusted implicitly to deal with the money wisely.

As time went on, the apostles found that practical issues

amongst the people in the church arose, which began to impact on their ministry. They were spending less time teaching and praying, which they felt was their main function, and realised that some administrative organisation was required. They therefore approached the believers in the church at Jerusalem and asked them to select seven men who were full of the Holy Spirit and wisdom to take responsibility for these practical tasks (Acts 6:1-6). These men are not referred to as deacons (servants) in this passage, but in the context of the rest of the New Testament, this is the ministry to which they were called. It is interesting again to observe the democratic style of leadership provided by the apostles. They were very focused on hearing God for all decisions; no individual dictated how things were to be done. This development helps to paint the picture of the non-authoritarian style of early church leadership.

The Development of the Church in Judea and Samaria

The success of the developing church in Jerusalem began to annoy the Jewish religious leaders. The Christians were often very forthright in their presentation of the gospel, and in many ways it was not surprising that there was opposition. One of the men who had been appointed as a deacon in the Jerusalem church was Stephen. He was full of the Holy Spirit and had been 'doing great wonders and miraculous signs among the people' (Acts 6:8). This had antagonised the authorities, and they had brought him before the Sanhedrin to try and show that his doctrine was unsound. Stephen was very outspoken in his defence, and he was condemned to death by stoning (Acts 7:51-60). Speaking forthrightly on the appropriate occasion certainly seems a characteristic of both Jesus' approach and that of the early church.

This event, which occurred in AD 35, acted as a trigger point for a general persecution of the church. Most Christians were forced to leave Jerusalem, and were scattered throughout Judea and Samaria.

This was obviously very difficult for them, but they turned it into an opportunity for the church to grow and spread further afield. Jesus commission to his disciples at his ascension was that they were to 'be his witnesses in Jerusalem, and in all Judea and Samaria and to the ends of the earth' (Acts 1:8). The persecution in Jerusalem led to phase two of the commission taking place into Judea and Samaria.

The spread of the gospel took place in two ways. First, individual Christians just talked abut their faith as they settled into their new surroundings. Acts 11:19-21 reads:

> Now those that had been scattered by the persecution in connection with Stephen travelled as far as Phoenicia, Cyprus and Antioch telling the message only to Jews. Some of them however, men from Cyprus and Cyrene went to Antioch and began to speak to Greeks also telling them the good news about the Lord Jesus. The Lord's hand was with them and a great number of people believed and turned to the Lord.

Secondly, those with a preaching ministry began to spread the good news in a more public way through speaking and through signs and wonders. Philip, for example, another of the seven deacons appointed in the Jerusalem church, went to a city in Samaria and began proclaiming the gospel to crowds of people.

At this stage the apostles were still based in Jerusalem, but when they heard of the developments taking place else- where in Judea and Samaria, they visited them to give support and direction. Peter and John went to Samaria to stand alongside Philip in the work he was doing there. The ministry of the apostles in supporting the establishment of churches thus gradually began to take shape.

Conversion of Saul

There were other significant developments during this period, one of which was the dramatic conversion of Saul. He had been a leader of the Pharisees and one of the driving forces behind the stoning of Stephen and the persecution of the early church. However, his life was totally changed when God spoke to him in a vision. He was on his way to Damascus to punish any people who had become Christians there, when he heard a voice explaining to him the truth about Jesus, which totally changed his way of thinking. Being blinded by the vision, he was taken to Damascus by his fellow travellers. Whilst there, he met up with some Christians, and his sight returned. He was baptised and began to preach the good news about Jesus. The hunter now became the hunted, and he had to escape the Jewish author- ities by being smuggled out at night in a basket through a gap in the city wall. He briefly met the apostles in Jerusalem, but they soon sent him back to his home-town of Tarsus for his own safety. However, he wasn't forgotten, and several years later, Barnabas went to Tarsus and invited Saul to join him as part of the leadership team at the growing church in Antioch.

Saul, who was later renamed Paul, made a dramatic impact on the leadership scene of the early church. He was very different from the disciples who had been with Jesus, none of whom were particularly intellectual. By contrast, Paul had been a Pharisee and had studied Jewish law extensively. This background meant that he had a reasoned approach to his understanding of the gospel. This was complementary to the other apostles, and brought a different dimension to the expression of early church doctrine.

The Church at Antioch

Several local churches became established in the region of Judea and Samaria. One particularly strong church emerged at Antioch in Syria, a large town about 200 miles north of Jerusalem. A number of believers scattered after the stoning of Stephen had ended up at Antioch and many people there became Christians. The converts were from both the Jewish and gentile communities. The Jerusalem apostles sent Barnabas to help the development of the new church in Antioch. This is significant in that it suggests that they were recognising an apostolic calling in someone other than the original twelve. Things went very well in the church and Barnabas felt he needed some help. In AD 43, he went to nearby Tarsus and found Saul who he obviously felt had leadership qualities. They worked together for about a further year in the Antioch church, and saw the development of emerging ministries of prophets and teachers. Individuals with particular gifts were identified as having a ministry in that area. Antioch was developing into what we would now refer to as a resource church, where such ministries have a chance to be nurtured. It is interesting to note, that although Barnabas was sent to oversee the development of the church in Antioch, he is only named as one of the leaders; church leadership appears to have been corporate. The leadership team sought direction together from the Holy Spirit.

Peter's Dream

God also spoke to Peter through a dream. Peter was beginning to travel around Judea and Samaria at this time and was in Joppa, a coastal town about 40 miles from Jerusalem. He fell into a trance and saw a large sheet being lowered from the sky to the earth with all kinds of animals. A voice told him to kill the animals and eat them. Many of the animals were unclean to the Jews, and Peter replied that he had never eaten anything unclean. The voice told him to not refer to anything as unclean that had been made clean by God. This was repeated three times. At first he didn't understand what this meant, but the meaning soon became clear.

Some men arrived at the house from Caesarea about 40 miles north of Joppa. They had been sent by a Roman centurion called Cornelius. He was keen to hear more about the gospel, and had commissioned his men to ask Peter to come and speak to him. The next day Peter started out for Caesarea accompanied by Cornelius' messengers. When he got to the house where Cornelius was staying, Peter found quite a crowd had gathered to hear him. These people were gentiles and it would normally have been against the Jewish law to visit the house of a gentile. However Peter now began to appreciate the meaning of the vision of the sheet of animals – that God intended the gospel not only for the Jews, but for the gentiles as well. He declared to the gathered crowd: 'I now realise how true it is that God does not show favouritism but accepts men from every nation who fear him and do what is right' (Acts 10:34-35).

Peter explained the gospel to them and many responded. The Holy Spirit fell on them, and they began praising God and speaking in tongues. This put the seal on the message that the gospel was universal.

After spending a few days with the new Christians, Peter returned to Jerusalem and shared what had happened with the other apostles. Although some of them initially had trouble coming to terms with this paradigm shift in their thinking, it paved the way for the next phase of church growth – *to the ends of the earth.*

Reference

1. Phillips, J.B., 1955, *The Young Church in Action*, Collins, London. Quotation reprinted by permission of HarperCollins Publishers Ltd © J B Phillips 1995.

CHAPTER ELEVEN

TO THE ENDS OF THE EARTH

Things were going well in the church over the first ten years since Jesus had died. Life had not been without its problems, but 'the Word of the Lord continued to increase and spread' (Acts 12:24). Many people were becoming Christians and local churches were being established. Individuals with different types of ministry were emerging – apostles, prophets, teachers, evangelists and elders. The church was ready for its next phase, and it began in the emerging resource church at Antioch.

The First Apostolic Team and its First Mission Trip

The church at Antioch had recognised four men as having prophetic and teaching gifts, including Barnabas and Saul. On one occasion when they were worshipping and fasting, God spoke to them through a prophetic word that Barnabas and Saul were to be 'set apart for the work to which God had called them' (Acts 13:2). They had already been thinking about how to spread the good news about Jesus to new areas. The Holy Spirit was saying that it was now time to begin. It was obviously helpful to have a clear word from God to confirm their calling. It was also good to be sent out on behalf of a church with its support, and not just to be doing their own thing.

After praying, fasting and laying-on of hands, Barnabas and Saul were duly sent off on their first missionary journey. They went first to Cyprus, and then on to the mainland of Asia Minor or what is now Turkey. They covered the areas of Pamphylia and Pisidia, which made up the southern part of Galatia. They visited several towns over a period of about two years between 46 and 48 AD. During this time Saul adopted his new name of Paul. The use of a second name was not uncommon in those days. Perhaps the adoption of the Roman name, Paul, reflected the fact that they were aiming to reach Gentiles as well as Jews with the gospel. There was also a change in the dynamics of the relationship between Paul and Barnabas. Whereas Barnabas was the senior one of the pair at the beginning of the trip, Paul began taking on a much more prominent role as their journey progressed.

The usual strategy of Paul and Barnabas in presenting the gospel was to go first to the Jewish synagogue in the town and explain the good news about Jesus. Paul would have access to synagogues as he had the status of a rabbi. There was a varied response from the Jews, with some people accepting their teaching, while others were quite opposed to it. Paul and Barnabas made it clear that the message was for Gentiles as well as Jews, and this sometimes caused Jewish people to turn against them. Despite the difficulties in some of the towns, we read that many believed and that the 'disciples were filled with joy and with the Holy Spirit' (Acts 13:52). Paul and Barnabas were clearly anointed by God for this task of bringing the gospel to completely new areas. They were gifted in preaching, and backed this up with miraculous signs. They were successful in making a big impact wherever they went.

After their adventures in preaching the gospel in these regions and surviving an attempt to kill Paul, they re-visited the disciples in each of the towns where they had been before. They were keen to ensure that the groups of disciples were formed into local churches, and appointed elders in each place to help this process.

Appointing of elders

The concept of elders came from Jewish society, and was also common in other nations in that part of the world. They were a group of leaders who were recognised as having wisdom and experience in life. They had responsibility for ruling in a town or area where they lived. This was sometimes proactive in setting the rules of their society, and sometimes reactive in settling matters of controversy that were brought to them. In Israel, it appears they worked alongside the religious leaders in carrying out their duties (Matt 21:23). This was important for them as a nation, who were specially God's people. For them, all social and political matters were linked to their spiritual life. It was therefore a natural development for the early Christians to use this model for church leadership. The precedent had been set in the Jerusalem church, where there were already elders working alongside the apostles (Acts 11:30, Acts 15:2).

Paul's letters to the churches contain quite a bit of detail about the qualifications and roles of an elder (1 Tim 3:1-7). They were primarily to be men of good character. They would usually be married with a family and have a good standing both within the church and in society. There were usually several in each church (Acts 14:23). Decisions about the organisation of the church and its direction were taken together as a group, seeking guidance from the Holy Spirit. There are no examples of there being a central or senior leader.

The New Testament uses two Greek words to describe this leadership position in the church. *'Presbuteros'* is usually translated as elder whereas *'episkopos'* is rendered overseer or bishop. However, the terms are used interchangeably (Acts 20:17,28, Tit 1:5-7) and therefore appear to refer to just one type of leadership role. Eldership functions involved overseeing the church and caring for the people. Their role is described as being like shepherds caring for a flock of sheep, an analogy that Jesus also used to describe his own care for his people.

Connection to resource Church

After revisiting the churches in Asia Minor, they returned to Antioch in Syria and to the church that had sent them out on their journey. It was natural that they would want to report back to the people who had commissioned them, and who had no doubt been praying for them while they were away. Paul and Barnabas demonstrated a great sense of loyalty and accountability in their ministry. They were clearly very gifted men, but they didn't go off and do their own thing. They were careful to preserve connections to the rest of the church.

The Question of Gentile Christians (Acts 15)

While they were back in Antioch, the first signs of disunity in the church began to appear, with the emergence of false teaching. Some men from Judea were suggesting to the believers in Antioch, that it was necessary to be circumcised under the Law of Moses to receive salvation as a Christian. This was a heresy that had arisen among Jewish Christians, particularly promoted by some converted Pharisees. They felt that Christianity had emerged in the context of Judaism, and therefore gentiles who became Christians had to go through the process of becoming Jewish proselytes first. They did not appreciate the full acceptance that was available for gentiles to become Christians under a completely new covenant. By this time, Paul's understanding of the relationship between the Jewish law and the message of Christ was quite clear, and so he and Barnabas refuted this false teaching. The leaders at Antioch were so troubled by this dispute, that they decided to send Paul and Barnabas to the apostles and elders in Jerusalem.

They received a warm welcome from the brothers in Jerusalem, who had heard about their exploits in establishing churches in Galatia, and were really pleased to hear in more detail about what had been happening. However, the celebrations were curtailed by a group of believers that had developed in the Jerusalem church, known as 'the party of the Pharisees'. Like the Jewish believers in Antioch, they also felt that gentiles becoming Christians should convert to Judaism, and agree to obey the Law of Moses. They used the opportunity afforded by the arrival of Paul and Barnabas, to bring the issue to the attention of the apostles. A meeting was convened to discuss the issue, and the arguments from both sides were presented. However, it was difficult to dispute the message that God had spoken about the acceptance of gentiles. This had come first to Peter through a dream, and then confirmed through the experiences of both Peter in Caesarea, and Paul and Barnabas in Galatia. Both had seen gentiles clearly become Christians and be filled with the Holy Spirit. James, the brother of Jesus, had the task of chairing the meeting, and summed up the proceedings by making it clear that gentiles wishing to become Christians did not have to convert to Judaism first. However, he did encourage gentile believers to adhere to a few basic rules. This probably did not go far enough for Paul, who saw a clearer distinction between the old Law and the message of grace through Christ. Nevertheless, it seemed a reasonable compromise in the circumstances, which went at least someway to preserving unity within the church. Unfortunately, it did not finish the debate, which continued for quite some time. The Jerusalem church decided to send two of their own leaders, Judas and Silas, back to Antioch with Paul and Barnabas, to help clarify the decision on the issue.

This interesting event shows how the early Christians dealt with what was the first of many doctrinal issues faced by the church. It cannot really be taken as the scriptural pattern of approaching doctrinal conflict, as there are no similar 'church council' meetings referred to elsewhere in the New Testament. However, there are some principles that can be taken from the approach used by the apostles. The matter was discussed initially among the leaders of the church rather than before the whole congregation. Throughout the process there was a clear desire to come to a place of unity about the issue. There appears to have been a genuinely open and full discussion, in which respect was shown to those raising the issue. Several factors seem to have influenced the final decision: (i) what God had spoken, (ii) the evidence from scripture (iii) the evidence from events and (iv) a consensus opinion. Finally, from the scriptural record, there is no evidence of any dispute about the consensus decision, even though it is almost certain that not everyone would have agreed with it. It appears that there was a spirit of submission here, which is spoken of extensively in the New Testament writings. Once the decision was made amongst the leaders, it was brought before the church, and discussed further in that context. Clear communication of the matter was also sent to the church in Antioch, and to churches elsewhere through the visits of the apostles.

The message from the apostles and elders in Jerusalem was well received back in Antioch. Judas and Silas stayed there for a while, enjoying fellowship with the folk in the church, before returning to Jerusalem. Paul and Barnabas continued for a further time in Antioch, where we read that they and many others taught and preached the word of the Lord. We again see, very clearly, the concept that bringing God's word to the church was not the remit of a selected few. The body ministry was genuinely functioning here in Antioch.

Personality issues in the leadership

Paul then decided to visit to the churches that had been established in Galatia, to share with them the message from the Jerusalem church. Barnabas was to accompany him, but wanted John Mark to join them. Mark had come with them part of the way on their first missionary journey, but had returned early, much to Paul's displeasure. Paul was not happy with him joining them on this second trip. This caused a sharp disagreement between Paul and Barnabas. Paul set off for Galatia with Silas, while Barnabas returned to Cyprus with Mark, presumably to visit the churches there. This is an example of human frailty creeping into the church, in the form of personal disagreement. The clash of personalities, particularly amongst leaders, who tend to be strong-minded people by nature, is an issue that the church has had to face throughout its history.

From Paul's writings, it appears that the disagreement was resolved with time. In his first letter to the church at Corinth, written some four years later, he speaks encouragingly about Barnabas (1 Cor 9:6). Then again, when he was in Rome writing a letter to Timothy, he requests that Mark should come and join him there (2 Tim 4:11). It seems that, even though the disagreement was initially strong, it was not allowed to continue. If it had, it would have been to the detriment of the church as a whole. Forgiveness and reconciliation are so much a central part of the gospel. It was important then, as it is now, to preserve unity in the church

The Second Mission Trip

Paul and his team's second missionary journey started in 51 AD. They visited the churches that had already been established in Galatia, and told them about the ruling regarding gentiles becoming Christians, which had been made by the Jerusalem church. Their visit helped the 'churches to be strengthened in the faith and grow daily in numbers' (Acts 16:5). One thing that seems to characterise the whole history of the early church, is the unity they experienced, and their joy at being together. Visits from the apostles were times of great rejoicing and encouragement. Even though there were issues of unity of the faith, regarding the details of the gospel and how Jesus' teaching should be interpreted, there was an amazing unity of spirit among the believers.

Paul, together with Silas and a young man called Timothy, then moved on, aiming for Bithynia, a province north of Galatia. They were always open to the Holy Spirit to guide them, and on this occasion they were directed away from Bithynia, but towards Macedonia. They established groups of believers in the area, notably at Philippi, Thessalonica and Berea. Life was never dull in breaking new ground with the gospel, and Paul and his companions were regularly getting into trouble. Some things don't change! Although Christianity is now known around the world, its spread is still contested 2000 years later, either ideologically in the west, or physically in several Asian countries. Paul would describe this later in his letter to the Ephesian Christians as being in a spiritual battle, warring against spiritual powers that we can't see, but are nevertheless very real.

The team then moved down into Greece. Initially, Paul went on ahead on his own, and was not joined by Silas and Timothy until he got to Corinth. In between, he broke new ground in bringing the gospel to the Athenians. However, while they were interested in the intellectual debate, it appears that only a few believed. He then moved on to Corinth, where he found a different situation. There were already some Christians in the city, notably Aquila and Priscilla. Like Paul they were tentmakers, and he established a strong friendship with them. He stayed at their house and 'worked with them' (Acts 18:3). This probably means both as a tentmaker, and in building the church. As in previous places, Paul had opposition from the Jews, but God made it clear to him that he was to remain there. In one particular vision, God spoke about there being many people in the city that he wanted to become Christians. Paul stayed there for about 18 months and, despite the opposition, many people believed in the gospel and were baptised.

An important principle here, is that where Christians were already established in a town, Paul did not set up a separate work, but rather got alongside the existing group. This is consistent with all that happened in early church history, and all that Paul taught about unity in the church. The leaders did everything they could to ensure that God's people in a locality were one in Spirit and in practice.

Expanding the apostolic team

Paul then decided that he would return to Syria, and report back on his progress to the church at Antioch. For the first part of the journey, he took Priscilla and Aquila with him. This gives insight into how new people were raised into leadership in the early church. As Paul went on his travels, he was keeping his eyes open for those he felt God had equipped for particular tasks. He had already called Timothy from the church at Lystra in Galatia to join his travelling team. Now he recognised in Aquila and Priscilla a couple who were suited to a different type of ministry. They were people who were used to moving. They had previously been in Rome, when the Jews were expelled by the emperor Claudius. Paul saw that they were good at providing a church based around a welcoming home. He therefore felt it was a strategic move to take them from Corinth to Ephesus, to support the church that was emerging there. When they settled in Ephesus, they established a church meeting in their house. Among other things, they helped Apollos, who was an enthusiastic new Christian and gifted preacher. He had only heard about the baptism of John when they first met him, and they were able to give him a good grounding in the whole gospel. After a while he wanted to travel, and the believers in Ephesus were keen to send him out with their blessing. He had proved himself in the local church setting in Ephesus, and he provided similar encouragement to the church in Corinth, to which he moved.

Meanwhile, Paul went back to Antioch by way of a brief visit to the Jerusalem church to update the leaders there. He then spent some time in Antioch. It seems that even though his apostolic ministry was by now well established, he still felt the need to spend time with the church that had originally sent him out.

The Third Mission Trip

Paul set out on the third missionary journey of his team in 53 AD. As on his second trip, he re-visited the Galatian churches, encouraging the Christians there. He then moved on to Ephesus, where he stayed for around two years to help build up the church. He also preached the gospel, both in the town and the whole surrounding region, and a good number of people became Christians. As in other towns, he initially used the synagogue as the place where he shared the gospel, but when the Jews started opposing him, he moved to an alterative venue, the lecture hall of Tyrannus. Paul did use buildings for the public proclamation of the gospel to non-Christians, but there are very few occasions where we read of the church itself meeting anywhere other than people's homes.

After his time in Ephesus, Paul felt God was guiding him to return to Jerusalem, which he did via visits to the churches in Macedonia and Greece. As always, Paul's journeys were full of incident. One of the places he visited was Troas. On the night he was due to leave, Paul had so much he wanted to share with the church, that he went on talking till midnight. One of the believers, a young man called Eutychus, was sitting in a third storey window listening. As Paul continued speaking for so long, he dosed off to sleep, and accidentally fell out of the window. The folk from the church thought he was dead, but Paul went down to where he had fallen, gathered him in his arms, and declared that he was alive. Eutychus duly recovered, and the believers took him home, greatly relieved that he was all right.

This story gives insight into the development of church life by around 55 AD. The same enthusiasm and commitment that characterised the beginning of the church in Jerusalem was still here in Troas some twenty years later. They carried on their meeting all through the night! They also seem to have got into a routine – it appears that on the first day of the week, they regularly made a point of meeting together specifically to break bread. Incorporated into that gathering, they included other aspects of coming together as the church, such as in this case, a time of teaching. Even though Paul was keen to proceed with his journey, he obviously really wanted to stay with the believers in Troas long enough to share with them the special occasion of breaking bread together.

Meeting the Ephesian Elders

Paul and his team then started the journey back to Jerusalem by sea. On the way he wanted to speak to the elders of the Ephesian church, but rather than break the journey by travelling over land from the port of Miletus to Ephesus, he asked them to come to Miletus to meet him. The content of Paul's message to them is recorded in some detail. It gives useful insight into the role of elders in the early church. Paul refers to them as shepherds of the church of God. He indicates that they are appointed by the Holy Spirit to be overseers of the flock. He sees one of their key tasks being to protect the flock from 'savage wolves' who will come to destroy it. He warns them to be particularly careful of individuals who will come and distort the truth and draw people away after them. He encouraged them to continue the hard work required to support the weak. Finally he prayed with them.

It is interesting that Paul should pick on these aspects of the role of elders. He is particularly keen to avoid the emergence of individual leaders. Corporate leadership operating on a spiritual consensus of 'what seemed good to the Holy Spirit and to us' (Acts 15:28) appears to have been one of the key principles of local church government for the early Christians.

Paul's parting with the leaders is also significant. There was much weeping and embracing, as the elders feared they might not see Paul again. Luke writes of Paul and the team having to tear themselves away from them. The intensity of the love between the early Christians is clear. No wonder it was said of them that they were known for their love for each other. Similar scenes followed as their ship stopped over at Tyre where they met with the group of believers there.

They also called in on Philip the evangelist at Caesarea, where Agabus prophesied over Paul that when he went to Jerusalem he would be bound by the Jews and handed over to the Gentiles. This word prepared him for what was ahead.

Trouble at Jerusalem

Eventually Paul arrived at Jerusalem. He was warmly received by the leaders there, who were delighted to hear what God had been doing. However, it was clear that the issue regarding the relationship between the gospel and the Jewish law had not been cleared up. The elders of the church were worried that Paul was regarded as being extreme on this issue. Word had got round that he was preaching against the Law of Moses. They feared there would be trouble now Paul had arrived in person. They persuaded him to show his willingness to uphold the Law by supporting some young men who were taking a vow as part of the Jewish legal system. Although Paul complied with this request, the Jews at Jerusalem were so convinced of his opposition to the Law, that they abducted him. They were just about to kill him, when the Roman soldiers heard the uproar, and rescued him from the marauding crowd. Paul got permission from the soldiers to speak to the people, but this only further antagonised them. The Romans took him into custody for his own safety. They found out that he was a Roman citizen, and as a result began treating him with a new level of respect. They didn't fully understand the religious issues that caused the Jews to be so opposed to him, and so the commander decided to send him to the governor Felix in Caesarea, where he could be tried in safety. Felix heard the case against Paul, and also Paul's defence. He didn't come to any firm conclusion regarding Paul's guilt, but kept him in prison to appease the Jews. Paul remained imprisoned there for two years (57–59 AD), until Felix was replaced as governor by Festus.

These were important times for the church, in that its relationship with Judaism was being clarified. Christianity had developed from Judaism, and there was no inconsistency between the two faiths, provided the validity of Jesus as the Messiah was accepted. However, it was becoming increasingly clear that the majority of Jews did not accept this, and so the development of a deep division between the faiths was inevitable. Paul's assured adherence to what he saw as the truth, ensured that the issue was brought out into the open and clarified, even though the personal consequences were very difficult. The ability to tackle contemporary doctrinal issues and bring God's wisdom, is clearly an important part of an apostolic ministry, which Paul was demonstrating in these events.

And so to Rome

When Festus replaced Felix as governor, it was an opportune time to re-open Paul's case. Festus tried to encourage Paul to return to Jerusalem to be judged by the Jews. However, Paul didn't feel he had done anything against the Jews, and so appealed to Caesar. This meant that he had to be taken to Rome. As usual, his journey was full of incident, and there were many opportunities to preach the gospel and demonstrate it in different practical ways. When he finally reached Rome, Paul was placed under house arrest, but was free to have people come and visit him. He was still hoping that the Jews would believe the truth about Christ, and he tried his best to convince them, but only a few believed. Paul spent at least two years in Rome from 59–61 AD. From here he wrote letters to several of the churches that he had helped to establish.

The record of the history of early church development in Acts stops at this point. However, as we have seen, there is much to learn about the principles of church life, both from this book, and from the letters that Paul wrote to the churches.

CHAPTER TWELVE

CHARACTERISTICS OF THE EARLY CHURCH

What can we learn from the way the early church operated that is applicable to church life today? What are the ongoing principles? We can go some way to answering these questions, by looking at those features of church life that are consistently found during the first thirty years of church history, which are recorded in the New Testament.

Sharing Life Together

One of the key aspects of Jesus' life with his disciples and that of the early church, was the way they shared life together. Jesus made it clear to his disciples, that while he wanted them to understand his divine nature, he also wanted them to be his friends. He demonstrated this by sharing all aspects of life with them. This same ethos carried over into the early church, where they met together daily in their homes, both for spiritual and social interaction. Right from the early days in Jerusalem, the togetherness of the Christians was clear. They were described as being devoted to meeting together for mutual encouragement in their faith, and also to eating together on a regular basis (Acts 2:42-47). The joy of sharing life was one of the characteristics of the church, which carried on through the rest of the New Testament. Paul's writings positively ooze with the joy of his relationships with other Christians. The people in the church in the New Testament clearly enjoyed spending a lot of time together.

One feature of these early days was that people sold their possessions and gave the proceeds to those who had need. They developed a lifestyle of having everything in common. The disciples would have picked up from Jesus' teaching that wealth was not something to be sought after, and could even be detrimental to their Christian lives. They would have remembered his words to the rich young ruler about selling his possessions (Matt 19:23-26). These ideas were in the minds of the apostles as they sought to lead the new Christians into all that Jesus had taught. This mode of living certainly persisted in the Jerusalem church for some while.

All the believers were one in heart and mind. No one claimed that any of his possessions was his own but they shared everything they had. With great power the apostles continued to testify to the resurrection of the Lord Jesus and much grace was on them all. There were no needy persons among them. For from time to time those who owned lands or houses sold them, brought the money from the sales and put it at the apostles' feet and it was distributed to anyone as he had need. Joseph, a Levite from Cyprus, whom the apostles called Barnabas (which means Son of Encouragement), sold a field he owned and brought the money and put it at the apostles' feet. (Acts 4:32-37)

As the church grew, the administration of distributing resource and ensuring this was done fairly became quite a task. Leaders were appointed to be responsible for handling some of the practical issues associated with the 'daily distribution of food' (Acts 6:1-4). The organisation of the Jerusalem church seems to have been successful in facilitating the lifestyle of sharing everything in common. After the 'deacons' were appointed we read: 'So the word of God spread. The number of disciples in Jerusalem increased rapidly and a large number of priests became obedient to the faith' (Acts 6:7).

However, this same type of lifestyle does not seem to have become a central or general theme of church life throughout the New Testament church. Paul refers, in his first letter to Timothy, to caring for people who are widows in the church (1 Tim 5:1-16). Here, he is giving instructions on church life, some thirty years after the establishment of the Jerusalem church. It relates specifically to the church in Ephesus, where Timothy was working with the leadership team. Practical support was being given to widows. However, there seem to be quite tight conditions associated with this support, and the impression given of the lifestyle of the church in Ephesus seems generally quite different to the early days in Jerusalem, where the believers shared everything they had.

The first apostles had just come from three years of the most incredible life with Jesus, and one can imagine that they wanted to reproduce as much of it as they could. This included a community lifestyle where they shared everything and spent much time together. They obviously managed to introduce this reasonably successfully in the early days of the Jerusalem church. However, one can imagine that this was something that was not going to be easily reproduced in every church that they established. People had jobs to do, so could not necessarily devote themselves to daily meeting together, and to the high organisation required to make community life work.

I think the conclusion on this issue is that full community lifestyle in which there is sharing of possessions, is a valid operation of church, perhaps an ideal to which we should aspire. However, it is not something that is a mandatory part of church life. The important principle is that community life in some form or other is a vital part of being church. It is an integral part of the heritage that Jesus and the early apostles left. It is surely a key part of the church that Jesus wants today.

Informality

The nature of life in the early church seems to have been quite informal. It was characterised by the life between people rather than organisation. Jesus himself had taught almost exclusively about relationships, relationships of people with God and relationships of people with each other. By contrast, there is much less emphasis on instructions about how the church was to be organised. This was very different from the religious life that the early disciples were used to as Jews. In the Old Testament God had laid everything out so specifically. The design of the tabernacle and the Temple were given in great detail. The way in which people were to worship and the sacrifices to be made were clearly defined. There must have been a temptation for the early disciples to impose a similar organisational structure on the way things were done. But they didn't. Rather, they let the life of God flow. People who became Christians wanted to meet together, and they wanted to know what the apostles were teaching. They did what was natural – they met in their homes. Throughout the New Testament record, the same ethos of informality remained within the church. Some organisational structure was introduced at a local level to ensure that church affairs were done 'decently and in order' (1 Cor 14:40). Elders were appointed to be responsible for local churches, and deacons to be leaders in serving the church. There were also general guidelines on the content of church meetings. However, there was no overall organisational structure, and there were no prescribed orders of service.

There were very few official ceremonies in the early church. In fact there were really only three: baptism, breaking of bread and laying on of hands, and even these weren't exactly formally regulated occasions. Jesus was baptised in a river and he instituted breaking of bread as part of a communal meal. Formal ceremony is conspicuous by its absence in the New Testament church. This is something that is reflected throughout the history of the early church as we have it recorded in the scripture.

Structure and Leadership

Unity across the whole church was one of its essential characteristics. However, for practical purposes, there had to be subdivisions to enable church life to be worked out in local communities. The New Testament speaks of two types of subdivision, both of which are geographical, the church in a town or city (1 Cor 1:2) and the church in the house (Rom 16:3-5). This arrangement gave rise to various types of leaders in the church.

First, there were the travelling ministries, the apostles and their teams. They spread the good news to new areas and established churches, including the appointment of local leadership teams. They also supported the churches that had been established by regular visits. This served to bring a sense of unity between the churches in different towns. They communicated news from other places, and also passed on any consensus decisions resulting from discussion among the senior apostles. The culture of the early Church was not of a heavily organised structure, but rather an association of independent churches in the different towns. The apostles had a key role in determining direction and vision for the overall church, and communicating this to the local churches. They did not however, get heavily involved in church management at a local level.

For members of local church communities, the personal visits from the apostles and their associated teams were very important times. The people were glad to be encouraged by the apostles and receive news of what was happening in churches in other towns. The visits provided Christians with a sense of being part of something bigger than their own local fellowship. This was more than a theoretical sense of belonging; it also worked out in practice. An example is the support provided to the Christians in Israel in a time of famine, by those in the Asian and Greek churches.

The second type of leader was an elder. Local churches were run by a group of elders, recognised by the church for their qualities of character and leadership and approved by the visiting apostolic team. Advice and guidance were provided through the team but it was the elders who ruled in the local setting. An attitude of mutual submission, rather than an assertive authority structure, was the ethos encouraged by Paul and Peter throughout their letters to the churches. David Pawson puts this succinctly: the scriptural pattern is to have several leaders over one church, not one leader over several churches.

The third category of leadership in the early church was the deacons. These were people that had a leading role within the church in practical serving. The seven men who were appointed to administer the distribution of support in the early days of the Jerusalem church, are not actually referred to in the New Testament text as deacons. However, an understanding of the function of deacons inferred from the rest of the New Testament, would suggest that that is exactly what they were. The word deacon means servant, and service was clearly the role of these seven men. In a sense, all of us in the church are servants. Jesus calls us all to serve him and one another. This is a key characteristic of the Kingdom of God. Deacons are particularly gifted in this way, and lead in the church's provision of service. In the New Testament, the qualifications for a deacon were high, in fact almost the same as those of an elder, the main difference being that there is no requirement for a deacon to be able to teach. Among the seven prototype deacons were some quite exceptional men. Stephen, for example, was described as being 'full of faith and of the Holy Spirit' (Acts 6:5). It was a very important role in the early church.

The final category of leaders consisted of those who hosted a church in their house (Rom 16:3-5). We are not given a specification of this ministry, as we are for elders and deacons. However, it was an important role, and Paul mentions several people who served in this way in different locations. Both men and women are recognised as being house church leaders. This is in contrast to the role of eldership, which appears to have been for men only. Aquila and Priscilla were particularly gifted in running a house church (1 Cor 16:19). The role was clearly vital to the functioning of the early church, as most meetings were held in homes. People who were welcoming and hospitable, as well as being gifted in hosting meetings and teaching, would have been needed for this ministry.

There is another description of the types of leaders in the church found in Paul's letter to the Ephesians

> It was he (Jesus) who gave some to be apostles, some to be prophets, some to be evangelists and some to be pastors and teachers. (Eph 4:11)

There is obviously some overlap between this description of leaders and the four categories mentioned already. Prophets were often based in local churches (Acts 13:1), but were also particularly seen as supporting apostles (Eph 2:20). Similarly, evangelists worked alongside apostles (Acts 8:1-25), but would also have had a useful part to play in the local church. Pastors and teachers were generally locally based, with their role very much overlapping with that of the elders.

It is clear that there were quite a variety of leadership roles, and that all were important in the development of the early church. Groundbreaking apostles with energy and ability to communicate were needed to get things going and to provide an on-going sense of vision and direction. However, equally important but with a different function, were those required to maintain life in the local churches once they were established.

Leaders in the church were not to be the ones who did everything, with other members simply attending meetings. The intention was for leaders to equip all Christians to contribute to the ministry. This is very clearly illustrated in the picture of the church as a body in which every part has a useful function to play. The continuation of the above passage from Ephesians categorizing the different leaders in the church emphasizes this point:

> . . . to prepare God's people for works of service so that the body of Christ may be built up until we all reach unity in the faith and in the knowledge of the Son of God and become mature, attaining the whole measure of the fullness of Christ. (Eph 4:12)

This ethos is reflected in the style of meetings of the early church in which all were encouraged to take part (1 Cor 14:26).

Leadership was obviously an important part of the early church, but it was not authoritarian, and it was not the focal point of church life. Leaders were there to help lead all people in the church to find their place of ministry.

Succession of Leadership

Succession of leadership in the church was to be by personal discipleship. Paul taught Timothy to pass on what he knew to faithful men, who then in turn taught others (2 Tim 2:2).

New leaders naturally emerged from within local churches. They could prove their calling in a local setting, in the presence of both existing leaders and the rest of the congregation, before being recognised in leadership. The input of itinerant apostles and prophets was sometimes useful in the evaluation process.

The apostles also got to know the people in the congregations they visited. When they saw someone they felt had God's calling for an itinerant ministry, they called them to join the team. This is really quite reminiscent of the way Jesus called his disciples. No systematic teaching in Bible schools was used; succession of leadership was based on a mixture of gifting and relationship. The same was true within local churches. The call to a particular ministry within the church came from the people of the church.

Church Councils

There was also a role for gatherings of senior leaders such as apostles and elders, as happened with the Council of Jerusalem. The purpose of these gatherings was twofold: to discuss how the Christian message should be applied in the context of particular issues of current interest, and to ensure that apostles had some level of accountability. There was a recognition that they would not get agreement on everything, but through discussion they arrived at decisions that they were all willing to stand by. It seems unity was more important to them than being right. They did have their disagreements, but from what we can understand these were usually temporary and much effort was put into resolving them. The desire to move towards the unity of the faith was there, even though they had not yet achieved it.

Unity

We have already seen how keen Jesus was that his followers should be one. The theme of unity in the church is followed up strongly throughout the Acts and the epistles. A very clear message emerges that there is only one basis of unity in the Church. In his letter to the Corinthians Paul writes: 'For no one can lay any foundation other than the one already laid, which is Christ Jesus' (1 Cor 3:11).

God has placed Jesus Christ as the one and only foundation on which our lives as Christians should be based, and this applies to us both as individuals and as members of the Church. Paul speaks against those who were claiming to be part of a group related to a specific leader, as an example of how it was possible to start using a different basis of unity (1 Cor 1:10-17). He uses the way that Christ had brought together Jew and Gentile, the most basic division as far as a Jew was concerned, to emphasise the unifying nature of the work of Christ (Eph 2:11-22).

There are two aspects of unity that we read about. Paul describes them in Ephesians 4 as the unity of the spirit and the unity of faith. He wrote these words when he was under house arrest in Rome.

As a prisoner for the Lord, then, I urge you to live a life worthy of the calling you have received. Be completely humble and gentle, be patient, bearing with one another in love. Make every effort to keep the unity of the spirit through the bond of peace. There is one body and one spirit – just as you were called to one hope when you were called – one lord, one faith, one baptism, one God and father of all who is over all and through all and in all (Eph 4:1-5).

The message is very clear. We all have one father who lives in all of us by his Spirit. Therefore we have unity of the spirit. We are urged to maintain this through living in humility with each other, and supporting each other in love.

Jesus demonstrated this in practice with the way he devoted so much time to being with his disciples. This included teaching, but he also enjoyed just being with them doing natural things. When his disciples started the church, they created a similar ethos by meeting together daily. Paul too carried on in the same way. He was always with his brothers and sisters. Throughout his writings it is clear he loved people. He mentions many individually by name and is familiar with detailed aspects of their lives. Being together and talking together is a key aspect of loving and understanding each other, and therefore of maintaining the unity of the Spirit.

A few verses after mentioning the idea of unity of the Spirit, Paul introduces another aspect of unity. He talks about the various ministries in the body of Christ working to bring the church to a unity of the faith, 'where we all have a common understanding in our knowledge of the Son of God' (Eph 4:13). It was clear even at this early stage of church development, that this was not as readily achievable as unity of the Spirit. It could not be assumed that all Christians will understand Jesus and his teachings in exactly the same way. However, unity of the faith was something that was worth working towards. Paul himself put this into practice with his usual vigorous approach. He was very keen to ensure that people grasped the essential truths of the gospel. He went round visiting and re-visiting all the churches he had planted, explaining the truths. He also had regular visits to other church leaders, to talk through any controversial issues. He was desperately keen that the church should get as close as possible to a unity of the faith. He boldly tackled the key issue of the day about the relationship between the Jewish faith and Christianity, despite the great difficulties and differences of opinion. He wanted the definition of the differences to be as clear as possible, so that the pure gospel would not be diluted. He recognised that false teaching was one of the key weapons of the enemy to lure people from a pure devotion to Christ. He equates unity of the faith and knowledge of the Son of God with a mature church, 'attaining to the whole measure of the fullness of Christ' (Eph 4:13). His letters contain warnings to be on guard for people who would try to lead believers astray with false teaching. One of the key responsibilities of elders was to protect the members of the church from such people.

The Council of Jerusalem was another example of attempting to preserve the unity of faith. The senior church leaders of the day got together to try to come to a unified understanding on the relationship between the Jewish faith and Christianity. A position was arrived at and then communicated to the churches through apostolic visits.

The achievement of unity of faith was clearly a struggle for the early Christians. In addition to dealing with the relationship of Christianity with Judaism, they had to be concerned about the development of new religions such as Gnosticism. This had some similarities with Christianity, but was clearly a different faith. The keys to the success of the early church in holding the faith together were (i) the clear adherence to the centrality of Jesus and his teaching and (ii) the unity of spirit which bound the believers together despite differences of opinion over certain issues.

One thing that isn't clear from the scriptures, is how much uniformity there was in the style of gatherings between churches in different cultures. There is one reference to 'the churches of the gentiles' (Rom 16:4). This might be taken to suggest that there were two types of church, those for the Gentiles and those for the Jews. However, this is very unlikely, as there is no other reference to separate churches in the New Testament. Also there is much teaching on the principle that Jesus came to bring unity between Jews and Gentiles. Referring to the relationship between the two groups Paul argues in Ephesians 2:

> For he himself (Jesus) is our peace, who has made the two one and has destroyed the barrier, the dividing wall of hostility, by abolishing in his flesh the law with its commandments and regulations. His purpose was to create in himself one new man out of the two thus making peace, and in this one body to reconcile both of them to God through the cross by which he put to death their hostility. (Eph 2:14-16)

The message is clear. People groups who were previously opposed were now to come together as one under Christ. There would not have been two separate groups of churches. The reference to 'churches of the gentiles' probably refers to churches in which most members were Gentiles.

Meeting Together

In the very early days of the church, it is recorded that the believers met daily, either in the temple courts or in their homes. From the scriptural record, the type of place where

believers met did not change over the rest of the New
Testament period. Most times we read of the believers themselves being together, they met in each other's homes. This
is interesting, as the apostles had a Jewish background, and
it might have been anticipated that they would use special
places for worship. They did occasionally meet in synagogues or hired halls. However, these occasions seem mainly
associated with evangelistic events when Paul first went to
a town to introduce people to the gospel. The most common
place for Christians to meet together was in homes.

It is significant to note the absence of any reference in the
New Testament to purchasing a place of worship or of any
formal order of service. Jesus would talk to people where they
were. When he got the disciples together it was sometimes in
someone's house, sometimes it was outside. Jesus said of
himself that he had 'nowhere to lay his head' (Matt 8:20).

The teaching of the apostles regarding the importance of
buildings was very clear. Under the Old Covenant God was
especially present in his Temple. However, everything in the
Old Covenant served to illustrate and look forward to something better and more complete in the New Covenant. The
fulfilment of the temple picture in the New Covenant was
that the believers themselves were the stones that made up
the temple (1 Pet 2:4-5). God's dwelling place was not in any
special building, but rather with men (Eph 2:19-22). No
wonder there is no mention of buying property or building
churches. The apostles were shaping the early church to be
a people, not a building.

The style and content of the early meetings of the church
had the same ethos of informality as the location. The apostles must have derived this from the way Jesus had shared

life with them. He spent a lot of time teaching them about spiritual things, but they also lived together, went for walks together and had meals together. Jesus described them as his friends. The informality of style did not mean there was anything casual about the teaching. This came across with great fervency and power. The content of the early church meetings reflected this mixture of social and spiritual. They shared meals together and had fellowship. They really enjoyed one another's company. They also discussed the apostles' teaching. It was really important that all Jesus had taught them and was fresh in their minds, would not be lost. This style of church life did not appear to change through the early years of the church recorded in the New Testament. Maybe the frequency of meetings did not continue at the same daily rate that occurred in the large Jerusalem church in the early weeks following the Day of Pentecost. Smaller local churches in other towns where people had jobs to go to, would probably have met less frequently. However, there are encouragements throughout the New Testament to 'not forsake the assembling of yourselves together' (Heb 10:25), and on the love of the brethren being shown in real tangible ways (1 John 3:18). Jesus' words about the importance of love and unity between believers (John 17:20-23) must have been echoing loudly in the ears of the apostles, as they sought to direct the life of the early church.

This atmosphere of informality clearly continued for the New Testament period. When describing the nature of early church meetings, Paul writes:

What shall we say then brothers? When you come together everyone has a hymn, or a word of instruction, a revelation, a tongue or an interpretation. All of these must be done for the strengthening of the church. (1 Cor 14:26)

The picture is of everyone at the meeting having the opportunity to contribute something. This style of meeting is very much in keeping with the concept of the church as the body of Christ, with each member having a part to play. The home was clearly a natural venue for gatherings of this type. One danger of such a meeting is that things could get out of hand. This appears to have happened in the Corinthian church, which led to Paul covering some principles on the way the meetings should be organised in his letter to them. He was keen that people should be given the opportunity to use their spiritual gifts, but also keen that there should be a good order to the meetings (1 Cor 14:40).

It is interesting to consider the extent to which there were different styles of meetings in different places. There are no predefined forms of service laid down in the New Testament. Therefore it is not unreasonable to expect that churches in different places would have developed different ways of meeting together, and that these would reflect to some extent the background of the majority of people, which made up a particular church. Thus, a church in a town in Israel, where most people were Jews, would probably have developed somewhat differently to a church in Greece, where most were Gentiles. However, there would have been common ingredients to the meetings. Fellowship, prayer, teaching and breaking of bread would be part of the gathering. Most meetings were in homes, and would have been quite informal. Everyone would have the opportunity to take part, and was encouraged to do so. There was also the teaching of Paul about our sole foundation being in Christ, and the importance of not allowing anything else to become our source of unity. This would all suggest that the style of meeting and ethos of the early Christian communities, would be geared to being open to all types of people who wanted to come along. I think they would have bent over backwards to ensure that people of all backgrounds would not feel uncomfortable, due to some particular form of service.

Signs and Wonders

Miraculous events were very much part of early church life. It had been a central part of Jesus' ministry, and his own teaching was clear that these gifts were meant to be available to his disciples as well. His commission to them, just before he ascended to heaven, included reference to healing the sick and casting out demons (Mark 16:15-18). Right from the beginning of the early church, when the Holy Spirit came on the disciples in Jerusalem and they spoke in tongues, its life was characterised by miraculous signs and wonders. In the early days, these appear to have been initiated mainly through the apostles. Wherever they travelled, miracles accompanied the preaching of the gospel.

However, it is clear from the teaching in the New Testament, that signs and wonders were not only to be carried out through apostles, and were not only to be used in the context of evangelism. Paul's teaching regarding the body of Christ, refers to speaking in tongues, prophecy, words of knowledge, discernment, healing and miracles all being part of the life of the church (1 Cor 12). Different people will have different gifts and different measures of the gifts given to them. They are to be used both as an encouragement to those within the church, to help build them up as Christians, and also as a testimony to those outside. There is nothing in scripture to suggest that the miraculous was only intended for the initial setting up of the church. Simple interpretation of the New Testament teaching, is that it was intended to remain as an integral part of church life.

Righteousness

Righteousness is one of the central characteristics of the Kingdom of God. In Romans we read 'For the kingdom of God is not a matter of eating and drinking but of righteousness, peace and joy in the Holy Spirit' (Rom 14:17).

Central to Jesus' message was that we were made to live righteous and holy lives. A good proportion of his teaching was in this area. This was mainly directed to individuals, to encourage them towards a godly lifestyle, but also inevitably had an impact on the life of the church together. The church as a whole was to be characterised by righteousness.

Righteousness was one of the key aspects of the life of Jesus. There is a wonderful phrase in the King James Version of the Bible encouraging us to worship God in the 'beauty of holiness' (1 Chron 16:29). There is something so clean and pure about the holy life of Jesus that is really beautiful. That beauty is also meant to characterise the church, which is to be the bride of Christ 'without spot or blemish' (Eph 5:25-27).

In the real world, of course, this presented the early church with significant challenges. It was bringing a message of welcome and forgiveness to people, but was also to be a place of righteousness. What was to be done when people belonging to the church were persistently unrighteous, possibly leading others astray and bringing the church into disrepute? The scripture gives quite clear guidelines on the process to be followed. In fact, in one of his only two direct references to the church, Jesus himself deals with this issue (Matt 18:15-17).

If your brother sins against you go and show him his fault, just between the two of you. If he listens to you, you have won your brother over. But if he will not listen, take one or two others along, so that every matter may be established by the testimony of two or three witnesses. If he refuses to listen to them, tell it to the church and if he refuses to listen even to the church treat him as you would a pagan or tax collector.

The first important principle is that something has to be done. When we are aware of an obvious sin in the life of a fellow believer, it needs to be brought to their attention. This is part of our love towards that person. The aim is to bring them back close to God. The second principle is that it is initially to be a personal approach. For most people this is not easy to do; we need a good measure of God's grace and wisdom to do this in love, to win the person without devastating them or driving them away. In Galatians where Paul teaches on this, he talks about being careful to restore people in a gentle forgiving manner (Gal 6:1), recognising that we are all together in need of God's forgiveness. John Ortberg refers to this willingness to confront as 'truth-telling', and while recognising it is not an easy thing to do, considers it to be one of the hallmarks of an authentic community[1].

If the person does not respond to the personal approach, it is to become a church matter, first with one or two others, usually church leaders. Finally, if there is still no repentance, the matter is to be brought before the church as a whole, and the person formally recognised as being excluded from the church fellowship. This was a rare event in the early church, and obviously one that was taken with great reluctance. However, it was there for the purpose of standing firm on the principle of righteous living being an important characteristic of church life.

It is interesting that Jesus said that after this has happened, we are to treat such a person as a pagan or tax collector. This does not mean that we cast them off totally and never speak to them again. Jesus loved pagans and tax collectors, and spent time with them trying to bring them into his kingdom. When someone is excluded from the church, there may be an initial period of separation, but that person is still a special individual made in the image of God who, by showing love, may eventually be won back into the kingdom.

Passion and Joy

Passion was clear characteristic of the early church that was maintained in the hearts of believers throughout the New Testament period. The rapid spread of the gospel and the wholehearted commitment of Christians, with several being called to sacrifice their lives for the gospel, is clear evidence of this. Jesus was filled with passion himself, and he wanted his followers to share the fullness of his joy, and to love God with all their hearts. The disciples caught this ethos of enthusiasm from Jesus. He had given them purpose in their lives. It was natural for them to be passionate about their relationship with God, about their life together with other Christians, and about sharing the wonderful good news they had with other people. The good news hasn't changed. It is still wonderful in the twenty first century. This wholeheartedness and sense of vibrant life is surely one of the ongoing features of our lives as individual Christians, and therefore of the church as a whole.

Alongside passion, a characteristic of the early church that seems to leap out of the pages of the New Testament is their joy. There was the joy in the good news of the gospel. As individual Christians they had been released from the punishment they deserved for their sin, and made right with God. They were experiencing the abundant life that Christ had promised. This was fresh and it excited the early believers.

Then there was the joy of being together. Belonging is something for which we humans are made. The joy of togetherness in a crowd when their local football team scores a goal, is an example that I can easily relate to. The togetherness of God's people is of course something much more special that this, for where just two or three are gathered together in his name, he is there 'in the midst'. David considered this in the Psalms when he declared: 'Behold how good and pleasant it is when brethren dwell together in unity. For God commands his blessing there' (Ps 133:1).

The sense of togetherness was a source of great joy even in the difficulties faced by the church as it sought to establish itself in an often hostile environment.

This joy resulted in there being much time devoted to worshipping God. It has been said that praise is the language of the Kingdom of God. For the early church I'm sure this was true.

Commitment

The sense of commitment to the church seen in these early days is also a consistent feature of New Testament teaching. We often speak nowadays of 'going to church' as if it were something we do on certain occasions like going to the cinema. The challenge of the story of the early church is not just to 'go to church', but to become 'part of a church', to join with other believers and to commit oneself to belonging. The concept is illustrated in the pictures of the church being a family or being like a body. Both these analogies illustrate the level of commitment between believers that Jesus wants within his church.

Jesus had taught his disciples much about the Kingdom of God. He had encouraged them to 'seek first the Kingdom of God and his righteousness' (Matt 6:33). The growth of the early church was a key part of the development of God's Kingdom, and so the disciples were naturally very committed to being part of it. It was a high priority in their life. The early believers shared life with one another, not just meeting on one day of the week, but in a deeply committed relationship, which affected all aspects of their lives.

Forgiveness and Service

I think of these characteristics as the fresh air of the Kingdom of God. They arise from that beautiful quality of humility, about which there is so much both in Jesus teaching, and in the letters to the churches. In church relationships, this comes out in two ways, an attitude of forgiveness and service.

Forgiveness is of course at the centre of the gospel. Jesus forgives us and we are to forgive others. This is actually one of the hardest aspects of Jesus teaching to follow. Resentment about the way we are treated by others is one of the enemy's prime strategies for preventing us from realising the fullness of Christ's presence in our own relationship with him. Bitterness towards others eats us up inside and is most debilitating from a spiritual point of view. Jesus taught a lot on forgiveness. He told us to forgive and keep on forgiving (Matt 18:21-22). The freedom that comes when we do this is tremendous[2].

Life in the early church certainly threw up examples of difficulties in this area. We described earlier the rift between Paul and Barnabas over Paul's refusal to take John Mark on their second missionary journey. Was Paul right not to take Mark? Should he have forgiven Mark and let him come, or was it that Paul felt Mark was not yet ready to serve God as part of the apostolic team? Perhaps it was wise to let Mark have some time to get more established in his Christian life in a local setting, before re-joining Paul on his travels. We will of course never know the answer to these questions. However, it is interesting to note that the discipline of excluding Mark from this trip, ultimately resulted in him finding a role in a travelling ministry, which Paul describes as 'being of great value to him' (2 Tim 4:11). Whatever the rights and wrongs of the cause of an initial rift between brothers, it can be healed over time, if there is a humble and forgiving attitude on both sides. This appears to have been the case in the relationship between Paul and Mark.

In addressing this issue, it is interesting that Jesus says on one occasion that it is the responsibility of the one who has sinned against his brother to make the first move in reconciliation (Matt 5:23), and then on another, he puts the same responsibility on the one who feels he has been wronged (Matt 18:15-17). That way, both parties should be making moves towards each other and meet in the middle. Christian reconciliation often establishes a special bond between two people for the rest of their lives. It is a great example of how in Christ we can overcome evil with good.

Jesus had described himself as a servant and had demonstrated this practically by washing his disciples feet. This concept features strongly in the way the early church was organised. All members of the church were to consider themselves servants of Christ, and therefore to share in the role of serving the church. In all the teaching about leadership, there is an emphasis on the leader serving the people. When describing the ministry of Christians in the church the Greek words 'diakonia' and 'doulos' are frequently used. These both mean 'servant'. There are other Greek words for people in official positions, but these are never used of church leaders.

Being a servant also worked out in practical ways. There was a genuine desire to help other people in the early church. Those who owned houses or land often sold them and gave the proceeds to the church, so that the money could be used to serve others. When Christians in one area were doing well and heard about those in a different location who weren't, support was sent. The disciples were known for their love for one another, which wasn't just in word alone, but also in practical expression through the provision of support.

Involvement in the World

Another aspect of the life the apostles had experienced with Jesus, which carried on into the early church, was of involvement in the world around them. Jesus spent a lot of time teaching his disciples. He clearly had a special relationship with them. But he also spent a lot of time with those outside this group in the world around. He spoke to crowds, attended social events and had individual conversations. He mixed with all sorts of different people, including the influential, the poor, and the outcasts of society. He was interested in the details of their lives. He told his disciples that they were to be 'in the world' (John 17:18), 'but not of the world' (John 15:19). He taught them to remember that it was not those who were well that needed a doctor, but those who were ill (Matt 9:12). His commission just before he ascended, was that they should be his witnesses in the world, bringing the good news of the gospel (Acts 1:8). Earlier he had used the parable of the Good Samaritan to illustrate how their responsibility was to care for all those they met along life's way (Luke 10:25-37). Jesus' life illustrated how these principles worked in practice. One of the keys to his demonstration of love to the people he met, was that he was filled with a heart of compassion for them. He felt for them in their situation, and from that position of understanding was able to reach out and help them. He recognised the image of God in each person, and taught the disciples to understand that whatever they did to another person they were doing it to him as well (Matt 25:31-46). He wanted them to see that he cared for and felt for each one, even those regarded as the least important. He encouraged the disciples to have the same heart of compassion in their interaction with others.

With the words and example of Jesus still fresh in their minds, the apostles did their best to ensure that the early church mixed with the life going on around them. They were building an alternative society, but not one that was distanced from the rest of the people outside. Like Jesus, they saw their task to bring the good news to the world. They reached out in faith to pray for people's healing, and used every opportunity to share the good news about Jesus. They were determined to make sure the outside world knew they were around. The people recognised that they were a separate group, and were even somewhat daunted by the dynamic lifestyle of the new believers. However, it was clear that much good was being done, and we read that the early Christians were 'highly regarded by the people' (Acts 5:13). This type of interaction with the world carried on throughout the New Testament church. When the church in Jerusalem was scattered by persecution, we read that 'those who had been scattered preached the word wherever they went' (Acts 8:4). Some time later Paul, describing the characteristics of an elder, says he must 'have a good reputation with outsiders' (1 Tim 3:7).

There were, however, two sides to the relationship between the early church and the outside world. While some people respected them, others were strongly opposed to everything the church stood for. This applied particularly to their relationship with the authorities. The Jewish leaders in Jerusalem were naturally 'greatly disturbed because the apostles were teaching the people and proclaiming in Jesus the resurrection of the dead' (Acts 4:2). This cut across the message they were bringing. They arrested Peter and John, and told them in no uncertain terms to stop preaching about Jesus. This brought a conflict between the word of God and the word of earthly authority. The disciples were clear in their response (Acts 4:19-20): 'Judge for yourselves whether it is right in God's sight to obey you rather than God. For we cannot help speaking about what we have seen and heard.'

They complied with earthly authorities except where there was conflict with what God was saying to them. They remembered Jesus' example. He had been fearless in proclaiming the truth of the gospel, even when this meant rubbing the authorities up the wrong way. For Jesus and many of the early disciples, this ultimately meant giving up their lives for the principle.

The Presence of the Holy Spirit

This characteristic has been left to last, not because it is the least important, but because it is the most vital part of life of the New Testament church, which undergirds all the other aspects of church life that have been discussed. When we read of the early Christians meeting together, we often find phrases such as 'they were all filled with the Holy Spirit' (Acts 4:31) or 'filled with awe' (Acts 2:43). It characterised the way they were together as God's people. The sense of God's presence was particularly real when the believers met together, but it was based on each of them having a vital relationship with God themselves. In Paul's letters to the churches much of the teaching is about ensuring that each person in the church is continuing to walk close to God, living by the Holy Spirit who is in us (Gal 5:16-26).

It was clearly possible, even in New Testament times, for churches to lose that sense of the presence of the Spirit. In Revelation, John writes to several churches that for various reasons were struggling (Rev 2-3). The principal reason for losing the sense of God's presence in these churches, was that they had forsaken their first love for each other and for Christ. It was a priority for leaders in the early church to encourage everyone to maintain a clear walk with God, in order to ensure the continuing sense of God's Spirit among them.

Concluding Remarks

This chapter has tried to provide an analysis of life in the New Testament church. It is an exciting picture of a vibrant community. In a later chapter, we will look at how the modern day church compares to that in the first century. However, before that we will conclude this part of the book by attempting to pull together what the scripture teaches on church structure and organisation.

References

1. Ortberg, John, 2003, *Everybody's Normal Till You Get To Know Them*, Zondervan, Grand Rapids, Michigan.
2. Gruen, Ernest J., 1976, *Freedom to Choose*, Whitaker House, Springvale, PA.

CHAPTER THIRTEEN

A MODEL OF THE CHURCH

As a scientist, I often use the idea of models to help explain physical phenomena. Complex scientific concepts can be more easily understood if they can be described as a model, which we can visualise as a picture. An example is the model of an atom consisting of a heavy nucleus at the centre with electrons spinning around in circular orbits. It is now known that this is not a very accurate description of what the atom is really like, but even this simplified model is very useful, and goes a long way to explain many of the physical and chemical properties of matter. This chapter presents a model of the church that has emerged from Restoration teaching. It isn't perfect, but it does give some good points of insight into how the New Testament church operated.

The model is very similar to that described by David Lillee in his book *Beyond Charisma*[1], which was published in 1981. David had been one of the early pioneers of the Restoration movement. He was concerned that the movement had drifted somewhat from its original principles, and wanted to

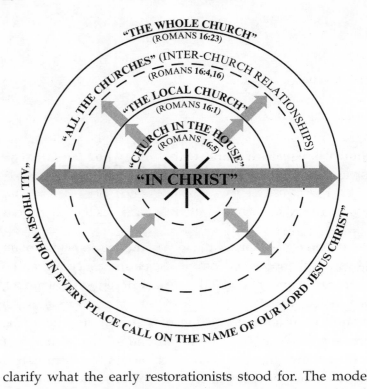

clarify what the early restorationists stood for. The model tries to encapsulate what the Bible teaches about church structure.

The church is described as being composed of four concentric circles: (i) the whole church, (ii) inter-church relationships, (iii) the local church and (iv) the church in the house. A diagram illustrating the picture is shown below. The case for this model is argued from the study of the church in the New Testament, presented in the previous chapters of this part of the book.

The Whole Church

We considered earlier that a church is a group of people called to be together in Christ. The whole church is therefore made up of all those who are Christians. To define the extent of the whole church, we need to be clear on what it means to be a Christian. When Jesus talks about the basis of the church, he equates it simply with people who confess that he is the Messiah, the Son of God (Matt 16:13-18). In the context of the rest of the New Testament, this is not someone who simply says these words, but who also lives their lives in a manner consistent with that confession, in a true relationship with Christ. In writing to the Corinthians Paul addresses himself to the whole church as follows:

> To the church of God in Corinth, to those sanctified in Christ Jesus and called to be holy, together with all those everywhere who call on the name of our Lord Jesus Christ – their Lord and ours. (1 Cor 1:2)

In this verse, Christians are described as being those who are set apart to live holy lives, and who recognise that Jesus is their Lord. To be part of the whole church, the outer circle of the model, is to have the focus of our lives on being a follower of Jesus.

The Bible, however, rarely uses the word 'church' to apply in this broad context. When the people of God within a large region are being described, it is usually in terms of the 'churches' (plural) in that region. The global church is more of a concept than a functional unit. We will never actually meet up with most other Christians. Nevertheless, it is a very real concept, involving a real unity of Spirit. There is a very special bond between all Christians, even those we have not yet met. Importantly though, there is nothing to suggest in the New Testament that the global church was intended to function as an organisational unit. While the apostles tried to maintain the unity within the church through meeting together from time to time, it did not operate as a global organisation with a hierarchical structure.

The Church in the House

All the subsequent sub-divisions of the church in the New Testament are geographical. The smallest unit is the church in the house, the inner circle of the model. In Acts, we read of the early church meeting together from house to house, and this pattern continued during the whole period covered by the New Testament. In many ways, it is rather surprising that this was the case. The first apostles were Jews, and the whole of their religious upbringing had been based around strict rules, with formal ceremonies held in special buildings. The initial developments of the church were in marked contrast to this, being focused on informal meetings in homes. We have already considered how this change must have resulted from the disciples trying to put into practice what they had learnt from the teaching and example of Jesus. He had been the perfect model of a small group leader. He had spent a lot of his time leading the disciples' own small group. He taught them about the good news of the New Covenant, but also shared life with them, walking and talking with them in the fields, and eating with them in homes. They had seen this concept of community worked out in the way Jesus had been with them. They wanted to reproduce this in the early church, and having small groups in homes was the ideal way this could be achieved.

Different house churches were identified by the person or couple in whose house the church met. We have previously mentioned Aquila and Priscilla, who were examples of people whose special ministry was hosting and leading such house churches. The meetings covered the areas of fellowship, breaking of bread, prayer and apostles' doctrine (Acts 2:42). At the relatively small gatherings, everyone was encouraged to contribute (1 Cor 14:26). However, life in the early church was not only about attending official meetings; it was about sharing life on a day-to-day basis. In Acts we read that 'they broke bread in their homes and ate together with glad and sincere hearts' (Acts 2:46). They found that being together as Christians was very special, even when doing natural things such as sharing a meal together. They had discovered the synergy that exists between Christians as they encounter the presence of Christ in each other. Jesus had expressed in this way: 'When two or three are gathered together in my name there I am in the midst' (Matt 18:20).

In the small house group setting, each individual was important, and each also had a part to play. This picture seems to reflect the heart of God as a father. In the natural world he had arranged for people to be in families, which are small enough for each member to be significant and to be loved as an individual. The small group structure in the church similarly allowed the love of the father to be expressed between Christians in tangible ways.

Small house groups represent the inner circle of the model. They did not exist in isolation from the rest of the church, but rather operated within the next circle of church organisation, the local church.

The Local Church

There was a strong emphasis in the teaching of Jesus on the unity he desired between those that would come to follow him through the message of his disciples. This is reflected in the practice of the early church. All Christians in a given locality were considered part of the local church. We read of the church in Antioch, the church in Corinth and the church in Ephesus. These local churches were initially set up through the ministry of apostles or apostolic teams. Once the church had taken shape, elders were appointed to ensure that affairs were organised in the area. After this the apostles generally moved on to the next location to which God was directing them. The elders were left to run things in the local church themselves. Occasional follow up visits by the apostles served to bring connection with churches in other towns, and also to bring teaching and direction.

It is interesting to note that in all the New Testament examples, several elders were appointed to each local church. Local churches were always referred to by the locality, and never identified by a single leader, either an apostle or elder. When this did begin to happen in the Corinthian church, Paul warns against it in no uncertain terms (1 Cor 1:10-17).

The local church appears to have been the essential organisational unit of the church. In most cases when scripture mentions church in singular form, it refers to a church in a city. Within each local church there were several house churches and these were the principal meeting places for the church. The apostles also often used synagogues (Acts 17:1-4) and sometimes hired halls (Acts 19:8-10) for meetings. However these tended to be used for evangelistic purposes, rather than meetings for existing believers. The case for the local, city church as the organisational unit is strongly argued by Watchman Nee[2].

The leaders of the local church were a team of elders. Others with a leading role were deacons, who helped administer church organisation, and house church leaders. The degree of independence between house churches within the local church is not clear. However, the implication is that the house church leaders would have considered themselves part of the local church and therefore subject to the rule of the elders of the church. This seems a sensible safeguard, in that there would be the possibility for a powerful personality to lead a small isolated house group in the wrong direction. Paul's instructions to the elders at Ephesus were to be on their guard to see that this did not happen (Acts 20:28-31).

Inter-church relationships

The final circle is rather more difficult to define, and in David's model he depicts it with a dotted line instead of a continuous one. This is based on the fact that there is very little detail on church organisation given in scripture beyond that in the local church. The singular form of church nearly always refers to a church in a city, whereas mention of a larger geographical area refers in plural to the churches in the region. For example Paul's letter to the Galatians was addressed to the 'churches in Galatia' (Gal 1:1-2). David argues that local churches in the New Testament were essentially autonomous. They were each led by a team of elders, under the headship of Christ. No hierarchical structure officially connecting churches appears in the New Testament, and there is therefore no evidence that this is how God wants to operate in this way in the modern day church.

Nevertheless, each local church was part of the universal church and was therefore related to other local churches, as part of the same family. The key to understanding how this circle of inter-church relationships functioned in the New Testament is in the travelling ministry of the apostolic teams. David's description of this part of the model seems incomplete, in that this important aspect of the way the early church functioned is not included. The apostles had a key role in communicating between the local churches. There was no organisational structure beyond the local church, and yet there was a good level of unity and mutual care and support between churches, particularly when one considers the relative difficulty of communication and transport in the first century. These strong links between local churches were facilitated by the apostolic teams.

These teams were based around strong churches such as Jerusalem, Antioch and Ephesus. They went out with the aim of establishing and supporting other local churches. In the initial stages of setting up a church they took a lead, but they saw this aspect of their role as only transitory. Once the local church was securely in place, they appointed elders, and left it to run under its own steam. They did however come back and visit from time to time. The difficulty of transport meant that these visits were not regular, but they were often prolonged, up to more than a year. Paul spent time with each of the churches he had planted, first, because he simply loved being with the people and second, because he wanted to do all he could to help them grow. The main emphasis of the visits was to encourage and build the local church; it was to impart wisdom, not to impose a rule on to the church. The apostolic ministry did have authority, but this was not forced on the church. Rather the churches gladly accepted the advice that was given, out of respect for the anointing that was on the apostle and on his team. The visits also gave the opportunity to share what was happening in other places, to bring greetings from fellow Christians, and to communicate news of any policy decision that had been made in meetings between apostles and other senior leaders.

To summarise, interactions between local churches were based on relationship rather than organisation, and were facilitated by the ministry of apostolic teams.

Concluding Remarks

This completes the description of our model of the church. It seems to be consistent with the New Testament account of the early church, and to provide a good summary of what can be gleaned from taking a purely scriptural view of the subject. Several questions arise. To what extent is this view of the first century church relevant to us in the twenty first century? Given that the current situation in the church is very different from this model, should we be trying to revert to it? In the last part of this book we try to address these questions.

References

1. Lillie, David, 1981, *Beyond Charisma*, Paternoster Press, Exeter (Permission to use the diagram of the model of the church obtained from Paternoster. Copyright © 1981).
2. Nee, Watchman, 1997, *Further Talks on the Church Life: Confirming the Truth Concerning Church Life*, Living Stream Ministry, Anaheim, California.

Part 3
The Path Ahead

In this final part of the book I am looking forward and asking the question, 'How can we become the church that Jesus wants?' The church is in preparation as the bride of Christ, and it's important that we make every effort to look our best for the wedding day. Traditionally, evangelicals have focused much more on our individual walk with God. While this is of course important, it needs to be balanced by considering how we are together as God's people. It's encouraging that God is stirring a number of people to specifically consider this issue. Significant books by James Thwaites[1], Michael Moynagh[2] and John Noble[3] have recently been published on the subject. These all contain useful and thought-provoking views on the future of the church. I hope that this book will add to these, and provoke further investigation of what God wants for his church. Please test what I have written according to scripture, and accept what you find is consistent with the Bible and seems right to you and the Holy Spirit. Please discard anything that doesn't pass these tests.

Many things are being suggested regarding the future of the church. My heart is that we should not just try new things because they sound like good ideas. The scripture has much to teach us about how to be church together, and although there is not a lot of specific teaching on how it should be structured and run, there are a number of guiding principles. These have been considered in some detail in the previous part of the book. As we look forward to how the church will develop, we need to have our foundations firmly built on these principles. But that doesn't mean we can't be creative. The New Testament gives generous guidelines and there is plenty of scope for originality.

We will first consider the current state of the church in the UK by comparing it with the biblical picture. The renewal and restoration movements have highlighted a number of aspects of church life found in scripture. How are we getting on with implementing them? The final chapter will then look at the specific challenges that the church faces in its objective to become the bride of Christ, the church that Jesus really wants.

References

1. Thwaites, James, 1999, *The Church Beyond the Congregation*, Paternoster Press, Cumbria, UK.
2. Moynagh, Michael, 2001, *Changing World Changing Church*, Monarch Books, London, UK.
3. Noble, John, 2002, *The Shaking: turning the Church inside out to turn the world upside down*, Monarch Books, London, UK.

CHAPTER FOURTEEN

HOW IS THE CHURCH GETTING ON?

One of the 'joys' of working in our day is the individual performance review. Each year we sit down with our boss or mentor, and review how we're getting on. The usual reaction on having to face the ordeal is to heave a big sigh. However, I think that secretly most of us don't really mind it too much. If it's used well, it's actually a great idea. First of all it gives the message to the employee that what he or she is doing is important – important enough for someone to come a spend time talking to them about it. It is also a chance to review – to celebrate the successes and to analyse areas where things went wrong. We can then look to the future, getting a vision of where we're going and planning how to get there.

There is a scriptural precedent for doing this in the church as well. In Revelation chapters 2 and 3, seven local churches in Asia Minor (modern day Turkey) undergo a very searching performance review. It is clear that God wanted these churches to seriously consider their corporate life, and take steps to remedy those areas in which they needed to change.

This chapter reviews the current state of the church in the UK with respect to the characteristics of the early church covered in Chapter 12. It will focus particularly on those aspects of church life with which God has challenged us over recent years through the renewal and restoration movements.

Sharing Life Together

The idea of the church as a vibrant and caring community of people was one of the emphases of the early restoration movement, which has carried over into other parts of the church. There has certainly been a lot of progress in this area. There is now a much better understanding that the church is a gathering of Christians sharing life together. The Alpha course description makes this point very clearly.

Two aspects of our life together that were part of the developing restoration movement, were the ideas of shepherding and submission, both of which are valid scriptural principles. Care for fellow Christians was a characteristic of the early church, and pastors were appointed as leaders in the area of caring. Church members were also encouraged to submit to their leaders (Heb 13:17).

Caring for one another

The emphasis on relationships in the early days of the restoration movement was greatly facilitated by the introduction of house groups. Individuals could find a place of belonging in the church that was not always easy as part of a large congregation. The prayer to 'bind us together' was worked out in practice with people visiting each other, making each other meals and generally sharing life together just as Jesus had done with his disciples. Church was not only about coming together on Sunday, but about being part of each other's lives every day of the week. Pastoral care was worked out through house groups, with leaders often taking responsibility for the people in their group. However, the idea of sharing the task of looking after one another, went even further than this. While there were individuals with specific pastoral ministry, mutual care was everyone's responsibility – all were to look for opportunities to show love in practical ways. This was a very positive outcome of restoration teaching.

The implementation of house groups in churches across the denominations, has helped to foster this ethos of friend-ship on a wider scale. However, some house groups focus only on one aspect of church life such as Bible study and do not always develop the rounded community aspects of the New Testament picture, where the meetings in homes were referred to as house churches. In the early days of restora-tion, Arthur Wallis described house groups as microcosms of the church as a whole, having all the features of church only being smaller. Ideally house groups should provide the mix of social and spiritual life outlined in Acts 2. The current ideas of meetings containing elements of welcome, worship, word and witness seem to provide this balance quite well[1].

There are also particular challenges to the practice of house groups in restoration churches. As some have grown into city-wide organisations with big buildings to look after, house groups have tended to be sidelined and treated as an optional extra, rather than being seen as the building block of local churches. I think we need to revert our focus to the original concept of house groups, and promote them as centres of belonging, care and growth.

Having the right structure of house groups is good, but does not guarantee a caring community. We have to develop an ethos in which we are genuinely looking out for one another. We need to be like a family, where this sense of care is seen as our responsibility.

The church as a whole, and in the western world in particular, has a great opportunity in this area, as there is general lack of care in our society. Mother Theresa noticed this in her travels in the west to raise money for the poorest of the poor in the developing world. She observed that while there was little real material poverty, there was a tremendous poverty in love. She saw many lonely people. As the church, we have a great opportunity to show love and welcome people into our family. Belonging is what we were made for, and contributes enormously to our physical and mental well-being. There is a great line in the first *Crocodile Dundee* film, where Mick's reporter friend talks about someone she knew having to visit a psychiatrist to talk about her problems. Mick replies, 'Didn't she have any mates?' Having close friends to talk to and communicate with is great fun, and also great therapy. John Wimber is quoted as saying that the biggest factor in determining whether people stay in a particular church, is whether they find friendship there.

There is much emphasis in the church at the current time on reaching out to be a positive influence in society. The Evangelical Alliance, the central voice of evangelical Christianity in the UK, has started several initiatives along this line. Typical of these is the 'Movement for Change' where the focus is on how church can change society. The phrase 'the church is the only organisation that was created for the benefit of its non-members' is very often used in sermons these days. In our own church we had a significant prophetic word about being a wagon train camped with the wagons arranged in a circle. We were looking after each other well within the circle, but now God wanted us to turn around and look outward and seek to help others outside. Outreach is obviously an important aspect of church life, and one in which we all need encouragement. However, in everything there is a need for balance. While the church is for the benefit of outsiders, its primary aim is to fulfil the purpose and heart of Jesus. It is also meant to be a great place for those who are in it. We have to keep all these things in balance. At the beginning of the restoration movement, we probably concentrated too much on building our own relationships and not on reaching out. My own feeling is that the pendulum has, if anything, swung the other way. We need to ensure that people in our churches are continuing to be loved and cared for.

Submission

This is another area of church life that is a clear scriptural principle. There are several verses about people in the church submitting to the leaders of the church (Heb 13:17, 1Pet 5:5). However this is balanced by the warning to leaders to avoid 'lording it' over their people (1 Pet 5:1-4) and the general encouragement to 'submit to one another' (Eph 5:21). This idea of mutual submission is based on the recognition that Christ is in each of us. Elsewhere Paul speaks about 'in honour preferring one another' (Rom 12:10). The nature of this relationship has been described by Philip Iszatt as 'voluntary mutual submission'[2]. It is a beautiful concept bringing security to both family relationships and the church. Again Mother Teresa gives us a good example[3]. She operated as part of the Roman Catholic Church where submission to leadership is very much the order of the day. When she first felt God speaking to her about caring for the poor, she shared her vision with the leader to whom she was accountable. Initially he told her that she should wait. She did this without question, but God continued to speak to her. When she shared it with her mentor again he gave his approval, and the rest is history! She went on to do an almost unparalleled work for good among the poor around the world. This is a great example of patient submission reaping its rewards in the end.

The perfect example of submission is of course Jesus himself. He subjected himself to the will of the Father while he was here on earth (John 8:28). He had every right to claim equality with God (Phillippians 2:5-11), but he chose to give up that right, so that he could play his key role in the plan of the Father to restore mankind to him. This led Matthew Baker to describe the concept as 'voluntary submission for the sake of purpose'[4].

Unfortunately, the implementation of shepherding and submission in the early days of restoration did not always adhere clearly to these principles. There was sometimes insufficient emphasis on the responsibility of leaders to temper their position with an attitude of mutual submission, which led to an abuse of authority in some cases. This wrong emphasis has now been acknowledged, but the result is that a perfectly valid aspect of church life has been rather put to one side. The word submission is now very rarely heard. It seems to be a case of the alternative to abuse being disuse. As is the case with pastoral care, I feel we need to revisit the topic, and reverse the swing of the pendulum, to recover the right balance in this important characteristic of our life together.

Informality

Moving away from rigid forms of meeting to a freer and more relaxed style has been one of the contributions of the restoration movement. It has been commented that people going to restoration church meetings look like they're dressed for a barbecue. I feel this is actually a good aspect of church life today, as it probably reflects both the way that Jesus met with his disciples and also the meetings of the early church. There is no indication that they put on special clothes to discuss teaching or pray together. I expect it is almost certain they did so in their ordinary day-to-day attire.

This practice has impacted many of the other denominations, even those with greater levels of formality in their services such as the Church of England and Roman Catholic Churches. Nicky Gumbel presents his Alpha courses in an open-necked shirt, and formal vestments are conspicuous by their absence at the New Wine gatherings. However, despite these changes, set forms of service and clothing for leaders of meetings are still an important part of church for many Christians. They represent a desire to do everything in good order, and also to honour God by making meeting with him something special.

I feel it is important for those of us in the 'freer' churches to respect our brothers and sisters who feel this is the best way to approach God. I think there is also something to be learnt from one another in this. My son and his wife recently had their twin daughters christened in an Anglican church. The words of the christening service are excellent. They include a prayer of blessing on all aspects of the lives of the children, and also serve as a reminder of the responsibilities of both natural and church families in caring for them. It felt that we were making an appropriately big thing of welcoming these new lives into the church.

I have recently started to attend a communion service run by the chaplains at the hospital where I work. This is exciting for me, as it brings together chaplains and other Christians in the hospital across the denominations. It consists of a very fixed form of meeting with a written order of service, which is not terribly natural for me as a restorationist, used to meetings with opportunities for spontaneous contributions. I just feel at present that I need to get down off my high horse, and acknowledge the unity of spirit that I have with these brothers and sisters by joining them in breaking of bread. I hope it will help to develop the link that already exists between our church and the chaplaincy at the hospital. Two people from the church are currently supporting the chaplains' contribution to the hospital by working as volunteers.

At these gatherings, the set forms of service have some great content. However, there can be a tendency to go through the words rather too quickly. Shouldn't we spend time to savour the great thoughts we are listening to and speaking? If we are to use set forms of service, it's important to let the words touch our hearts and spirits as we read them.

Structure and Leadership

A radical look at church structure and leadership was one of the features of the restoration movement. The early restorationists felt clearly from scripture that the role of apostles should not have died out with the early church, and that there was still a place for them today. This was contrary to popular belief in evangelical circles at the time. Several of the restoration leaders were recognised as apostles, and they created teams to help the growing number of groups seeking to establish restoration-style churches in their locality. In each new church, they appointed a leadership team consisting of a group of elders. This kept in line with what we can learn of the role of apostles from the New Testament.

However, as time went on, some of these apostolic teams developed into large hierarchical organisations. In other parts of the world, some were claiming to cover thousands of churches. Peter Wagner's book on the New Apostolic Churches paints exactly this picture[5]. These groups of churches have often spread out on an international scale. Instead of apostles fitting the scriptural pattern of being basically church planters, they had become effectively 'archbishops' of a large family of churches.

This operation of inter-church relationships was a significant change from the original restoration ideas, which had focused around the establishment of local churches. These would welcome the support of an apostle and his team for advice, but were to be essentially independent. In the New Testament, the local churches were simply part of the universal church. Their basis of relating to other churches was their unity in Christ. This vision had no place for the denominations that characterise the modern day church. Churches in a denomination have an additional basis of belonging together. Paul speaks against this in 1 Corinthians, where divisions were being created in the local church by people aligning themselves with particular leaders (1 Cor 3:1-11). Denominations result in division of the true local church, and the early restorationists were clear that they wanted to see this situation rectified. However, as restoration developed, churches relating to a particular apostle became part of his family of churches, many of which might be distant geographically. They had therefore effectively become part of a denominational-like organisation. What the movement had originally set out to counteract, it was to some extent becoming part of.

This change in apostolic role is a clear case of history repeating itself. For some reason, the scriptural model of apostles seems very hard to maintain. In the first century, the apostles had travelled from town to town, first founding and then supporting churches. They appointed teams of elders in each church to take responsibility for day to day organisation. Apostles supported and advised the elders, but did not manage them. However, within a relatively short space of time there were subtle changes to the leadership style. Local leadership began to focus around a single bishop rather than a team of elders, and the bishops also began to take responsibility for smaller surrounding churches as well. Apostles weren't needed any more, and the ministry faded from view. The dynamic, fluid arrangements of the early church had been replaced by a static structure. To some extent this process has been repeated in the twentieth century restoration movement.

Nevertheless, there are several examples where the development of church families has proved very successful. Many vibrant churches have been established, and many people have become Christians. The Kingdom of God has been extended. Vineyard in the UK is an example of an apostolic team that has become a network of churches and could easily be labelled as a denomination. There is a hierarchical structure headed by a national council[6]. Each pastor has an overseer who is another Vineyard pastor and who is also responsible for several other pastors. However the ethos of the operation of the structure is not strong on authority but rather on giving good support to the local pastors. They have an annual national meeting of the leaders. The provision of good support has proved very successful in seeing of a significant number of Vineyard churches established around the country.

Terry Virgo's Newfrontiers is another excellent example of a successful restoration family of churches. All Newfrontiers churches are clearly associated as being part of the family. This important principle was established when the team changed from being the loose association of churches, Coastlands, to become the Newfrontiers church family. This had worked well because the support given is excellent. My observation of the limited sample of Newfrontiers churches that I have visited, is that they go a long way to fulfilling nearly all the qualities of biblically based churches outlined in Chapter 12. They make a clear statement of their values of loving God, loving one another and loving those in the outside world. They stand strongly on biblical teaching, and there is a good sense of the presence of the Holy Spirit in their meetings.

Newfrontiers has always emphasized the importance of the local church and has avoided being dominated by a strong central organisation. As it has expanded, apostolic teams have been established to plant and serve churches in different areas of the UK and in other countries. Each church has good fellowship with the local apostolic team. The central administration of Newfrontiers acts as a hub to organise conferences and produce publications, which are geared to encouraging the development of new apostolic teams and hence churches. Their leaders gatherings for prayer and fasting have been significant times. The purpose is to genuinely seek direction from God together. Interpretation of prophetic words brought at these gatherings has shaped several key developments amongst the family of churches. The ethos is one of providing an environment for hearing God together and inspiring people, rather than imposing a rule from a central organisation. There are clear echoes of the way things were done in the New Testament, where decisions were made on the basis of what 'seemed good to the Holy Spirit and to us' (Acts 15:28).

In the New Testament, the apostolic teams were clearly strongly involved in the churches with whom they were working. However, the work of the team was organised separately from that of the local churches. The teams acted as a means of communication between churches in different localities, but did not set up any official organisation between them. The group today, which probably expresses this most clearly, is New Covenant Ministries International (NCMI), which is based in South Africa. They are quite clear that they regard themselves as an apostolic team, rather than an organisation of churches. They aim to support churches, rather than to govern them. Their website describes the role of team members and the team as follows[7]

> There is however no hierarchy in these teams. No one is at the top or at the bottom and these teams are not above the leadership of the churches that relate to them. They are men and women who have been anointed by God, and who we have been able to release in a way that enables them to give the benefit of that anointing to more than just their local church.
>
> We see the Church as local and the work of the team as translocal. Trans-local teams enable local churches to link responsibly and effectively with others in doing the work of the Kingdom.

This philosophy of the relationship between apostolic teams and churches seems very consistent with the New Testament model.

Having compared the philosophies of Newfrontiers and NCMI, however, it is worth noting that in practice their operation is actually very similar and the two groups have joint leaders meetings where they enjoy good fellowship[8]. I think it is important not to become too prescriptive in dictating the way apostolic teams should work. One cannot use scripture to define their operation exactly. What seems important is that the church clearly still needs apostolic teams whose primary function is to plant churches, and who do not get overburdened with organisation of churches at a local level.

Despite the good work that has been done in developing these families of churches, there is, to my mind, one

drawback. The close connection of each church within the
family means that they generally do not see it as a priority
to build links with other churches in their locality. Terry
Virgo, for example, argues that to plant biblically-based
churches at this time, it is still necessary to build independently from other denominations[9]. He has good relationships with leaders from other streams within the
church. He speaks, for example, at the New Wine conferences, and organises leaders' gatherings, which are
attended by people from a wide range of backgrounds. He
also meets with Christian leaders in his own locality of
Brighton. Despite these developments, he feels at this stage
there is insufficient ground on which to build together. He
may well be right for the present. My hypothesis is to question whether today might be the right time to consider how
we start laying that common foundation on which we can
build together in the future. I believe that we now need
apostles who can see the way forward to drawing God's
people together from across the denominations and planting unified local churches.

In addition to the question of inter-church organisation,
there are also challenges to the operation of leadership
within local churches. In the early days of restoration, there
was general adherence to the principle of plurality of elders.
However, in many cases, this has reverted to a situation
where one person becomes recognised as the pastor. It is so
natural for us as humans to look to having a single leader.
In the Old Testament, the people of Israel wanted a king,
when really God wanted them to see him as king, not a
single man. The New Testament is also absolutely clear on
plurality of leadership. I think it is worth persevering with

this scriptural model. Again the NCMI web-site echoes this concept

> We have given ourselves to see strong and healthy, eldership-led local churches established and nurtured. Believers in these churches will be trained, equipped and released to grow into their full potential and maturity in God. Our objective is that the priesthood of all believers will be exercised fully and freely. In this context, it is our desire to nurture elders to become skilful shepherds who lead with integrity of heart.

Many people would argue for the need for a single leader of a local church, and again one cannot be prescriptive from scripture about whether this is right or wrong. The important principle is that one person should never be allowed to dominate things, and there should always be a group of wise, respected leaders who govern the church as a team.

Unity

It is clear from scripture that Jesus longs for unity among his people. This is to be worked out both on a small scale, in loving relationships between individuals, and also on a large scale, between Christians across a locality and between churches. There are many scriptures about God breaking down dividing walls, even between such fundamentally different groups as Jews and gentiles (Eph 2:11-22). Probably the clearest statement of this ultimate unity is in Ephesians 1

> And he has made known to us the mystery of his will according to his good pleasure which he purposed in Christ to be put into

effect when the times will have reached their fulfilment – to bring all things in heaven and on earth together under one head even Christ. (Eph 1:9-10)

This is definitely one of my 'wow' verses. It's stating something of the whole purpose of everything. That is to bring all things together in Christ. This is certainly something to muse on. It's great to have the big picture in mind. In my work as a scientist, I am sometimes asked to examine PhD students on their research work. Almost inevitably the first question we ask the student, is to describe the context of their work. It's so important that they have not just being working away for three years trying to solve a problem in isolation. They need to have understood why they have been doing what they have been doing. I think it's good to try to do the same with what's happening in the church.

It's also good to consider how these wonderful global concepts translate into real life in the modern day. No one does this better than Juan Carlos Ortiz. In his book *Disciple* he has a short chapter entitled 'Mashed Potato Love'[10]. Here are a couple of excerpts.

God is regrouping us. He has already begun. He is not using our categories (denominations), however, God has only two groups – those who love one another and those who don't.

With all the reverence possible, I say to you that the Father, Son and Holy Spirit are three potatoes made into mashed potatoes. And Jesus is hungry for mashed potatoes. He is going to have them. He is already doing something very profound in his church.

Juan Carlos describes the process that potatoes go through from being separate entities in the ground. They are grouped together in sacks. Then they are washed, peeled, cut into pieces and mixed. They are all put in the same pot and cooked, finally being fully mixed together to make mashed potato.

It's certainly true that over the last thirty or forty years, the church in the UK and worldwide has made some important strides along the path to becoming mashed potatoes. First, there is a much-improved recognition of one another. All over the country, people are much freer to visit one another's churches. When our church, for example, was recently being refurbished, we were encouraged to visit other local churches. This extends right across the whole Christian community, with Catholics and evangelicals alike writing books where they clearly acknowledge what is happening in other parts of the church[11]. In Southampton, there have been a number of inter-church initiatives, and there is a general groundswell of desire to recognise one another, and work together for the furtherance of the Kingdom of God. Some of the ministers in the city have resolved that if they are asked about their church, they will refer to being part of the church of Southampton, rather than talk about their own congregation. Another exciting development has taken place in Stoke-on-Trent. A few years ago, a national survey was carried out to compare lifestyles in different towns in the UK. A wide variety of aspects of life were evaluated, and the quality of life determined from the total score. Stoke sadly finished last in this list. This stimulated local Christians to do something about it, and since that time there have been gatherings of Christians for prayer from across all the church in the city, as God is drawing his people together.

The rise of the Evangelical Alliance is one of the encouraging aspects of church development over this period. It has done much to make those of us who believe the biblical gospel message feel at one with each another. Nevertheless, despite the progress, there are still a number of key issues that divide us both in what we believe and how we practice our faith. One of these issues is that of ethnic differences. How do we deal with the corresponding differences in culture? There is hardly anyone better placed to give an opinion on this than Joel Edwards, the General Director of the Evangelical Alliance. He came from a West Indian Pentecostal background, and in his book entitled 'Lord make us one but not all the same', he describes his experience of relating to the predominantly white evangelical church in the UK[12]. He also describes some of the other tensions, facing the evangelical church of today that he has had to deal with as leader of the EA, such as the charismatic issue, prosperity teaching, and general way in which we interpret the Bible. His conclusion is that in the church we need to recognise one another and 'celebrate our diversity'.

'Celebration of diversity' is a helpful concept in calling Christians to recognise one another, but I feel that God wants to take us on further than that. If I were looking for a phrase to summarize God's heart for his people, it would be: 'recognise our diversity but celebrate our unity'. God shows himself in different ways through the variety of people in the church – we all have different characters, different talents, and different backgrounds, which have shaped us. We all have a significant contribution to make. However, we are called to be one, not only recognising one another as part of the same family, the unity of the Spirit, but also in what we believe about Jesus, the unity of the faith. We are called to a oneness like that between the Father and the Son – that is really something to celebrate!

Meeting Together

The restoration movement has introduced several new aspects of meeting together, that have been more generally adopted by other churches in the UK. We now meet informally in small groups, often in homes, and have an emphasis on everyone having the opportunity to take part. These developments have helped us to move back to the heart and style of New Testament descriptions of church gatherings.

Another area of meeting together that has changed, is in the nature and style of worship. This was one of the three areas highlighted by George Tarleton in the paper he presented to the South Chingford Congregational church in 1971, which appears in Appendix 1. It has been one of the major areas of impact of the restoration movement on the church. But what exactly do we mean by worship?

It seems to mean different things to different people. To many it would mean the time we spend on a Sunday singing praise to God, and indeed that is surely part of worship. However. the concept of worship in the Bible is somewhat broader than that. The Greek word 'leitourgeo' is translated either 'worship' or 'service', and is used in a variety of contexts in the New Testament. It appears that the concept of worship was to do with all aspects of our lives being focused on God. Therefore when the early church came together, their meetings reflected this attitude of worship. Acts 2:42 records the purpose of believers coming together as being for teaching, fellowship, breaking of bread and prayer. Worship is not mentioned as a specific component of their meetings. I believe this is because worship was understood to be the basis underlying everything they did. The passage in Acts goes on to say that 'everyone was filled with awe'. Their meetings had a tangible sense of God's presence. One of their prayer meetings is recorded in Acts 4:23-31. You can almost feel the presence of God as you read this prayer. At the end it says 'After they prayed, the place where they were meeting was shaken. And they were all filled with the Holy Spirit and spoke the word of God boldly'.

A. W. Tozer attempts to describe worship as 'To feel with the heart and express in some appropriate manner a humbling but delightful sense of admiring awe, astonished wonder and overpowering love'.

Although the term 'worship' is not used specifically to describe what the disciples were doing at that time, their hearts were surely filled with worship as defined here by Tozer.

Worship is part of our whole life, and so it is natural that it will also be part of our church meetings. When we consider the greatness of our God and the sense of well-being that comes from knowing him, it seems so natural to be excited about it and want to express our joy. Throughout scripture, part of God's people coming together was to express their gratitude to God for his greatness and goodness.

Music was a means of worship in the early church. In Ephesians, Paul encourages the believers to be full of thanks to God in their heart, and express it together in song:

> Speak to one another with psalms, hymns and spiritual songs. Sing and make melody in your heart to the Lord, always giving thanks to God the Father for everything in the name of our Lord Jesus Christ. (Eph 5:19-20)

Evangelical churches have had rousing hymns for hundreds of years. In Wesley's times these hymns raised strong emotions; Wesley himself describes his heart as being strangely warmed as he met together with other Christians[13]. The charismatic movement has re-emphasised the expectation of a spiritual dimension in our worship. We sense a tangible presence of God in our meetings. We are overwhelmed with thoughts of his awesomeness, but also of his love, and we hope to make a personal encounter with him. There is a new sense of joy and excitement in our worship. It is acceptable to clap, to raise our hands and even to dance, as we are filled with the excitement of knowing God. These are of course natural expressions of joy, and have been used throughout history, from Old Testament worship through to crowds enjoying success in a football match.

A desire for this new reality in worship has extended across the different denominations. There are many new songs, which reflect what God is doing in the present day. Worship is now often led by a band of musicians, rather than a single organ. However, changing the type of songs and the style of worship, do not guarantee that the congregation will experience a vibrant sense of God's presence. I have visited churches where the songs have been great, and I've been longing to clap or raise my hands or do something to express my excitement in the presence of God, but haven't felt free to do so because no one else was. We need to create a culture where people are expecting to sense the nearness of God. We are encouraged to draw near to God, so that he will draw near to us (Jam 4:8). Where better than when together with his people, remembering his goodness and love to us?

I guess that there are a number of churches in transition in worship. There is sometimes a reluctance to open up in this area, due to the possibility of people of an extrovert nature going 'over the top' in their expression of worship. This is quite understandable, but is not really a valid reason for suppressing the development of a real sense of God's presence in worship, which can do wonders both for individuals and for the church.

The effect of exuberant worship on outsiders is also something to consider. Certainly, there are many who find it a pleasant surprise that people can actually enjoy themselves in church. Others are naturally perplexed by shows of emotion and strange phenomena, such as speaking in tongues. I always think that a word of explanation from the front at the beginning of any meeting where there are likely to be visitors, is useful to put their minds at ease. Paul recognised the possible negative effect of speaking in tongues on the outsider, and in his letter to the Corinthian church advises the Christians there to be mindful of this in their meetings (1 Cor 14:22-25).

Worship in which the believers sensed the presence of God, was a way of life for the early church. Perhaps our 'worship' times in church have become a little one-dimensional, focusing too much on singing. There are many other ways of expressing our appreciation of God. Some people are exploring the use of different art forms as means of encouragement to worship[14]. God has made us creative beings, and it would seem entirely reasonable to use alternative approaches to help us sense the reality of God with us. Whatever way this is achieved, the important thing is that we are drawn closer to God, and that we sense his presence, as did those in the early church.

God loves us to worship, and this has been an important area of growth in the church over recent years. Let's ensure that we continue to place it at the centre of what we do as a church, and that we are sensitive to God to grow in our understanding of the best ways to join together in worshipping him.

One question regarding worship has always intrigued me, as no doubt it has many others. Should we all be looking to worship in the same way? I think of Jesus' prayer about being one as he and the Father were one (John 17:20-21) and in my heart I say, yes, I really would love to have a situation where all God's people, young and old, extrovert and introvert, black and white would be happy to worship together. I can't see the Father, Son and Holy Spirit going off to different places to worship because they each liked their own style. They are three different persons but they are one. Their harmony is one of the beautiful things about the nature of God. Surely then, in principle at least, it is reasonable to aspire to reach a place where we can all worship together.

How can this happen in practice, when we have exuberant Pentecostals at one end of the spectrum and contemplative Catholics at the other? Isn't it possible to have both? I love both exuberant singing and quiet meditation. To me the key quality that can draw us together in worship is 'respect'. This is a great word used frequently in the Bible about inter-personal relationships meaning 'esteem felt or shown to another person'. If we could really learn to respect one another, to honour the style of worship each other likes, I think we could achieve it. Perhaps the young people would-n't mind having the music volume turned down a few deci-bels if they knew it was causing grandma to have a 'hot flush'. Perhaps the older folk can learn to enjoy 10 minutes of action songs when the focus is on the children. . . . I have a dream!

However, I have to admit that, as I have talked about these ideas with Christian friends, and as I have read what others have written, I cannot find many folk with the same heart. The usual response is that we want 'unity but not uniformity'. Christians generally seem happy to accept that we can all worship God in our own style in our own place. The argument is that God loves people to worship him, and that he is at home with the exuberant Pentecostals and with the contemplative Catholics. I'm sure this is true. He has made us creative beings and worship in a local church will naturally reflect how that particular group of people prefer to worship. I just wonder whether there is a better place for us with more recognition of the value of one another's styles.

Signs and Wonders

The supernatural gifts of the Spirit were brought to the atten-tion of the twentieth century church through the Pentecostal and Charismatic movements. The majority didn't hear the message first time round, but a good proportion of us did at the second attempt. The last thirty years of the century saw a great increase in the expectation of the supernatural gifts of the Spirit. Many individual Christians speak in tongues in their own times with God. Meetings often include prophetic words and people pray for one another to be healed. All these gifts have been a source of blessing and encouragement to the church. However, I think it is also true to say that we are not seeing them in the full flow that is implied in the scriptures. There have been cases where prophetic words have been given which have not been from God, and caused confusion. The issue of healing has been discussed earlier. We have seen a few wonderful healings, but most times when we pray for someone to be healed, it doesn't happen. What should our reaction be to this?

Our response should certainly not be to give up on the gifts. We should rather be seeking God, 'earnestly desiring the best gifts' (1 Cor 12:31). There is helpful advice in this area in the writings of some of the early Pentecostal pioneers. R.A. Torrey argues that scripture points to answers to prayer being related to the closeness of our walk with Jesus and to each other[15]. He takes all Jesus' words on the subject to build up a full picture of the keys to praying prayers that get answered. John G. Lake was mightily used by God in a ministry of healing in the early years of the twentieth century both in the USA and South Africa. Reading his biography, it is clear that these gifts were based on a deeply committed walk with God[16]. He talks about the need to have a close relationship to God, and a genuine sense of the fact that Christ is in us so that 'as he is, so are we in this world'

(1 John 4:17). He interprets that as meaning that we can share in the full nature of Christ in the world today. While this seems to be too much for any of us as individuals, surely it is not too much for us as his body together. Jesus said that we would do greater things than he was able to himself (John 14:12) and the epistles speak repeatedly of us being the body of Christ in the world. I feel we need to take John Lake's advice, and rekindle our spiritual hunger for Jesus to move in more power through his body.

However, our expectations need to be realistic. R.A. Torrey[17] argues that we cannot just pray for anything and expect Jesus to answer it, as some preachers today would have us believe. If we took this suggestion to its extreme, with enough faith, everyone would become Christians, no one would get ill and no one would die. We believe that heaven is going to be something like that, but it doesn't seem feasible for things to be like that now. It's important that we don't have unrealistic expectations that will end in disappointment. Nevertheless, we can increase our faith from where it is today, and believe that God does want the miraculous to be a significant part of his church in the twenty-first century.

The general question of why some prayers get answered and some don't, has intrigued Christian philosophers over the years. C.S. Lewis uses the example of the responsibility of a headmaster in a school to explain how he feels God responds to prayer[18]:

God has retained a discretionary power of granting or refusing it. Except on that condition prayer would destroy us. It is not unreasonable for a headmaster to say, 'Such and such you may do according to the fixed rules of the school. But such and such other things are too dangerous to be left to general rules. If you want to do them you must come and make a request and talk over the whole matter with me in my study. And then – we'll see.'

It is surely reasonable to trust God to know how to deal with our requests, but it doesn't stop us from asking.

Righteousness

There is a real challenge to the church today in the area of righteousness. The morality of modern day society is no longer based on the teaching of the Bible, but rather on what seems right to the majority. Moreover, the new morality is not shy in promoting its own doctrines, and those who fall short, commit the heinous crime of political incorrectness. As Christians, we need to be aware of where the spirit of our age diverges from what Jesus and the Bible teaches. We need to be on guard that we are not led astray by its ideas. When so many people adhere to a particular attitude with regard to homosexuality, for example, we must take care we are not swayed by weight of opinion. In the church today, we have not always managed to hold unswervingly to biblical truths.

One of the problems with promoting righteousness in areas that others don't consider being wrong, is that we can be perceived as being self-righteous. As many Christians are pointing out, we must follow Jesus' example in this by not condemning or rejecting people because of their sin. We have to achieve a balance where we are clear about what we believe is right, but at the same time love individuals even though they fall short of God's standards[19]. This is sometimes a difficult line to find. John Ortberg helpfully considers the distinction between forgiveness and reconciliation[20]. Through forgiveness we keep on loving people despite their sin, but that person will never be properly reconciled to God or to us, until they have repented and turned away from that sin. The perfect example of finding this balance is of course, in the life of Jesus. He taught the truth fearlessly and uncompromisingly, but also showed a huge heart of compassion to those whose lives were not right. We as a church need to follow his example by holding on to the truth of the Bible, and declaring it with genuine love to our neighbours.

One excellent example of how this balance can be achieved, is the Firgrove Family Trust, which is an initiative originating from our own church[21]. It is a pregnancy crisis centre that has grown from our desire to respond to the issue of abortion. We firmly believe that legalising abortion is not God's best for our society, and Firgrove clearly proclaims this message. However, it also proclaims a message of hope to those are facing the dilemma of an unplanned pregnancy, or who have already had an abortion. The aim is to demonstrate Jesus' heart of compassion to these people as individuals, by standing with them at their time of need.

Passion and Joy

Passion and joy were not characteristics that people would have generally associated with the church early in the twentieth century. Even today, at the start of the twenty-first, many non-Christians still use the word 'boring' to summarize their view of the church. However, things have changed significantly in the past hundred years. The charismatic movement has brought a renewal of life to many individual Christians, which is reflected in a new atmosphere of passion and joy in many churches. The removal of set forms of worship in restoration churches has given opportunity for that joy to be expressed in church gatherings. However, having freer forms of worship does not guarantee the continuing presence of that joy and passion. The most common comment in the review of the churches in Asia Minor was that they had lost their first love (Rev 2:4). How easy it is for us to do that as individuals? It can also happen to congregations. In order to preserve that freshness of our passion for Christ, we need to be continually 'provoking one another to love' (Heb 10:23-25).

Commitment

A strong commitment both to God and to the church was another characteristic of the early believers. Individual commitment of our lives to God has been part of the evangelical ethos since the time of the reformation. The restoration movement has added to this an emphasis on the importance of commitment to church. I believe there are challenges to us in our level of both individual and corporate commitment.

There are many examples in the contemporary church of individual Christians being devoted and committed to Christ. However, I do not believe that developments over recent years have generally led to the level of devotion to Christ and to his body to which scripture points. It's as if we have been shaken but not stirred; shaken into life by the presence of the Holy Spirit, but not yet stirred into the full practical outworking of his presence. We do not see the devotion pictured in Acts, where people met together daily for prayer and teaching, and sold their possessions to give to those who were in need (Acts 4:32-37). The lifestyle of the western world seems to prevent us having quite that commitment of our time and resources to our spiritual life. Our work lives and family lives make heavy demands on our time. How can we break free to be the radical influence that was provided by the early church?

One area, which always challenges me, is the implementation of Jesus' teaching on possessions. There is such an emphasis on wealth and possessions in our society. How can we implement the altruistic lifestyle that Jesus both taught and demonstrated, in the light of the enormous inequality of wealth that exists throughout the world? Jesus taught that loving our neighbours included sharing our natural resources. It is encouraging to see many Christians involved in developing-world projects, but are we being radical enough? Are we really willing to sacrifice one of our two coats so that our needy brother or sister can have one, or are we too entrenched in the affluence of western society to fully take on board that teaching? Mother Teresa has demonstrated what can be done in this area in the modern day. The church has a great opportunity to demonstrate how the love of Christ can provide the answer to this very pressing global problem. The challenge of how to do this more effectively is great. I think we need to review our attitudes and lifestyle in this area in relation to Jesus' teaching.

There are challenges too in our commitment to God's people. The current ethos of society is to be wary of commitment. Young people are often reluctant to get married. Business agreements have become incredibly complicated with lots of clauses dealing with what happens if the agreement breaks down. The legal profession is having a field day! We, as Christians, have to be very careful not to get sucked into this way of thinking. The concept of covenant, where we enter into a committed relationship, is an integral part of the way God wants to be with us as his people. It's also the way he wants us to interact with one another. When we sign up to be a Christian we enter into a covenant with God, and also a covenant to belong to his people.

For the church to function successfully, we all need to be committed to provide our contribution consistently. This involves sacrifice. We will not be able to do some of the things that we would otherwise enjoy doing. Of course there has to be a balance in life. If we have a job to do and a family to care for, then these are priorities, and our work for the church must fit in with these. However, we also need to understand that our service in the church is an important part of our lives as Christians. Do we know what that contribution is and are we committed to providing it consistently?

The issue of relationships between Christians in different 'streams' and denominations is a difficult one. The situation in the church today is a long way from the scriptural idea of geographically based local churches. I want to be loyal to the congregation of which I am part, but I also feel committed to other Christians in the local church in Southampton. This division of loyalties is particularly difficult for Christians in denominational churches, because of the commitment to the denominational organisation. I think for the moment we have to work with both connections, serving those to whom we are particularly joined, but also looking to forge relationships across the whole local church as opportunities arise.

Forgiveness and Service

Forgiveness is a topic that has come to the fore in the church today in a couple of contexts. We often hear talks on the importance of forgiving others and making peace with any people with whom we might have a dispute. This is important first of all from a personal point of view. It is now widely recognised that forgiveness and good relationships with others are needed for a clear walk with God, and both our physical and emotional well-being[22]. Good relationships are also obviously vital to the functioning of the church as the body of Christ.

Forgiveness has also appeared as part of the rather more controversial concept of identificational repentance. This process recognises that there are often deep-seated differences between groups of people that have been present for many years. The sectarian tension in Northern Ireland is a typical example. Even though current members of the groups are keen on living together in peace, the historical differences seem to make it difficult for this to happen. Identification with the sins of one's group in previous generations and repentance from them, is seen as a means of release from the bondage of the continuing antagonism between the groups. Although it is difficult to find specific scriptural texts for this approach, it certainly seems in keeping with the general philosophy of forgiveness in scripture. Christ came to break down barriers between people groups, and this seems a positive step in the right direction.

In general, there seems to be a good emphasis on forgiveness in the church today. We will continue to need to work on it, if the barriers that still exist in the body of Christ are to be fully broken down.

The idea of service in the church has certainly been highlighted by the restoration movement. 'Body ministry' in which everyone is recognised as having a part to play was a key component of its message. Whilst leadership is important, its goal is to bring each person to maturity (Eph 4:11-13). There has certainly been a development of this concept in the church in the UK over the last 50 years.

My wife and I occasionally visit our local Church of England congregation and have been struck by their efforts to get a variety of people involved in taking part in their Sunday meetings. They have around 150 people attending, and so this seems rather easier than in our own 500 plus congregations at Central Hall. They also have a strong emphasis on house groups. These are mentioned often in the main Sunday meetings and are obviously seen as a key part of church life together.

This pattern of change is common in many, if not most, evangelical churches. There is a growing sense that church is meant to involve every person and not just focus on a single pastor. It is also meant to be life together as Christians, covering every day of the week, and not just revolving round a meeting on Sunday. There is general encouragement in many churches for everyone to serve in some way or other. This has led to a diversity of service both to people within the church and those outside.

There is currently quite a lot of emphasis on the outreach

aspect of service. In Southampton at present, for example, there are 126 Christian-based social projects[23]. Many folk, particularly young people, have been touched by the problems of poverty and disease in the developing world, and have a real heart to reach out and help them. This is of course all excellent work and is to be encouraged.

However, a balanced church must also focus on mutual care. A body cannot be working all the time. There must be time spent on nourishment and care and this is a key component of church life. House groups have been a vital development in this respect. In a house group everyone is important and is missed if they don't turn up to a meeting. They give opportunities for love between Christians to be worked out in real ways by serving one another. Everyone plays a part in group life. They also give opportunities for Christians who feel God is calling them to a particular ministry to develop it in a small way in a loving context. From this sound base they can develop service both to others in the church and beyond.

Involvement in the World

Jesus lived in clear separation from the world system, and yet was intimately involved with its people. He described it as being in but not of the world (John 17:13-19). The early church reflected these ideas in their relationship to the world around them. They were a community separated from the rest of society who were viewed with some suspicion by the general public, and yet they also had strong involvement with them. They sought to be salt and light to the people around, and also to share with them the good news about Jesus.

This is an area where Christians today are still very active. Most evangelical churches are also very evangelistically minded, and there are regular encouragements to look for ways of connecting with people around us. The Alpha Course is a great example of an imaginative way of reaching people in our day. The emerging church movement, in particular, has focused on looking for new ways of sharing our message. Many other initiatives are seeking to demonstrate practically the love of God by reaching out to disadvantaged people in society. Given the relatively small percentage of people who are Christians, we are having a very positive impact on society. Steve Chalke's 'Faithworks' and the 'Oasis Trust' are excellent examples of this[24]. The Evangelical Alliance is also regularly creating new developments to raise the profile of the Christian message and to encourage churches to look outwards.

But we shouldn't be complacent. We need to be continually provoking one another to love (Heb 10:23-25). We live in a society, which is becoming increasingly alienated from the truth of God. It is a society, which is asking us, as the enemy did to Eve, 'Has God said?' (Gen 3:1). We need to stand by the truth, even when it is unpopular and politically incorrect. We need to be clear about what God has said. At the same time, we need to be full of the grace of God, not condemning people but rather stressing the love and forgiveness of God. This kind of balance is not always easy and as individual Christians we need both wisdom and boldness to say the word both in season and out of season.

One challenge to the church is to look for ways of supporting individual Christians in their life in the real world. James Thwaites, in his book *The Church Beyond the*

Congregation, considers this as one of the important issues for the church in our day[25]. It is actually not very easy for most of us to be effective witnesses in our work environment. We long to be able to share the good news about Jesus, but to gossip the gospel in the coffee room will usually mean being regarded as something of a freak. For most Christians, it is not something we naturally warm to. As someone who clearly falls in this category, here are some thoughts, which I hope will encourage fellow strugglers.

We need to really love our neighbours, and the first thing we can do is pray for them – Arthur Wallis used to have a saying 'sacrifice sleep (for prayer) to save souls'. Another key to being able to share our faith, is keeping our own walk with Jesus alive. When we're excited about him, we will talk about him much more naturally. The next principle I always try to follow, is to simply be honest when people ask me questions. If someone asks me what I did at the weekend, I not only talk about enjoying the latest football match (or not if Southampton lost again), but I also mention that I went to church or house group. Most times people don't respond when you mention church, they look away or make an embarrassed grunt. However, it gives them the opportunity to respond, and sometimes they do. Finally, I try to share with people the practical things that churches do, as this is something they can more readily relate to. When we used to help run a gathering for elderly folk, people always seemed more interested in that than our normal church meetings. We are not seeking to impress them with what we have done, but we do want to use all means we can to get them interested in spiritual things. The natural can often lead on to the spiritual. The business of being effective witnesses as individuals is not easy, but gossiping the gospel is a vital part of today's evangelism, as it was in the early days of the church. It's good to think of ways we can do it more effectively.

Given that many people will never come to church, or may not even meet a Christian in their social circle, there is still a place for organised evangelistic events. There has probably been rather less emphasis on this mode of evangelism in recent years, as we have focused on lifestyle evangelism. However, the generally lower profile of the Christian message in people's lives, means that the need for evangelism outside church is somewhat greater. Evangelists are still therefore a vital part of the twenty-first century church in the UK. It's encouraging to see imaginative new ways of preaching the gospel emerge. The work from our own church of Miracle Street mentioned in Chapter 5 is a good example. I think we need to re-establish an emphasis on this type of evangelism, which worked well for the early apostolic teams.

Integration of non-Christians into churches is a very important area. It is one in which we do not always excel. Becoming a Christian is a difficult enough thing in our society; keeping the faith when the full life-changing implications of being a Christian become clear is often another ball-game. The message of the gospel is wonderful, but it is also incredibly challenging. As churches we need to do all we can to look after and nurture new Christians in the early days of their walk with God. We have already mentioned John Wimber's observation that the most important factor about people staying in a church was whether they found friends there. We have to be a welcoming people to those that come in. Sadly, I think we are not always that good at this. We are enjoying ourselves so much in our church fellowships, that we find it difficult to extend our friendship group to welcome newcomers. Let's ensure a genuine warm place of belonging is available to all those who God adds to us.

The church does not get generally a good press in the outside world, but then neither did Jesus or the early church, so we are in good company. However, there are some plusses. *Songs of Praise* generally continues to present a clear and relevant gospel message, and the public persona of the church is also helped by several celebrities like Cliff Richard, Paul Jones (of Manfred Mann) and international rugby player Jason Robinson, who are refreshingly open about their faith. God TV, although generally restricted to subscription TV, gives the opportunity for the gospel message to be shared. We have a great message, but one that is never going to be amazingly popular outside a revival. We need to continue to faithfully proclaim God's word by all means, both traditional preaching and new creative methods.

The Presence of the Holy Spirit

This key ingredient of a biblical church life has been highlighted by the charismatic and restoration movements. There is now a real expectation of sensing God's presence in our church gatherings. However, that sense of meeting with God is not something that can be taken for granted. We can have all the correct structures and functions in place, but this does not guarantee the presence of the Holy Spirit. Like the churches in the first century mentioned in Revelation, we can lose it through individual members losing the vitality of their own walk with God. Brennan Manning in the *Ragamuffin Gospel* encourages us to cry out daily for the Holy Spirit[26].

> Don't assume that the Holy Spirit will act in your life without you taking the initiative. Cry out for a mighty outpouring of the Holy Spirit. Wherever you are – in the church or at home, alone or with others, watching television, lying in bed or driving to work – pray continually for more of the Spirit of Jesus Christ.

We need to do this both personally and for our church. The Holy Spirit is living in each of us, but God wants us to be hungry for his presence. We need to be actively praying to God and stirring one another up to cultivate that vital sense of spiritual life among us.

Concluding Remarks

There are inevitably both good and bad points about the church today. I'm really glad I'm in it, and am proud to be part of it. But it's far from perfect and, as in our own lives we seek to become more Christ-like, so in the church we need to agree together to move towards maturity as God's people. The final chapter suggests some ways we might do this.

References

1. Withers, Trevor, 2004, *Help I'm leading part of my cell meeting: practical help in leading the welcome, worship, word and witness*, Cell UK Ministries, Harpenden, Herts.

2. Noble, John, 2002, *The Shaking, turning the church inside out to turn the world upside down*, Monarch Books, London.

3. Spink, Kathryn, 1997, *Mother Theresa: an authorized biography*, HarperCollins, London.

4. Baker, M., 2001, 'What does the scripture mean by "head"? A consideration of the voluntary submission of Christ within the Godhead'. Presented at a c-net Theological Forum, 10th May 2001, Southampton.

5. Wagner, C. Peter, 1998, *The New Apostolic Churches*, Regal Books; Gospel Light, Ventura, California.

6. Vineyard UK web site <http://www.vineyard-churchesuk.com>.

7. New Covenant Ministries International web site <http://www.ncmi.net>.

8. Virgo, Terry, Personal communication, 8 August 2007.

9. Virgo, Terry, Personal conversation, 23 August 2006.

10. Ortiz, J.C., 1976, *Disciple*, Lakeland, London.

11. Hocken, P., 1994, *The Glory and the Shame: Reflections on the Twentieth Century Outpouring of the Holy Spirit*, Eagle, Guildford, Surrey; and Scotland, N., 2000, *Charismatics and the New Millennium: the Impact of Charismatic Christianity from 1960 into the New Millennium*, Eagle, Guildford, Surrey.

12. Edwards, Joel, 1999, *Lord make us one – but not all the same*, Hodder and Stoughton, London.

13. Wesley, John, *The Works of John Wesley*, Journal 1 (1872 reprint, Schmul Publishers, Salem, Ohio n.d.).

14. Jones, Simon, 1998, *Why bother with church*, IVP, London.

15. Torrey, R.A., 1971, *The Power of Prayer and the Prayer of Power*, Zondervan Publishing House, Grand Rapids, Michigan.

16. Lake, John G., 1994, *John G. Lake: His Life, His Sermons, His Boldness of Faith*, Kenneth Copeland Publications, Fort Worth, Texas.

17. Torrey, *op cit*.

18. Willard, Dallas, 1998, *The Divine Conspiracy*, Fount Paperbacks, HarperCollins Publishers, London. Quotation reprinted by permission of HarperCollins Publishers Ltd © D. Willard 1998.

19. Clarke, Philip, 2006, *A Heart of Compassion*, Authentic Media Milton Keynes.

20. Ortberg, John, 2003, *Everybody's Normal Till You Get To Know Them*, Zondervan, Grand Rapids, Michigan.

21. Clarke, *op cit*.

22. Gruen, Ernest J., 1976, *Freedom to Choose*, Whitaker House, Springvale, PA.

23. 'Saints of a Different League: a report on church-based community activity in Southampton', 2006, The Shaftesbury Society, UK.

24. Chalke, S., and Watkis, A., 2004, *Trust: A Radical Manifesto*, Authentic Media, Milton Keynes.

25. Thwaites, James, 1999, *The Church Beyond the Congregation*, Paternoster Press, Cumbria, UK.

26. Manning, Brennan, 2005, *The Ragamuffin Gospel*, Multnomah Publishers Inc., Sisters, Oregon.

CHAPTER FIFTEEN

THE WAY AHEAD FOR THE CHURCH

I will build my church and the gates of hell will not prevail against it. (Matt 16:18)

This verse is a tremendous encouragement. When we look at the church as it is today, it's easy to feel that it is far from the way God wants it to be, even after 2000 years of trying to get it right. It's encouraging to know that Jesus is not going to give up on us. The church is right in the centre of all God has planned. I believe that the last 50 years of the church in the UK have seen significant steps in the right direction. It's obviously important that we keep on moving in the same way. What then is the right direction? How should we be looking to grow together as God's people? For those of us with an ongoing heart for restoration of the church that Jesus wants, these must be questions that are at the forefront of our hearts and minds.

A significant prophetic word came to our church a few years ago from Eric Tichbourne, who has faithfully sought to bring God's word to us over the years. It was a picture of a door through which God was wanting to bring his blessing to the church. It was currently shut and was proving very difficult to open, as the four hinges on which it hung were rather rusty. The four hinges were prophecy, worship, intercession, and evangelism. We needed to see these hinges oiled by the Holy Spirit, which would then allow the door to open and bring in a new wave of God's blessing. This caused us as a church to consider those issues, which are of course all important parts of our life together as church.

One day while I was musing on this word and what God was trying to say to us through it, I looked again at the picture of the door in my mind. This time I noticed that to open freely the door not only had to have good hinges, it also needed a good doorpost. A doorpost was in three parts, two vertical and one horizontal. The meaning of the three parts of the doorpost came to me immediately. The two vertical posts were the love of God and the word of God. The horizontal post was our love for each other. These key elements need to be in place and have a right relationship to each other for the door of God's blessing to be free to open. I shared this at our church, and hope it was a helpful contribution to what God was trying to say to us at that time. When I came to start writing this chapter on what God was saying regarding the future of the church, I was reminded of this picture. These three aspects of church life seemed to quite neatly sum up what was on my heart, and so the chapter is structured around them.

The Love of God

We've already noted that when God wrote his letters to the seven churches in Revelation, the most common problem was over whether they were continuing in their first love. Being rooted and grounded in God's love is foundational to our individual walk with God. Paul writes in his letter to the Ephesians

> I pray that out of his glorious riches he may strengthen you with power through his Spirit in your inner being, so that Christ may dwell in your hearts through faith. And I pray that you being rooted and established in love may have power together with all the saints to grasp how wide and long and high and deep is the love of Christ and to know this love that surpasses knowledge that you may be filled to the measure of all the fullness of Christ. (Eph 3:16-19)

Paul is absolutely overflowing with his thoughts on the comprehensiveness of the love of Christ. When we focus on this, the roots of our individual Christian lives will be strong. Claire Suffield once did a Bible study in our house group on these verses. She drew two pictures of a tree with its root system, each on a large sheet of paper. On the first tree we wrote into the different branches of the root system the words that came to mind when we thought about a life rooted in the love of God. We came up with words like refreshing, strong, compassionate, peaceful, and secure. We went on for some time meditating on how good it was to have a life rooted in the love of Christ. We then considered what words came to mind when we considered a tree not rooted in the soil of the love of God. The words were very different: perplexed, unloved, lonely, guilty and despairing. The concept was very simple but the impact very profound. It made us determined that we would make every effort to ground ourselves in the love of God.

The church is a body of people, and the basis of a good church is having individual people who are living an abundant life in Christ. The most important aspect of this is that we are rooted and grounded in God's love. We start by knowing that God loves us and being really secure in that. This then produces in us a love for God. Graham Cooke describes this as the love cycle, making an analogy with the water cycle. Water comes down from the clouds to the earth, nourishing it and helping to sustain natural life. It then evaporates from the earth back up to the clouds, and the whole cycle begins again. Similarly, God's love comes to us. We respond by loving him, praising him and demonstrating other fruits of love. This goes back to him and pleases him. This then prompts more love to flow back to us, sustaining our spiritual lives.

Love has always been the focus of God's covenant with mankind. Under the Old Covenant, the first and greatest commandment was 'to love the Lord your God with all your heart and with all your soul and with all your mind' (Matt 22:35-38). The New Covenant hasn't changed that central focus. It just makes it easier. God has always been the initiator in this love relationship. Under the New Covenant we can see that love for us more clearly, as it has been demonstrated in the flesh through Jesus.

Living in God's love is fundamental to our lives as individuals, and together as the church. Love is the first and foremost of the fruits of the Holy Spirit. It is the basis of good relationships within the church, and also provides the motivation for reaching out to others.

Sharing the good news to those outside is a key part of church life. Two recent books on the subject of church have a strong emphasis on this aspect of church life. In his book *Intelligent Church*, Steve Chalke gives very practical advice on how we can be a church that reaches out to the community around[1]. We bring the good news of the gospel in the context of showing God's love in practical ways. Rick Warren's *Purpose Driven Church* describes a whole church system that is geared both to reaching outsiders and ensuring that they are discipled and built into the church[2]. We have already mentioned in the previous chapter that reaching out to others is not always an easy task. Non-Christians do not naturally want to be challenged with a message that asks them to change their whole way of life. There's a great phrase in the Bible used by Paul in the second letter to the Corinthian church. He is trying to explain what makes him so keen to share the gospel and sums it up by saying 'the love of Christ constrains us' (2 Cor 5:11-15). People always talk with enthusiasm about the things or people they love. Being full of the love of God makes it a natural thing for us to want to do. It will also help us to get our focus right in bringing the gospel. While the message of the gospel is a challenge, it is essentially about bringing the love of God. As we are rooted in God's love ourselves, we can love others with the love God puts into us. This helps to put the challenging message of the gospel in its proper context of sharing God's love with the person.

Outreach to non-Christians is an important part of church-life, but it is not the central focus of the church. I've made the second part of the title of this book 'to be the church that Jesus really wants'. Isn't this our key purpose? Loving Christ is about seeking what's best for him, both in our own lives and in the way we are together in the church. There have been a number of prophetic words in recent years in which God is saying that he wants his church back. The main message of this book is to ask us to consider this challenge. I believe that if we are honest, we will recognise that we often have other agendas for our churches, and these prevent us from having this correct focus. The love of Christ should constrain us to seek with all our heart to be the church that Jesus wants. When we think about the future of the church, nothing can be more important than determining to keep God's love firmly at the centre of our consideration. Paul says to the Corinthian church that 'they may speak with the tongues of men and angels, but if they have not love they are like a tinkling cymbal' (1 Cor 13:1). We may have great wisdom about how to organise the church, but without love of Christ at the heart of it, the structure we produce will not be the church that Jesus wants.

The Word of God

God has given us scripture as an invaluable aid in learning his truth. It is not always easy to understand, and different people interpret it in different ways, but it is nevertheless very useful both in our individual Christian lives, and in determining how we should be together as God's people. Our enemy knows this, and over the years there have been many attempts to ridicule and invalidate its truth. In our current post-modern era, the prevailing ethos is that there is no such thing as absolute truth. Of course as Christians this is something we have to conclusively reject. Jesus said 'I am the way the truth and the life. No one comes to the Father but through me' (John 14:6). We have to accept that absolute truth exists, and although we do not fully understand what it is, it can be approached through Jesus.

If the church is to progress towards the oneness that Jesus desires, then an important key is to ensure we all have a common understanding of the extent of the church. Remembering that the church is a body of people, the question is not primarily about denominations or organisations, but about which individuals are part of the real Christian church? The church is described in scripture as consisting of all people who are Christians, so the question becomes: what makes a person a Christian? It is someone who has turned from their sin, trusted in Christ for forgiveness, and committed their life to following him. This commitment to Christ also includes adherence to the basic truths of the gospel. While there are a variety of interpretations of many aspects of Christian doctrine, the essentials are very clear. God created the universe and everything in it. He created man to have a relationship with him. Man was made in the image of God and this included having the ability to make moral choices. However, man abused this choice and sinned, which separated him from God. To rectify the situation, God came to earth in the form of a man, Jesus, to draw men back to himself. Jesus lived on the earth, was crucified, died and rose again. He died to pay the penalty that we deserved for our sins, so that we could be forgiven. This enabled us to enter into a new life in communion with God through the Holy Spirit, who is given to those who believe. Being a Christian means being committed to live pure lives that are pleasing to God, and also to be part of the community of believers, the church. The early Christians were very clear about holding on to these essentials of the faith. We must do the same in the present day.

Those who deny that Jesus came in the flesh or that he was raised from the dead, are not Christians in the true sense of the word, and are therefore not part of the church. Jesus didn't get angry with many people, but he did with religious hypocrites. I think he would be angry today with those who take the name Christian, but deny the basic truths of his message. Likewise Paul, in his writing, repeatedly goes over the basics of the gospel, to ensure that those who denied that Jesus came in the flesh or that he rose again, were clear that these were the essentials of the genuine gospel message. We need to recover this clarity of understanding of the extent of the church. It is vital to be aware of it, and declare our stance on it, if we are to become genuinely one in Christ.

This is of course a particular challenge to those in some denominations such as the Church of England, where there are clearly people holding positions of leadership, who openly deny both these essentials of the faith. In many ways, the Church of England would be an ideal focal point of unity for the church in the UK, with its parish-based system of locally based churches, which neatly cover the country. The development of its evangelical wing over the latter half of the twentieth century has been very encouraging. It has provided leadership to the church in the UK, with its introduction of the Alpha Course and New Wine Bible weeks. These have been valuable to both evangelical and charismatic Christians, and have been a means of drawing Christians together across denominational barriers. It is such a shame that the strength of Church of England's liberal lobby is holding it back. Despite these great developments in the Anglican Church, numbers are dwindling. In my opinion, this is clearly due to the mixture in the church. In recent days, when there has been controversy over the ordination of homosexual bishops, there were several letters published in the *Christian Herald* from people who were so frustrated with the inability of the Anglican church to remain true to clearly biblical principles, that they were being forced to leave. This is surely the tip of the iceberg. There would be many more Christians who would stay in the Anglican Church, and others who would join it, if it were to adopt a clear evangelical, bible-believing stance.

It is worth noting that the approach to understanding the Bible has changed over recent years, even among evangelicals. While the firm belief in scripture as the plumb-line of our faith is still very much in tact, there have been changes in the ground rules for interpretation of that truth. Essentially the change has been to take into consideration the cultural context in which the scripture was written. In interpreting the writings, it is necessary to evaluate the underlying principles of the teaching, and distinguish them from those aspects, which were simply the working out of those principles for the people of that time. It can be seen clearly in the writings of leading evangelical Christians such as John Stott[3]. I think this approach is fine, and with the guidance of the Holy Spirit can lead us into clearer understanding of the application of the scriptures to our lives today.

The approach is also clearly scriptural. Paul, in particular, makes several references to modifying his behaviour according to the context of his cultural background. When speaking to the church at Corinth he says, 'I have become all things to all men that I by all means might save some' (1 Cor 9:22).

On another occasion he advises the Romans that there are situations when it is good to modify their behaviour if it offends the sensitivities of people to the traditions of their time. Writing on the issue of eating food that has been offered to idols, Paul says:

As one who is in the Lord Jesus, I am fully convinced that no food is unclean in itself. But if anyone regards something as unclean then for him it is unclean. If your brother is distressed because of what you eat, you are no longer acting in love. Do not by your eating destroy your brother for whom Christ died. (Rom 14:14-15)

The danger with this approach to the scriptures is that we will discard the principles along with the details. It is therefore vitally important that we follow it with due care and prayer. The values of the world around us must not be allowed to influence our moral stance. We need to value righteousness and hate sin. The relative morality of the world is sinking sand, which we must make every endeavour to avoid. It will mean sometimes being made to look old-fashioned, or out of touch with political correctness. However, we are standing on the solid rock of God's word, will which outlive man's temporary current moral judgments, and we can commit ourselves to it with confidence.

The Bible not only gives us guidance on seeing what the church is and its extent, it gives us valuable principles on how it should organise and conduct itself. I have tried to look at this in Part 2 of this book. One of the keys to God's people coming together and being the church that Jesus wants, is to be willing to take a fresh look at the way we practise being church. Many people are arguing that this is vital if the church is to survive. It is really important that we don't just have our own good ideas on the way forward – we need to ensure that all our developments are aligned firmly with the principles given to us in the Bible. This is a key aspect of the way ahead for the church.

The focus of these two foundations of the love of God and the word of God, can be neatly summed up in the phrase being 'God-centred rather than man-centred'. David Lillie often used these words in describing the heart of the early restoration movement. It is still central to those who hold a vision of the full restoration of the church that Jesus wants.

Our love for each other

If we look at the world as a whole from a natural perspective, the biggest issue for us as a global community is the poverty gap between rich and poor. Other more local issues are important to us in our day-to-day lives, but when we take an overview, global poverty far outweighs these in importance. If we take an overview of the church, there are also many aspects of its life we have to consider, but to my mind, the biggest issue is our lack of unity. Over recent years, big strides have been taken to rectify this deficiency. However, there is clearly still a long way to go, and our lack of unity remains the biggest challenge for the church.

This brings us to the third element of the doorpost, which is the horizontal bar across the top, the lintel, which is our love for one another. Jesus spent a lot of time teaching his disciples on this subject. Paul in Galatians picked up the message, and gives us a clear clue to priorities 'Therefore as we have opportunity do good to all people, especially to those who belong to the family of believers' (Gal 6:10).

We do want to help people outside the church, but our priority in terms of care and doing good, is to look after those inside the church. How should we relate rightly together as God's people? How can we really love one another?

I live in the Shirley area of Southampton. Most people in our house group come from this area. Our mission statement is to be an Acts 2 group. We meet together in our homes for teaching, fellowship, breaking of bread and prayer. We aim to be an encouragement to one another and build each other up in the faith. We also aim to reach out with the good news to the different people we meet in our lives, both in our neighbourhood of Shirley and through our work. We are part of the Community Church in Southampton, which is a large church of around 1000 people. There are several con-gregations which meet weekly. Most of us in the group go to the Sunday morning congregation that meets at Central Hall, a large building in the centre of town. As explained in chapter 5, this is a good church. It preaches the gospel, cares for people and reaches out to those around. I love the folk in my small group, and have other good relationships within the church. Despite all these good aspects of the situation, my heart is unsettled, and I believe this reflects the fact that God's heart is unsettled as well.

Living along my road there are a number of Christians. Some are part of my church, but most go to various other churches. This troubles me. Although we see one another from time-to-time and have an occasional good chat, we are surely missing a great opportunity for really being together as a local community of God's people. When Jesus was here on earth, he prayed most passionately that his disciples would be one as he and the Father were one. We seem to be a long way from this level of unity. That's why we need to regard this lack of oneness as a serious weakness of the church, and why we should see this as the highest priority issue to be resolved.

We have very clear promises about unity. God will command his blessing where brethren dwell together in unity (Ps 133). Our evangelism will always lack credibility as long as we suffer from division. It is a remarkable evidence of God's love and power that, despite our divisions, people still get added to the church. One of the most common objections when we share the gospel with people outside the church is about the divisions within it. Getting together would improve our credibility rating enormously. Watchman Nee taught very clearly on the nature of church that Jesus was looking for. In his book entitled *Further Talks on the Church Life*[4], he observes that God is able to bless us even when we are not joined in right relationships with our brothers. He asks how much more would he be able to bless us if those relationships were right? In the door illustration, the door of blessing would not get stuck because the top door-post was crooked, it would be able to open fully.

How can we change this situation? The first and most important thing we need to do is to get the vision for where God wants to take us. A beautiful picture of the loving community is painted by John Ortberg in his book, *Everybody's Normal Till You Get To Know Them*[5].

In a world where shalom (peace) prevailed, all marriages would be healthy and all children would be safe. Those who have too much would give to those who have too little. Israeli and Palestinian children would play together on the west bank; their parents would build homes for one another. In offices and corporate boardrooms, executives would secretly scheme to help their colleagues succeed; they would complement them behind their backs. Tabloids would be filled with accounts of courage and moral beauty. Talk shows would feature mothers and daughters who love each other deeply, wives who give birth to their husbands children and men who secretly enjoy dressing as men.

To get the full impact of this picture I recommend reading the book, but suffice it to say that he includes 'churches will never split'. Perhaps he could have added to this picture that Christians in a locality would be together as one local church, loving one another, praying together and reaching out to the world together.

John Ortberg is painting a picture of God's kingdom. Jesus came to establish that kingdom and talked a lot about it in his teaching. It is coming in phases; it is not in its final form yet, but it is here now. But what exactly do we mean by the Kingdom of God? George Eldon Ladd describes it as the 'rule of God'[6]. The kingdom is the realm where the rule of God is recognised. It is therefore here on earth among all the people who accept that rule in their lives through Jesus. It is here in his church. We are the expression of God's kingdom on earth. We are a nation united under our king who is Jesus. What a wonderful picture this is. We are not experiencing this in its fullness at present, but it is a great vision to work towards.

Relationships between Christians are not only about getting together on this large scale. It is about living together and supporting one another on an individual basis. We need to see this as a really high priority (Gal 6:10). Normal life throws up all sorts of problems for Christians and non-Christians alike. As Christians we are amazingly privileged in that we have the presence of God's Spirit in us to help us. However, this spiritual dimension in our lives means that we are part of the spiritual battle that is going on over the earth, and therefore in some senses our task is harder. It is clearly feasible for us to be overcomers in this battle, but it is not always easy. Being together in the church, surrounded by people who are praying for us and encouraging us, is of great help in this respect. Of course this also means that we need to play our part in encouraging others. The picture we get of the church as a loving community, full of service, forgiveness and praise is a great one.

By focusing on having a healthy, loving community we can really provide something that is attractive. One of the things that non-believers noticed about the early church, was their love for one another. In present day western society, there are many lonely and isolated people. We have a fantastic opportunity to provide a loving society, which people can come into. However, while there are many attractions of becoming a Christian, the message of the gospel is also very demanding, calling people to commit their whole life to following Jesus. To survive in this challenging new life, we desperately need one another. We need to be part of a caring community, which demonstrates the love of Christ in practice, in supporting each person.

So where do we go from here?

For the church to progress, we need to ensure that all three parts of the doorpost are straightened up. While the most obvious distortion is in the horizontal support, the two vertical posts must also be straight.

Everything we do must be focused on expressing the love of Christ. We need to look for pure, selfless motivations in all our dealings with other Christians. We must allow the love of God to flow through us in recognising one another as our brothers in Christ. We will have a humble spirit, and will accord one another appropriate honour. Our determination to demonstrate the love of Christ, must transcend the loyalty to our denomination, however good, important or historical we feel it to be. Being rooted in the love of God is absolutely fundamental to us being able to relate rightly together in the body of Christ.

We must also be careful to ensure that in all considerations of how the church should develop, we judge everything against the plumb-line of God's word. We cannot hope to achieve genuine unity in the Body of Christ, unless we are clear on the basis of that unity. While we know that there are a variety of interpretations of many of the scriptures, we can surely be clear on the fundamentals. Beyond these, we need to have open minds to appreciate one another, and try to understand where each other is coming from and why they believe what they do.

Lesslie Newbigin was one of the great Christian thinkers of the twentieth century. (When someone says that of another person, it usually means they agree with them, and that is certainly true in this case). He writes with great enthusiasm about the unity of the church[7]. He sees the church at present as being divided up into three parts, the Catholic/Orthodox, the Protestant and the Pentecostal. He argues that all three have an important part to play in the make up of the church as a whole. The Catholic strength is on being a visible fellowship of God's people. Protestants focus on proclaiming the message of the gospel, and becoming members of the church through hearing and believing. Pentecostals remind us that everything in our Christian lives is done in and through the Holy Spirit, who is given to all who believe. If we take any one of these three on its own, we get a distortion of the true picture. At present, we do not fully accept one another in the church, and it is not as it should be. He argues that we should not see the church as something that is static, but something God is working on to perfect, and therefore we should be willing to adapt.

> We have too long devoted our strength to mutual accusation and to self-defence on the basis of what the churches are. Surely it is time to meet one another in penitent acknowledgement of our common failure to be what the church ought to be. On the basis of what we are, none of us can be said to possess the esse of the church. That is the real truth of the situation.

I believe that he has hit on one of the keys of the way forward for us as the church. That is humility. Jesus had this quality in abundance, and it is vital that we all adopt a humble attitude if we are come together the way that Jesus wants us to. Lesslie Newbigin was very involved with the efforts of the ecumenical movement to bring denominations together. He continues:

There was a stage in the ecumenical debate at which the formula suggested for our mutual acceptance was: 'All have won and all shall have the prizes'. Surely it is precisely the reverse of this that we must acknowledge. 'They have all turned aside, they are together become unprofitable.' The place of our meeting will not be the place where in our easy-going way we can decide – after all – to let bygones be bygones. It will be none-other than the mercy-seat where alone Christ meets with us, the place where we know that we are sinners against God. Nothing that the Church is can provide us with our basis of assurance. Our only basis of assurance is the mercy of Christ who calls His church to be his own glorious bride, without spot or wrinkle or any such thing. None of us has any standing save in the mercy. The mark of our calling will surely be a looking forward and a hurrying forward which are a sort of echo of the grace of God who quickens the dead and calls things that are not as though they were, a determination to cease judging one another for what we are, and to build one another up in faith and hope and love into what he has called us to be.

The whole message of *The Household of God* can be summed up in one word 'respect'. All the different streams need to have a genuine respect for their brothers and sisters in other traditions, to recognise their value to the church, and be willing to be joined with them. There are bound to be disagreements about details of how we can move to become God's people together. Respect will ensure that our belief in one and other's integrity will rise above minor doctrinal differences and styles of meeting together.

The recognition that we need one another and belong together is touching us in Southampton. Chris Halls, one of the leaders at Highfield Church in the town, has a clear vision for God's people coming together, and has written a paper on the way ahead for the church in Southampton[8]. This includes the following paraphrase of the passage in 1 Corinthians 12:12-27 about the body of Christ:

> For even as there is one church in Southampton and yet it has many different fellowships, and all these congregations though they are many, form the one body of Christ in Southampton, so also is Christ. For in one Spirit every believer in the city has been baptized into one church, whether Anglican or Pentecostal, Baptist, Methodist or Brethren, whether charismatic or evangelical; and we were all given the one Spirit to drink. For the church in the city there is to be no bland uniformity, but each has a unique way of expressing the life of God.
>
> If the Catholics should say, 'Because we are not Protestants, we are not part of the church in the city,' they are not for this reason any the less part of the body. And if the new churches should say, 'Because we're not part of any denomination, we don't belong with the rest, they are not for this reason any less a part of the body. If none of us had a building of their own, where would the ministries be that need them? If the church in Southampton only met in 'church buildings' how would we reap the benefits that come from meeting in one another's homes? But now God is overseeing the different expressions of church, each unique demonstration of his life, in the body of Christ, just as he desires. And if each was a copycat model of the other, how could the full life of Christ be expressed?
>
> So now there is a multiplicity of groupings, but only one church in the city. And denominational churches cannot say to independent ones. 'You don't belong with us'; or again the new churches say to the historic denominations, 'We don't need you!' Just the opposite, it is much truer that the traditional congregations in the body which may appear less demonstrative are vital; and those we

think are more orthodox, these we cherish – especially at certain times of the year and for special occasions, for their reverence and sense of stability whereas those we regard as 'going places' spiritually these we can sometimes take for granted. But God has so composed the church of Jesus Christ in Southampton, affirming and honouring those that seem to lack so that there should be no schisms in the body, but that each congregation and fellowship should recognise and have the same care for one another.

And if one local expression of Christ's body suffers ridicule or opposition, all the others suffer alongside. If one is strengthened and receives, for example, public recognition, the whole body rejoices. Now each grouping of Christians in the city is part of every other and we belong together in Southampton for Christ.

This gives us some very clear ideas on how we can practically move ahead towards the unity that Jesus longs for between his people.

A vision for the way ahead

The most important starting point in determining the way ahead for the church is to have a clear and unified vision. God has an incredible vision for his church and he wants us to share it. I believe the key points are:

1. That God is not finished with the church and is still working to perfect it. God's heart is for a bride without blemish. Consideration of the church as it is today, makes it clear there is need for improvement.
2. That he wants all his people to be in unity. Jesus' prayer in John 17 shows that this is a key aspect of the church that he wants (John 17:20-23). There is a great picture in Isaiah

looking forward to the type of life that will come in through the stem of Jesse, who is Jesus.

> The wolf also shall dwell with the lamb and the leopard shall lie down with the kid and the calf and the young lion and the fatling together; and a young child shall lead them. (Isa 11:6-9)

I'm really looking forward to see that vision fulfilled. God's overall purpose is to bring everything together in Christ (Eph 1:9-10). Church unity is a key part of that overall purpose.

3. That he wants just one church in each locality. I think there will be many Christians who would accept the principles of points one and two. This next point will, I expect, be more controversial. In Chapter 13 we considered a model of the church derived from scripture. In this model, the church in a locality is taken as being the basic unit defining a church. Within any locality there can only be one church consisting of all the Christians living in that place. We are not practising this model in the church at present. I believe we need to grasp the idea that this is the type of church that God wants.

Working out the Vision

Leadership

We have already acknowledged that working out this vision is not going to be easy. I believe that one of the keys will be the emergence of apostles, who will have both the vision and gifting to bring God's people together across the denominations. The role of apostles is to be first, the initiators[9]. They need to lead the way in taking the church on to the next step. I have tried to pull together the teaching and the various prophetic voices that are pointing the way. What we need now are the apostles who can lead us through this transition. Apostles in scripture were leaders, but they did not manage large church organisations. They established individual churches each with it's own leadership team. The apostles and their teams served the churches they had established with visits and encouragement, but did not govern them – that was the job of the local elders. We need men and women with vision for a unified church today, who also have a heart of service and are not builders of large empires. They will need to be winsome individuals who have the gifts of being peacemakers and bridge-builders. They will need to gain respect across the different streams, which currently comprise the church. This will not be easy, but if it is God's purpose for the church, then he will provide the right people for the job.

Locality

How can we move towards seeing visible local churches consisting of all Christians in the area? We first need to understand what we mean by locality. In the scripture it is usually equated to a city. Watchman Nee considers that this is a scriptural principle[10]. However, if this pattern were taken literally in the twenty-first century, there might be some practical problems. Large cities such as London are rather too big to be taken as localities, and in rural regions where people are spread over a wide geographical area it would be difficult to determine boundaries. A simpler alternative, which could be applied across the whole range of localities, is the parish system used by the Church of England. There can be several local parishes in a large town, whereas a rural parish can encompass several small communities. I don't feel we should be prescriptive about this issue; what is important scripturally, is that the locality is the unit of the church, however that is actually defined. The key to developing local churches would be flexibility, allowing local Christians to come to a decision about what they felt was the best definition of their locality.

If the parish idea were to be adopted, each parish would have only one church. Progress is already being made in this direction. In my own locality we have an organisation called Churches Together in Shirley. This expresses the desire of Christians in the locality to work together. I believe that the next step is to become the Church Together in Shirley. The name change is small, but the principle of change is very significant. Instead of being a loose association of independent churches, most of which had links to different denominations, we would become a single church governed by a group of elders. This will be a hard step to take. It would take some time to work out, and would involve some tough decisions to be taken in identifying with local Christians instead of the central denomination. However, I believe that this is a practical way ahead, which could lead us to a scriptural expression of church. We will properly be able to express our unity in Christ, and I am convinced that God will pour out his blessing on us as never before.

How good and pleasant it is when brothers live together in unity. It is like precious oil poured on the head, running down on the beard, running down on Aaron's beard, down on his collar robes.

It is as if the dew of Hermon were falling on Mount Zion. For there the Lord bestows his blessing, even life for evermore. (Ps 133)

God has a tremendous heart for his people. If we came together as unified local churches, we would give him the chance to pour out his blessing on us in much greater measure than we have experienced in the past.

One thing I think it would be really good to agree on is that no new churches should be planted in areas where genuine Bible-believing churches exist and are functioning. Church planting is an important principle of church growth, and it is great to see new churches established on new estates and localities where there is no church at present. However, I always find it rather sad to hear of a new church being started in places where there are already good vibrant churches. The apostolic teams of the restoration movement have exciting stories to tell of new churches being planted. However, in some cases, perhaps even more could have been achieved if those people who started off their new churches had instead joined the church that was already there, and combined their gifts with the other Christians in the locality.

Another practical way of Christians fostering the idea of unified local church, is to have 'cross-pollination'. I have already talked about our own visits to the local Anglican church, which have been very encouraging, and caused us to meet up with other Christians in our area. Others from our church have actually 'moved churches' to be more associated with their locality. In this way a quiet revolution is taking place. Christians on the ground are recognising more and more that the divisions between churches are artificial. They consider themselves to be part of the church in their locality, not particularly Catholic, Anglican, restoration or any other specific group. They are expressing their desire to be part of God's people as a whole. It is vitally important that church leaders in each locality realise this. They need to start talking to each other about how the concept of local church, which many Christians are looking for and the Bible teaches, can be progressed towards realisation.

Commitment to inter-church events and initiatives, as well as learning to respect and appreciate one another, are all really encouraging steps in the right direction. However, I don't believe these developments will be the final expression of our unity. We need to catch the vision that God wants us to join together in a full sense of oneness like that, which exists between Father, Son and Holy Spirit.

Logistics

There are a number of practical considerations in developing the church in the locality. If we consider the church in an area like Shirley, Southampton, there are probably several thousand Christians. If we decided to come together as the local church where would we all meet? There would probably be some difficulty finding a building in Shirley that was big enough to house everyone at the same time. The church in Jerusalem had a similar problem. It also consisted of several thousand believers and as far as we know, didn't own any buildings. Their main place of meeting was in homes, which meant they usually got together in small groups. As we have discussed before, this seems to be a clear scriptural principle on the way Christians should meet together. It therefore seems reasonable to propose that it still applies to local churches in the present day. The church of

Jerusalem also met together in the temple i.e. a public place, but this may not have been everyone at the same time. There is not a lot of detail given in Acts on how they organised these larger meetings. Therefore, apart from the principle of meeting in homes, I think it would be up to the local elders to work out how best to come together as God's people in larger groups. The local church in Shirley for example, would have access to several buildings where sub groups of the local church could meet together. For larger celebration style meetings, one of the local school halls could be hired. However, it is important to remember that the key to church life in the New Testament was of sharing life together, not just meetings. Whatever way a modern-day local church chooses to organise its official gatherings, it should never lose sight of the fact that church life should focus around people loving one another, and spending time with one another on a natural day-to-day basis.

Another question that would result from the formation of unified local churches, is what happens to all the denominations? How would Christians relate to a denomination, which had supported them faithfully over many years? These organisations have often been led by godly men, and they have provided churches with excellent help and guidance, in some cases over many centuries. Unfortunately, if we're honest, in their current form they don't really have a role in the structure of the church as it is described in scripture. Despite this, I think it would be important to recognise their value to the church, and not to lose their expertise and experience. They not only have a lot of natural resource, but also a lot of spiritual resource. There would be considerable potential for these organisations, in changed form, to support apostolic teams for example. Even if unified local churches were to be established, apostolic teams would still be an important part of the church on a wider scale, having a trans-local function. In the early church, they established new churches and supported existing ones. They provided vision, leadership and guidance on doctrinal questions of the day as well as links between local churches. The denominational organisations could still have an important role in helping these trans-local teams operate in these areas.

A further consideration is what would happen to people who were employed by their churches? What would be their place in the new local church? Some would clearly become part of the eldership team of the church. But perhaps not all would find the readjustment very easy. It is important that a compassionate and understanding approach should be taken to this situation. One would also hope that these men and women would be willing for an open and honest re-evaluation of their calling in the new context of the unified local church. A key attitude to the smooth operation of this transition would be respect on both sides. Combined with a genuine openness to hear from God, these difficult changes could be worked through in love.

There are clearly a number of questions in the detail of this proposal, and not all have easy answers. Fortunately that doesn't really matter too much to God. The way he operates is not based around us having all the answers. Rather, we have to hear a word from him, and then act on it in faith. If we really believe that God is calling us to form local churches, then we need to step out in faith in that direction, believing that he will be with us and will help us work out the details as we go along.

We will need above all, a spirit of humility. This was so much a central characteristic of the early church, and it is just as important in the twenty-first century. We need to be humble in recognising that our denomination or group has not got everything right. We need to recognise that God has put his Spirit into Christians in other local congregations. This will lead us to discover how we need each other to be the complete body of Christ in our locality. Nowhere will this attitude of humility be required more than in the lives of the apostles whom God calls to leadership. Church history is littered with stories of gifted men who start off in the Spirit, but then carry on in the flesh. Men always want to try to organise things and create big empires. We have to resist this temptation. There is one overall church with Christ as the head, but he has given us a structural pattern in which the basic organisational unit is the local church. We need men who are leaders, but who will also keep true to this principle. They will need to be humble, and not seek to produce great organisations beyond what God has ordained in a locality.

We will need both open minds and open hearts to see this vision develop. Please consider the picture I have outlined. Go back to scripture. Listen to God with an open mind. In the field of science, progress is generally made by people coming up with new ideas which, in themselves, are a small step forward. However, when that idea is shared it can trigger off another idea from another person, and in this way of mutual encouragement or synergy, progress is made. I don't believe that I have all the answers, far from it. However, I pray that you will listen to the arguments I have put forward, take what is good from them, and then add what God wants to say or do through you.

We also need to grow in our hearts to one another. Watchman Nee has described the situation between denominations in our day as 'holding hands over the fences'. This is a good description of initiatives like Churches Together in Shirley. We are agreeing together and recognising one another, but we are still content to live with the fences in place. Holding hands over the fences is a good start, and I believe that moves in this direction bring joy to the heart of God. But they are only a temporary staging post along the road that he is taking us. We need to move on from there to actually take down the fences, and live and work alongside one another in the oneness like that of the Trinity. In that oneness there can be no fences at all. Let's really open up our hearts fully to one another. We need hearts that respect and believe in each other even when we don't agree on every detail.

Concluding Remarks

The vision of the church we have in the Bible is tremendous. It is an exciting dynamic group of people with Jesus as our leader, working together in love and friendship to please him, serve one another and bring the good news of the gospel to those around. I'm so pleased to be joined with all of you who love our Lord. I am convinced that there has never been a time in church history since its early days when there has been a better opportunity for us to join together than now. Let's not be content to stay as we are, separated by these divisions. Let's all join together to be the church that Jesus wants. I pray that you will catch this vision and put all your energy into seeing it fulfilled.

References

1. Chalke, S., 2006, *Intelligent Church: A Journey Towards Christ-Centred Community*, Zondervan, Grand Rapids, Michigan.

2. Warren, Rick, 1995, *The Purpose driven Church: growth without compromising your message and mission*, Zondervan, Grand Rapids, Michigan.

3. Stott, John, 1992, *The Contemporary Christian*, Inter-Varsity Press, Leicester.

4. Nee, Watchman, *Further Talks on the Church Life: Confirming the Truth Concerning Church Life*, Living Stream Ministry, Anaheim, California.

5. Ortberg, John, 2003, *Everybody's Normal Till You Get To Know Them*, Zondervan, Grand Rapids, Michigan (Copyright © 2003 by John Ortberg. Used by permission of Zondervan).

6. Ladd, G.E., 2002, *The Gospel of the Kingdom – Scriptural studies on the Kingdom of God*, W.B. Eerdmans Publishing Company, Grand Rapids, Michigan.

7. Newbigin, L., 1953, *The Household of God*, Paternoster Press, Carlisle, Cumbria (Permission to use quotation given by Paternoster. Copyright © 1998).

8. Halls, C., 2006, 'Strategy for Southampton: A Christian perspective', 2006.

9. Breen, Mike, *The Apostle's Notebook*, Kingsway Communications, Eastbourne, England.

10. Nee, *op cit*.

EPILOGUE

On January 10th 2007 a meeting was held at Highfield church in Southampton to launch the Southampton Christian Network (SCN). For a number of years Christian leaders in the city had been seeking to work more closely together. However two different groups had emerged, the Southampton Evangelical Alliance, consisting of evangelical leaders and the Joshua Partnership, which had a more charismatic flavour. In a desire to express unity across the church it was decided to close these two organisations and merge to become one new expression of the church in the city. Around 300 people came to support this new venture. It was good to join in worship and prayer together. The guest speaker was Lloyd Cooke, one of the leaders from a similar initiative in Stoke-on-Trent. He encouraged us by relating the story of the way God had blessed their coming together in Stoke. At the end of the gathering around 40 leaders from different churches joined together at the front to express their desire to walk and work with one another in the future.

Jesus said that he would build his church (Matt 16:18). This development is an encouraging step forward for the local church in Southampton that reminds us that Jesus is still actively involved in this process. Hallelujah!

GLORY IN THE CHURCH
by George Tarleton

As I begin, the Lord's words to the prophet 'Write the vision, make it plain' (Hab. 2:2) are both my commission and my challenge. For the Lord has given me a vision, along with many others, concerning the church as she is meant to be – especially in the days just before Christ comes to take her to Himself. As there seems to be a universal awareness among those who search the scriptures that 'the coming of the Lord is at hand' I feel that the time has come to share this with you, praying that I can make it plain.

The Scripture informs us that the church that Jesus is coming for is not a weak, struggling thing but a 'glorious church' (Eph. 5:27 AV). What will be some of the characteristics of this glorious end-time church? Let's start with the well-known prophecy of Joel (2:28-32). The most striking thing about it is that the prophet foresees a profusion of charismatic gifts scattered throughout the age range on both sexes. Two groups are singled out – young people and the workers – both of them causing considerable concern at this time in the world. So we begin with:

1. 'The gifts of the spirit' (1 Cor. 2:14)

John Wesley's comment in his diary on the 15th August 1750 shows the outworking of this fourteenth verse. 'The grand reason why the miraculous gifts were so soon withdrawn was not that faith and holiness were well nigh lost – but that dry formal orthodox men began even to ridicule whatever gifts they had not themselves and to decry them all as madness and imposture'.

The doctrine of the gifts of the Spirit is not based on some obscure verse or on a few isolated texts but on three chapters of God's word, which are devoted to this subject – 1 Corinthians 12 to 14! In order to avoid the obvious implications of these chapters, some claim that the gifts were withdrawn at the end of the apostolic age.

The onus of proof lies with those who make this claim, for they have neither the support of history (Ireneaus and Tertullian quote them as operating in the second and third centuries); nor the support of Scripture for Romans 11:29 categorically states that 'the gifts and call of God are irrevocable!'

To any unbiased reader of the New Testament it becomes very obvious that the gifts were a part of the *normal* life of the church and not an optional extra. This is particularly true of the book of Acts where we see the young church in action. J.B. Phillips uses these very words as the title for his paraphrase of the book. In his preface he says that Acts shows us the church as she is meant to be: 'For it was vigorous and flexible, for these were the days before it became fat and short of breath through prosperity or muscle bound by over-organisation!'

There are those who speak of all that has been accomplished without the gifts. The only reply to such a negative statement is – think of how much more can be accomplished with them.

One is sadly aware that the charismata have been abused. Nowhere is this more painfully obvious than in the church at Corinth. However, it is to this church that Paul gives that striking piece of advice 'Do not forbid speaking of tongues' (14:39)! For the alternative to abuse is not disuse but proper use.

Finally, it seems clear from such scriptures as Acts 2:4, 10:46 and 19:6 that 'the baptism in the Spirit' is the gateway to the gifts. By this phrase we mean the experience which Paul had subsequent to his conversion in Acts 9:17. He received it through the laying on of hands, this appears to be the usual way whenever possible.

The second characteristic of the end time church will be the corporate life, summed up in that phrase Paul loved to describe the church:

2. 'The body of christ' (Eph 4:12)

The body is the best vehicle of expression that we have. That is why God chose it in order to display His glory (John 1:14). Now it was the Father's intention that what Jesus began to do and teach (Acts 1:1), should be continued through the ministry of 'the church which is his body' (Eph 1:23). There are only two ways in which the scripture looks at this body. One is from its universal aspect, the other from the local. Both have their origin in the teaching of Jesus (Matt 16:17-19 and 18:15-20). Denominations are neither one thing nor the other.

The unifying factor in the Body of Christ is the fact that we all share the same *life*, because we are born again by the same spirit into the same family. We find this in Acts 2 where they were drawn together not because of an agreed doctrinal basis, but because they had become partakers of the divine nature (2 Pet 1:4). We are commanded in Ephesians 4 to 'maintain the unity of the spirit (life) . . . until we *all* attain to the unity of the faith (doctrine)'. But we are not there yet!

As we look at the local aspect of Paul's teaching on the body we find he is intensely practical, for to him the term 'the Body' was a functional one describing a living organism (not organisation). Listen to what he says in Romans 12:4-5 'Just as there are many parts to our bodies, so it is with Christ's body. We are all parts of it, and it takes everyone of us to make it complete, for we each have different work to do. So we belong to each other and each needs all others. God has given us the ability to do certain things well . . .' (*Living Letters*). Then he explains exactly what he means in verses 6-8.

In the twelfth chapter of 1 Corinthians we see that there is a very real connection between the gifts of the Spirit and the body of Christ. For the Holy Spirit bestows gifts upon us to enable us to contribute something to 'the common good' (v. 7). It's in this chapter that the apostle outlines the principles on which the body works.

a. The Principle of Inter-relationship (vv. 15-16)

This is simply being satisfied with what we are (by grace not by nature), and not wanting to be like someone else. So find out what your ministry is and where you fit in to the body, for if one member stops functioning the whole body suffers.

b. The Principle of Inter-dependence (vv. 17-20)

This means that we all need one another and it is essential that we leave room for others to function. Verse 19 shows that it is impossible to have both a one-man-ministry and body-ministry.

In order for the latter to become a reality the church will need to centre more and more on the house-meeting.

c. The Principle of Integration (vv. 21-26)

We cannot say to another born-again member 'I have no need of you' – we need each other to keep us in our rightful place, for the Father has so proportioned the body as to make the weaker parts 'indispensable' (v. 22)! A body functioning properly bestows 'greater honour on the inferior part'. In order that there should be 'no discord in the body' He has blended us so that we feel for each other *spontaneously* (v. 25).

Finally, in vv. 27–30 Paul speaks of the various ministries of this body. The five main ministries are listed in Eph 4:11 as apostles, prophets evangelists pastors and teachers. We need them *all* if we are ever to attain 'to mature manhood, to the measure of the stature of the fullness of Christ.' If the Psalmist, when he considered his physical body, could say 'I am fearfully and wonderfully made' – how much more can we as we meditate on its spiritual counterpart.

3. 'Worshipping the Father' (John 4:23)

This is the last characteristic that I want to deal with but it is by no means the least for it is the Father's ultimate purpose that we should not only be a redeemed people but a worshipping people. That was, in fact, his original intention when he made us like himself (Gen 1:27) for himself (Col 1:16). For he speaks in Isa 43:21 of 'the people whom I formed for Myself that they might declare My praise.' We were made in his likeness in order that we would appreciate him enough to worship him. Because no one comprehends the thoughts of God except the Spirit of God (1 Cor 2:11), the Father placed His Spirit within us so that we could appreciate Him enough to admire Him and end up adoring Him.

The teaching of Jesus on worship in John 4:20–24 is the clearest statement that we have on the subject. Here we see that worship must not be governed by tradition (v. 20), nor is it to be confined to any place or building as in the Old Testament (v. 21). Although we agree with this in our heads, in our hearts we still associate worship with wearing special clothes to go to special places on special days!

Jesus went on to say that the object of all true worship must be 'the Father' (v. 23), however much of what passes for worship seems to be summed up by the previous verse 'Ye worship ye know not what' (AV). In verse 24 he categorically states that all 'must worship in spirit and truth', this means at least

a. It must be initiated and energised by the Holy Spirit; for 'when be cry "Abba! Father!" it is the Spirit himself bearing witness with our spirit that we are the Children of God' (Rom 8:15-16).
b. It must have its genesis deep within – in our spirit not our souls.
c. It must be governed by the truth found in the Word – not our own sentiment

d. It must have a touch of reality about it (truth – experience of real).

A.W. Tozer comes nearest to describing this kind of worship when he says 'it is to feel with the heart and express in some appropriate manner a humbling but delightful sense of admiring awe, astonished wonder and overpowering love.' For a description of worship in the New Testament church one needs to read carefully through 1 Corinthians 11 to 14 (see 14:26 in particular). The importance of worship is seen in John 4:23. How amazing that a self-sufficient God should actually 'seek' men and women like us to worship him – how inscrutable are his ways! Truly worship is the Christian's highest occupation.

Conclusion

I believe that God is looking for a church which will

Receive the power He has made available in the gifts of the Spirit;

Restore the pattern He has given in His Word for a functioning Body;

Realise that His ultimate purpose is that we should worship the Father.

'To Him be glory in the church and in Christ Jesus to all generations. Amen' (Eph 3:21).

George W. Tarleton, 1971